PRAYING FINGERTIPS

December 2009
Dear Kay,
Thanks for sharing this spiritual journey.
Terry

Terrence Douglas
312 Whiting Lane
Virginia Beach, VA 23456
757-650-3308
trdassociates@cox.net
www.rulesofengaging.com

ISBN: 978-1-60383-202-1

Published by:
Holy Fire Publishing
Unit 116
1525-D Old Trolley Rd.
Summerville, SC 29485

www.ChristianPublish.com

Cover Design by Jay Cookingham

Sketch by Betty Wells

Printed in the United States of America and the United Kingdom

Endorsements

My recommendation to all readers would be to pick this book up each morning and randomly select just one of the meditations to read for that day. I believe most readers will be surprised at how often that one meditation will fit so relevantly into their day, and actually inspire a course of action in many cases. If it does not, don't fuss it, because the next one undoubtedly will. I've saved every one of Terry's meditations on my computer, fully intending to recall some for another closer reading. To have 365 of them in a book, sitting next to my favorite reading chair, will greatly facilitate such review.
W.L., Retired senior CIA operations officer, NC

A mediation that focuses on God and the wonders of life brings me personal peace in a world filled with so much strife.
J.V., Educator and political advisor, Ottawa, Canada

"Terry Douglas' meditations are superbly selected and touch the intellect and emotions in a way that is both comforting and challenging. They make a difference in my day."
G.H., International corporate executive and retired USA colonel, Vietnam Veteran.

Terry's life experience has taught and guided him in unique ways, given him insights and through loss he gained strength and grew. During times of paradigm change and the unfolding economic and political meltdown, many people will be clamoring to find a way back to spirituality and a sense of being rather than having. Reading Terry's *'Daily Meditations'* might be a good start.
F.B., International Security Consultant, Toronto, Canada

After living with fear for a long time, Terry Douglas' meditations enlightened my heart, so I can seek and live my legend with the help of God; Who speaks the universal language of mankind.
J.M. International Marketing, Whitefish, Montana

Terry Douglas shares with us his soul-searching questions and meditative responses which shine like words of Spirit flowing from his keyboard. These messages are practical and inspirational, not sugar-coated platitudes but down-to-earth wake-up calls to live more fully within the love and joy which God showers on all of us, regardless of age or circumstances.
Keeping our faith alive and vibrant, we can become more aware of each gift and blessing sent by God, moving the mountains of our cares and concerns with His help and grace, always available to us, though sometimes forgotten in the daily challenges we face. Blessings on Terry Douglas for lighting our souls' path with his daily words of wisdom.
R.D. Former President and Executive Officer of International Association

Introduction

Raised in New York, attending college and graduate school there as well, I served with the CIA and the corporate world abroad. Among the cities where I resided are Warsaw, Delhi, Beirut, Berlin, Jeddah, and recently Kabul. My wife and I raised five children who accompanied us as we explored the world. We had been married for thirty-nine years, when my wife was lost in a tragic accident as she was walking to church.

For nearly thirty years I have risen before sunrise to spend time in a quiet place, most days praising God and seeking to know His will for me. Over the years, my quiet place moved from a cluster of Blue Spruce trees I planted behind our home in Vienna, Virginia; to a bench overlooking woods that surrounded our residence in West Virginia; to a hooch situated within a fortified compound in Kabul, Afghanistan; and most recently to my deck wrapped around my home overlooking the Atlantic Ocean in Virginia Beach.

In the last several years, I have incorporated in this routine the reading and reflecting upon Scripture. Most mornings when the weather allows I begin these mediations outside just as the sun is beginning to rise. I select a verse or a few verses from the New Testament or Hebrew Bible that I have come upon, realizing that there are no coincidences. I read the text slowly and pause when I feel a pull to explore further the message reserved for me that morning.

I then retreat indoors and sit before my keyboard. At the insistence of my mother, I took a typing course in high school and now, so many years later, am able to type at great speed without looking at the keyboard. This skill is what allows me with eyes closed to record in the stillness what I hear as the words flow freely through my fingertips. I have come to accept that the murmuring resounding in my heart as the response of the Holy Spirit to my daily prayer.

The format I use is the same for the meditations that follow. I record the verse(s) with the Scriptural citation; I offer a prayer, usually for deeper understanding; and then with eyes closed record what I hear. When the meditation is concluded, I open my eyes. I then read what I have typed and make only the most minor edits, such as adding a "y" to "ou" that my speed across the keyboard neglected to register.

It amazes me that minutes after the meditation session is concluded I am unable to recall what I typed. Later, I reread the writing, as if for the first time, amazed at the treasure contained therein.

The meditations that follow are clustered in twelve chapters. My suggestion to readers is that they use the meditations as a springboard for their own exploration of the anointed word of God.

Terrence Douglas
Virginia Beach, Virginia
March 14, 2009

TABLE OF CONTENTS

CHAPTER ONE --TESTIMONY

Giving testimony is more than verbal whispering what one believes is the truth. It is speaking aloud that truth – like placing the lamp on the lamp stand where it's light can shine for all to see; it requires us to support the words with action – action that might well put one in harm's way by a judgmental world we live in.

As I read the Scripture I see that it overflows with examples where Jesus, his disciples, and the prophets spoke boldly, but in quiet dignity, conviction, and courage to encourage us as we witness this truth to others.

I listen carefully each morning and pray for that same courage to speak and act openly.

#1

Scripture: *You are a mist that appears for a while and then vanishes. James 4:14*

Prayer: And there was a mist – a light rain had fallen during the night – when I went out onto the deck to read scripture at dawn. Help me to meditate on this verse and derive what I require for this stage in my life.

Response: At first glance James' words do not seem encouraging but they are. Why? Because I am turning, returning your attention to the present. Imagine if you can, the mist that you are sitting in, or were sitting in, is the present where all or much is not clear to you. Yet the mist is so attractive and comforting. Remember your drive through the morning mist on the West Coast and seeing the priest emerge from the fog on his walk to the country chapel.

You can either say that the mist is gloomy or enlightening. The mist gives you the present in which to allow my message to infiltrate each and every bone, vein, blood capsule that you ride around in. The mist protects you from what you are not ready to absorb. The mist protected you from your spouse's passing. So mist is good. It is the curtain that begins to part with your preparedness. Reading scripture, writing poetry, engaging everyone you meet gently is the parting of the curtain.

Before we go further, make a list of all those you can recall with whom you had contact yesterday and gently reassured with your words.

OK. Now let us return and speak about the scripture reading. You understand that mist is to indicate that what you consider so substantial is not, and what you fail so often to appreciate and reverence is. Your body will fade away and how often do you fail to appreciate deeply that the body is housing the immortal soul that is in the body to learn love and compassion in the conflict of daily life.

How do you like that? Love and compassion in conflict. That is the lesson of life, put so simply that all of you should be able to understand it. You are moving toward that understanding, even illumination, though only your losses over the years and most especially in the last years have contributed to the acceleration of your ascension growth.

Mist is also so temporary. Another good insight is buried here. Let's consider temporary in the sense that illumination is on the way, is just before you. What helps to speed the evaporation? Yes, the Sun, the light, the warmth of Love. So don't tremble with the thought that the mist (you) will disappear, vanish. Think more on what you become to replace that mist. Like a cocoon you will become a colorful butterfly.

I think I have given you enough. Finally, understand that I did not command you to pick that phrase on which to meditate; you chose it yourself. That is the freedom you have and I applaud your selection; it indicates your growth in spirit.

#2

Scripture: *[T]hrough faith [you] are shielded by God's power. 1 Peter 1:5*

Prayer: What does it mean to be shielded by your power?

Response: Envision if you will the fiercest battle where the enemy is intent on seizing your battle flag. All around you are besieged, yet you no less engaged are covered it seems in a mantle that prevents the enemy from seizing you or harming you in any way. And this is so though you walk in the middle of the calamitous scene not as an observer but one fully in engaged in defeating the enemy. That is what it means to be shielded by God. Keep in mind that you are fully engaged, you are a warrior that gives no quarter to this enemy that seeks to capture your fealty, and if not, then to destroy you.

And you are engaged in a purpose. And that is to share the victory that awaits you with those less aware of battle, and to do this sometimes quite subtlety as you witness the grief and aloneness that others experience. You especially have your voice in your poetry that gives voice to others who need the chord of the melody before they can go on.

Your shield is magnificent. It is of burnished silver and fits your body closely. I say burnished because each battle in which you have engaged has added a luster. The steel of your sword has been tempered through all the trials and grief you have suffered.

Today, I instruct you to feel in the depths of your body and soul the inexpressible joy you feel in this moment – not influenced by the cares and responsibilities of the world in which you sit. Feel the joy that surpasses any fear or anxiety of the battle. This inexpressible joy serves to enkindle your spirit and your sword glows in that awesome power of love from which the enemy flees into a darkness that diminishes.

You are shielded and realize that there would be no reason to shield you if you were not in battle. My love to you this day, gentle spirit.

Scripture: *Concerning this salvation . . . Even the angels long to look into these things. 1 Peter 1:10-12*

Prayer: And what about salvation?

Response: It is so often the case that a word is used and overused and one such example is salvation. Let me tell you something about salvation that even the angels wish to learn. You have seen the artistic depiction of God Divine touching the fingertip of created man. Salvation is that moment and process whereby your soul is lightened to a brilliance that outshines the brightest sunrise.

Salvation is the flame within exploding consciously with Divine Love. Salvation is occurring right this moment at the edge of your fingertips as you record the process. Salvation is the mystery that holds the intention of the angels and draws them to you in support and love.

Salvation is the remaking of all that constitutes your uniqueness into an exalted being that shares divine love so deeply and fully that you reflect in all you are a magnificent brilliance that can only be attributed to the divine grace that has imbued every element that names you; I am clearly not limiting this you to body form.

Salvation is a knowing with no dark corners of concern in spirit. Angels are attracted because they have not experienced this alchemy. Out of mud you became body, out of salvation you became spirit reflecting that brilliance of light.

Please reflect on these words that attempt to capture what cannot be captured.

Scripture: *For you have been born again, not of perishable seed, but of imperishable, through the living and enduring word of God. For all men are like grass, and all their glory is like the flowers of the field; the grass withers and the flowers fall, but the word of the Lord sands forever.* 1Peter 1:23-25

Prayer: Lord, what are you telling me this morning?

Response: Well, it is so obvious even you can see this clearly. You have been born again. And it is important to realize that born again is not some past event but is rekindled, reborn each day. This time of grief, rejection and healing have all set the stage for your rebirth that is occurring daily. You are the attentive student whom I am instructing. Were you to be complete and "reborn" as a past event there would be no need for the instruction that you are now receiving.

Remember how you learned a foreign language so well with one-on-one instruction given to you by a dedicated teacher. Well you are receiving the same intense instruction from me. And it is required of you to study at home and use what you learned in language lesson, so it is with my instruction. And do you see the correlation with the Word. You studied the language to be able to converse and convey ideas and thoughts and so it is with my instruction.

So the theme today is of being reborn over and over again. And each birth brings you closer to the essential divine truth, something you have been searching for in your travels, relationships, musings, prayers, through your poetry. You have been knocking on the door so vigorously we have not been able to ignore your pleadings, as if we would. What distinguishes you is your persistence. Continue to nourish that hunger and you will find that your lawn will withstand whatever the weather elements provide.

Scripture: *Therefore, rid yourselves of all malice and all deceit, hypocrisy, envy, and slander of every kind. Like newborn babies, crave pure spiritual milk, so that by it you may grow up in your salvation, now that you have tasted that the Lord is good. 1 Peter 2:1-3*

Prayer: Lord, teach me this morning.

Response: This is a good morning for you to take stock of who you are and how far you have traveled. It is with the confidence of my love that you truly have passed beyond malice, deceit, hypocrisy, envy. When you had not yet developed the confidence in your being, envy was a blemish that you worked on with my grace. You do crave the pure spiritual milk undiluted by watered-down versions offered by religious faiths that don't think that one can absorb the undiluted version.

Think a moment of India and water buffalo milk. Remember how thick and tasty it was, how the water buffalo did not get the diseases that require pasteurization, and yet how the Indians in seeking to spread the pure product further added water, unclean at that, to it, making the milk unsafe.

That is the thought for you to day. You are being encouraging to seek the unadulterated, pure milk of the Spirit and to convey the same to those around you. Remember how thick and rich it was. You used to say, and you were not far removed from fact, that one whisk and you had the sweetest thick cream. Yes, that is what we encourage you to seek directly, the pure white, thick, rich, unadulterated spiritual milk of the Father. You are to seek this beverage for sustenance, growth, enlightenment, enjoyment, pleasure, and as something that will sooth you in days when you might feel overwhelmed.

There will come a time when you will drink from this pure spiritual milk almost exclusive of your cares and concerns. And you will know this when your face reflects an easy grace that radiates the Father's love in whatever circle you dance.

For today take heart because this morning you drank fully of the pure spiritual milk described and you will notice how it affects your every moment, smile, gesture, written word, and prayer. Continue to search for deep meaning in every random phrase knowing that nothing is random.

#6

Scripture: *[T]he unfading beauty of a gentle and quiet spirit. 1 Peter 3:4*

Prayer: Less than five hours sleep, I read these lines this morning and thought of my spouse, long gone. Please give me guidance this day.

Response: Do you remember the words of the priest at the memorial service when he said that saintly people come among us not by accident, and your wife was one such person. She indeed was a gentle and quiet spirit. That is what is being developed in you, a gentle and quiet spirit. What is required for you to hasten those qualities within you – for you see they are the basis of faith?

Gentle is a characteristic filled with compassion. In fact compassion is its seed or spark, both seemingly contradictory aspects but they are one. For you to hasten gentleness you must continue to view the world with love and wrench from your heart any call to violence even verbally or in thoughts. Gentleness is found in the pause before speaking, the survey of the mind to uproot prime motivations that must be softened. Gentleness bespeaks the confidence that there is nothing to fear, that all is being made right; gentleness is accepting that around the corner just up the path in the gloom the fog is lifting and clarity prevails.

Quiet connotes that time or period of nurturing that allows me to reach you. It is a time like now that brings you to a quiet space where you hear my voice resounding in your heart. Quietness is reflected in stretching tension-free alone or in the arms of a loved one.

Hear me in this space. Reach this space daily and you will not be disappointed. There is no task or set of tasks that are not possible with you as a quiet spirit. It is in the quiet time that your Self, that silent observer, emerges and you recognize a union that is blurred when the ego strives to rule. A quiet spirit also hints to you of the divine union that you experience now but will fully comprehend in your ascension. You see there are not conflicting spirits packaged in your body but one whose union and integration reflects union with the divine – divine union.

So much is emerging to allow you to become the vehicle for divine love in your surroundings near and far. Cultivate this gentleness and quietude and you will be overcome with appreciation.

Scripture: *For Christ died for sins once for all, the righteous for the unrighteous, to bring you to God. He was put to death in the body but made alive by the Spirit, through whom also he went and preached to the spirits in prison who disobeyed long ago when God waited patiently. 1Peter 3:18-20*

Prayer: This is a difficult passage it seems. Please guide my spirit to comprehend the lessons and teaching for my journey.

Response: First understand that Christ came for all, not just the gentle souls who in their gentleness and compassion were already far along in understanding the love of the Divine. He came for you in the depth of your despair, and I do not mean this specifically for you. He came for you in your violence and hatred; he came for you in your loneliness. But the key is *to bring you to God.*

Notice, Peter did not write nor was he inspired to write *to force you to God.* You are responsible for saddling up as it were and traveling along that sometimes difficult traverse to Him. And what you must understand is that ultimately that journey is solitary. I did not say lonely though it could be. No, I said solitary because you travel alone in a crowd.

Rowing was such a good sport for you because you took in the aloneness on a rowing team – all assisting the others with their strength and rhythm but all responsible for themselves. So the tragedy, if there is one, is that some (despite the clarity of the path laid out before them) are still determined to reject the path, but only they know it. And the path is not a religion. Religion is like the crowd with whom you are rowing. No the path is your solitary participation within a community or team that might be quite unbeknownst to the crowd at large.

Now what is particularly difficult for scholars to understand is he *preached to the spirits in prison who disobeyed long ago.* Please put aside the time dimension and consider their rejection of God's love as present. Of course the prison is the prison of their rejection of God's love whenever in your time dimension that it occurred. The prison is one of hopelessness and it is a prison without walls or time. He preached the good news of redemption and some still do not direct their attention and will to his words and still do not hear though the message is ever "broadcast" as it were on the wings of angels and in the words and gestures of those who accept the truth.

So Peter wrote not to confound the scholars who would be confounded and puzzled by his meaning. He simply wanted you to understand that in the final analysis you can still will not to listen and wallow in a self pity of despair.

All for now. You are present to this teaching that will deepen as we progress.

Scripture: *[T]he gospel was preached even to those who are now dead, so that they might be judged according to men in regard to the body, but live according to God in regard to the spirit. 1 Peter 4: 6*

Prayer: Dear Lord, I am listening.

Response: It is at times like this that I reach you most deeply. And it is for a purpose. Be calm and listening.

The Word, and I capitalize the word, is me reaching you right now just as I reached those who were to be responsible for recording the word of God in the scripture. They did not realize what was happening to them at first. They would reflect on their experiences with Christ, how simply telling, you would say preaching, had such an effect on people. And it was not the effect that passed over once they left for another town.

Peter especially reflected on these things, that is, his life that began with Christ and the events that he experienced up until Christ's death and resurrection. And to think he thought it would end then, not that its impact was life transforming, but he had the glory of experiencing Christ during the time of the resurrection. Perhaps, we would clarify that he considered the era even more filled with power at the time after Christ ascended. Wondering if he would have to rely on his memory, Peter found that Christ in the Spirit was just as present even more so.

So this morning you are wondering the where's, why's, wherefores of your life and here you sit listening to the word as if dead. But you are not dead, overwhelmed perhaps, but not dead. And the Spirit is saying to you *Trust, listen, and all will be made clear.*

You see there is no time dimension when it comes to hearing the word. There is no space dimension either. You are as present as if you were in the field hearing Christ talk about love and compassion; you are as present as if you were at the crucifixion; you are as present as if you passed on and heard the message ringing in the chambers of an empty soul.

The message is one of joy and love, the message reminds you over and over again that you alone cannot construct the sense of hope, purpose, joy, love, compassion that you desire without returning over and over again to the source.

All for now. Watch the unfolding that occurs today in all aspects of your life.

#9

Scripture: *Cast all your anxiety on Him because he cares for you. 1 Peter 5:7*

Prayer: I feel anxious today. Let me throw all that anxiety upon you. Give me the will and the confidence to do so.

Response: Mornings like this are so special. You are reminded of the need to let go. You are dropping out of the plane and awaiting your parachute to open. It is in that period that you are and it is a time of great growth for you. You are in a life-changing period. The gears are changing down, or should I say shifting. You are making a turn to the left and in the turning radius all is not familiar to you. You must trust and follow the instructions that you have already received and will continue to receive.

It is in the chopping of wood and drawing of water, that is, the mundane tasks, that cover you so, that you discover the inner observer who rises so far above the mundane.

Do not be hard on yourself. All is on schedule.

#10

Scripture: *And the God of all grace, who called you to his eternal glory in Christ, after you have suffered a little while, will himself restore you and make you strong. Firm and steadfast. To him be the power forever and ever, Amen. 1Peter 5:10-11*

Prayer: Lord, I don't feel so strong today. My anxiety about finances, my aloneness, affect me this gray morning. Please give me your guidance.

Response: You have a direct line to me. You are secure. In the stormiest sea I have secured your craft with the most secure line. You seem to be jolting up and down but that is only because I am holding this line firm against the storm sea that seeks to drive you out beyond the buoys.

You are to be kept warm and dry though the rain will sweep across your face and hands. Oh, you are set to comprehend how secure you are, and not to remain stationary, frozen in fright of the storm, but to engage the elements of life as you do – with your children, grandchildren, and those you love. It is important as you seek that special way to further my word and the hearing of that word in your poetry and writing.

Do you think that I would not send a legion of angels to be at your side to advance your mission? Do not doubt they are at your side. And your loved ones who have passed on are all in agreement that "You are the one" as anyone is who is fully committed to the Light.

I laugh at your anxiety and concern as a father confronting a son who wishes to open his present early. Yes, patience even patient endurance are those magical traits that I am testing and refining in you.

But all is not lost – Your impatience masks energy unrivaled among so many. We are simply – though the process is far from simple – harnessing that energy. Think of that quote from Teilhard about harnessing the power of love. Here is a truth – harnessing the power of love is harnessing impatience. Think of one of those huge horses pulling a wagon – the power of those horses. You are one of those horses. And the beauty and freedom is that you are driving that wagon into regions of the heart within and in your environment that I applaud and await.

#11

Scripture: *Grace and peace be yours in abundance through the knowledge of God and of Jesus our Lord. 2 Peter 1:2*

Prayer: Winds gusting to fifty miles-per-hour, rain in sheets, losing power a couple of times, no school. Lord, grant me the grace and peace that Peter blesses us with. Please give me guidance this morning.

Response: Let me talk about grace and peace. First grace. Grace is that unsolicited touch that you felt and remember first when you were nine years old and the touches that occur constantly it seems on your road. You have always been "touched" by the story of the disciples on the road to Emmaus. Grace is what Emmaus is all about. Two disciples leaving Jerusalem, walking briskly, trying to put as much distance between the sad events and themselves, wrestling with their doubt and disappointment, on a journey with a destination only to discover at the deepest level that there is no destination.

Grace is the "chance" encounter with the resurrected Lord. Understand there are no chance encounters. Grace is that gift of insight, expression of love, gift of the spirit that you receive on a daily basis and too often dismiss as the passage of life. Instead of the passage, think of it as the essence of life.

Grace is all around you and within you. It is the quiet in the next room of your son reading, your dog at your feet, the storm subsiding, the light emerging outside and within you. Grace is the filament, like gauze, that protects you. You cannot wander anywhere without this filament wrapped around you like the Saudi cloak you don.

Peace. Oh there is a word for you to consider. Peace is harmony of the spirit. Peace reigns supreme within even though outside is tumultuous – in chaos. Peace is kind of a disconnecting from what would ordinarily disturb you. Even those who most love you can interfere with your peace and they do not even realize it. That is why you are responsible for receiving the gift and allowing it to work its purpose in you.

Why is this so important? Peace, I mean. Peace is your confirmation and affirmation that you have accepted the gifts and you show your acceptance by allowing them to work their magic within you. Peace is your thank-you in praise. And for those observing peaceful action it is a stunning reversal as to what the world expects. At court the other day you witnessed the peace of a spirit in harmony and those present sense what it means to be peaceful.

So peace and grace shower on you from me and your thank-you is measured as you calmly accept the rain and wind in praise, and I mean the rain and wind in your life.

#12

Scripture: *His divine power has given us everything we need for life and godliness through the knowledge of him who called us by his own glory and goodness. 2 Peter 1:2*

Prayer: Lord, this gray, cool, cloudy morning, I feel expectant. It's a strange feeling for me because I am unaware of what you intend and I don't see a whole lot of control over my destiny. Destiny seems to be such a loaded word and portends a future so far removed from this present moment. Lord, please guide me today with your wisdom and please direct my feet and in doing so the feet of my son and those I love.

Response: If you can stay present you will look back in a present time of the fashioning, refining, defining that is taking place within you. All of what concerns you is like the wrapper of a candy bar that blows off in the wind, the skin left in the darkness as you emerge in the Light, the brightness that affects you as you awake from a long slumber. Yes, some will hardly recognize you when the process is complete and there are those who will wonder why it took so long for you to emerge free of all the constraints of what he should *do* with his life, forgetting for themselves as well as for you the critical query what he and they should *be* with or in their lives.

The steps for you are becoming clearer yet you are hesitant because the path is unfamiliar. You have been on unfamiliar paths before but this one is dramatic because this path is taking you home. To help, please repeat a mantra when you are befuddled and questioning *I am going home.* Enough of wandering and you all must wander to gather the experience and to expand your awareness, but now it is your consciousness that is being called to rise. Like an eaglet you have been led to the edge of the cliff and it is time to leap off the cliff and fly even soar. It will be good for you to take your son to North Carolina to view the hang gliders off the tall sand dune, or return to Sedona and capture or recapture the feeling as you stood above the red rock.

You are going home and let me assure you there is no rush. You are not leaving soon. You are in that beautiful phase of life and you have been granted this experience where you are called to speak with clarity about this journey and the preparation required. Not everyone is so called, but you are and in the silence of your soul that call is quite clear to you.

One thing I should mention about such an important journey, it begins with one step. The one step tells me that you are willing, that you have faith, that you are brave and courageous, that you are patient and can endure in adversity, that you are loving and generous, that you are committed, and that you are a little mad – I want to emphasize that the world opinion that sizes life down to instant gratification will think you mad but it is that madness that overcomes the doubt.

22

So for today, and by now you realize that you are on a daily program, try to pull some time away from your hectic life to reflect. I bless you even anoint you today. Feel my touch, experience the soul expansiveness of my love.

#13

Scripture: *[Jesus'] divine power has given us everything we need for life and godliness through our knowledge of him who called us by his own glory and goodness. Through these he has given us his very great and precious promises, so that through them you may participate in the divine nature and escape the corruption in the world caused by evil desires. 2 Peter1:3-4*

Prayer: My attention was caught by *you may participate in the divine nature.* It seems that we have a condition to meet – *through our knowledge of him.* Please enlighten me as I move forward into another day – one that seems to be a harbinger of sunlight following the storm of the last days.

Response: You are seizing on the right phrases for where you are in your life. Your real question is related to participating in the divine nature. What does that mean, you ponder?

Divine nature, what you become conscious of in a halting fashion, is hidden in the pause you experience looking at a thick brush of dwarf pine trees, a recollection of a run along a solitary path, quiet that almost thunders, a touch that needs no return. What I have just described are the finger events that point your attention to the divine and in doing so you are pulled in a rush, even if only momentary in a temporal sense that is actually eternal.

Divine nature and participating fully in divine nature knows no time or space. The ego's concerns of what would I do there is absurd because there is no "doing" or "there." There is no "will my best friend be there to share the experience" because there is only Now and as I just said there is no there.

Participating in divine nature is the ultimate test of faith because all else, those foundations upon which you build your life are absent. The ultimate act of faith is that you are willing, you will, to know me at the risk that there is no one else. All the mind's efforts to make sense out of this in a linear sense are subject to failure. A hint of the state is your son's comment to you in church that Mom was busy else she would be here to tell him that she loved him.

Participating in divine nature can only be explained in allegories. You put on a mantle of gold and fire and hear the resounding hymn of praise and joy that sounds like claps of thunder on a day when the sky is clear and the sun golden. Participating in the divine nature is union to consider the most essential level and you must try to understand that there are no levels.

And now here is something to puzzle you even more. To participate in the divine nature – one has the potential of not participating at all or choosing to participate sufficiently. And this is what you are to ponder: once you participate in the divine nature you are free, you remain free to elect otherwise. That is why it is so important in this life for you to become absorbed in the divine light so that you enter the next phase totally imbued with the light that is unceasing.

So much have you received today. Do not be troubled but absorb my message as you are able, as you grow to understand.

Scripture: *We did not follow cleverly invented stories when we told you about the power and coming of our Lord Jesus Christ, but we were eyewitnesses of his majesty. For he received honor and glory from God the Father when the voice came to him from the Majestic Glory, saying, "This is my Son, whom I love; with him I am well pleased." We ourselves heard this voice that came from heaven when we were with him on the sacred mountain. 2 Peter1:16-18*

Prayer: Instruct me this morning when I am so tired after getting to sleep late and wakened too early.

Response: You are hearing my voice more clearly each day. Put yourself, if you can this morning, into the scene where Peter with all his flaws is in the company of the disciples, actually James and John, when they accompany Jesus to the mountaintop and see Jesus conferring with Moses and Elijah. How unworthy he felt to witness and observe the happenings; and to break the solemnity he suggests building three tabernacles for each. And overcoming them is that cloud, deep, dark thick cloud, almost like a storm cloud or a fog hinting of rain. Then it lightens and this voice anointing Jesus. In a real sense Peter was anointed in that moment with all his failings and frailties. So much lay before him.

So this morning, your willingness to stand before me in your weariness, fragility, anxiousness, confusion is a sign, or should be to you that you are anointed. Feel my warmth and comfort that I offer you this morning in the quiet of your heart. There is nothing that I would not do to bring you closer, to encourage you, to cause you to see that all your experiences, the challenges, the loneliness, the uncertainty are all designed precisely for your transformation into the Light. How will I know you, or better will others recognize you. as this transformational process goes further in enriching you?

Well, let me say that you will be marked with a patient endurance and perseverance that will astound you. Yes, I use the word *astound* to impress upon you the transformation in process. You will become single-focused in knowing me at a level so deep that you will have to choose your words carefully so that others will come to this truth. You will move off the cross road where you now stand and the direction you choose will astound you. I use that word again, for its clarity and simplicity; your relationship in love will know no bounds in revealing a soul dimension that is every bit as astounding as my revelation to you – at least in the process unveiled. Your work will become clear and I will sustain you. Do you understand what I am saying? I will sustain you. You will be just as amazed as others, like Peter even, who discovered in letting go and trusting all becomes manifest.

For what purpose? That you might bring the Light of Love among you in an abundance and clarity that has been confused of late. Today, no sleep and all, you will make enormous strides in approaching your writing project. Just trust your inner voice which is my voice that embraces you at times of confusion. You are on the brink of furthering my word amongst those who thought they understood and soon will understand better, and among those who have not heard the words. Your only requirement right now is to listen quietly and with peace because it is my peace that I give you.

#15

Scripture: *And we have the word of the prophets made more certain, and you will do well to pay attention it, as to a light shining in a dark place, until the day dawns and the morning star rises in your hearts. Above all, you must understand that no prophecy of Scripture came about by the prophet's own interpretation. For prophecy never had its origin in the will of man, but men spoke from God as they were carried along by the Holy Spirit. 2 Peter1:19-21*

Prayer: Sitting with my son on the deck just before dawn and reading in the gray light and he with a chess book these words caught my attention. Can you guide me in my understanding of the dawn star and what it means to be carried along by the Holy Spirit?

Response: Let me start with the dawn star, a symbol of first light, the light of Christ. The dawn star symbolizes also return of light to a world overcome with darkness. I can tell you that a dawn star is emerging once again as the violence of this world seems so evident. The dawn star shines alone and lights the sky as the sun emerges behind it. The dawn star is the precursor as Christ was the precursor of a new dawn. Search for the dawn star when you are up before dawn. Stir that degree of anticipation and excitement. You will find that you take this into each day

Now what does it mean to be carried by the Holy Spirit? You are being carried by the Holy Spirit, so ask yourself what does it mean to you, how do you feel about it? Clearly, I sense your excitement holding on and I also feel or sense your anxiety because you don't want to fall off the wings of the Spirit.

Carried along means that you can sit as you are now and hear me so distinctly as if I am sitting before you and instructing or mentoring you – and I am. In addition to the knowledge and understanding that you are receiving, I am also nudging you to a path of opportunity that will fulfill your passion and your meaning. Not all are so favored because they often times do not take the time to listen so intently. There is a way that consciousness will be raised among so many once a critical mass of listeners gathers to hear my word.

If there is one charge I would give you today is to listen, listen deeply and attentively, listen with ease free of anxiety. It is so simple. Listen.

#16

Scripture: *You ought to live holy and godly lives as you look forward to the day of God and speed its coming. 2 Peter 3:11-12*

Prayer: It seems that we have something to do with or at least influence the coming. Can you provide me what I can understand today?

Reponse: You are correct in detecting Peter's hint of your influence in bringing in the future that you envision. Interesting is it not, that your writing of visualizing a future is supported by this line? Prayer, deep generous prayer is a redirection of one's attention for a future that transforms a present.

This does not mean as you know living in the future or neglecting the present. First you must realize that time considerations do not exist except in your dimension. By looking forward you are really looking within and there you connect with the divine murmuring, if I can say, that sings a melody that can be audible in each moment.

So indeed you can hasten the advent of peace in our world, you can experience peace in regions of the world that have only known war and famine, rape and pillage. It requires you to look forward which is another way of visualizing a greater peace that of course begins where you started the visualization that is within.

So begin each day with a visualization – or visualizations – and carries through each day until you close your eyes in the evening; you will find that you are hastening the coming of the Lord in his majesty which is love, peace, compassion, and generous spirit. Visualize diligently in your prayers, writings, actions and you will contribute to that hastening that all wish for but lacking confidence do little to hasten.

You see, and this might be difficult for you to understand, there is no prescribed answer to what is being brought forth. You are responsible for hastening the coming with your pure and intent desires.

Scripture: *We proclaim to you what we have seen and heard, so that you also may have fellowship with us. And our fellowship is with the Father and with his Son, Jesus Christ.* 1 John 1:3

Prayer: Lord, do you see my weariness?

Response: Yes, and that is a primary reason for you to seek, pursue, enrich your fellowship with me, and my grace is causing your soul to break up and to see that union and fellowship.

I see your tears and your fatigue. How you desire to make things right, to be right in your love, and I know you feel the pressure of time. The time that you feel though is the past. Do you, can you see this it is the past and haunts you – were you a good father, what should you have done differently, and on it goes.

You could fill up a page and more with such regrets and I ask you simply to be in fellowship with me as you now are in fellowship with those you love and who love you.

Focus today on your friendship with me. I am the one you want to be with when there is a crisis and when there is much joy to share. See me present in your every moment of the day, and you will experience a day that shimmers light like a kaleidoscope.

And your prayer must be for those who are close and far to feel my presence as you do. My presence in your life is the fellowship I offer and which John is telling you this morning.

And yes you are hearing me when I ask you to share these readings with others.

Scripture: *This is the message we have heard from him and declare to you: God is light, in him there is no darkness at all. 1 John 1:5*

Prayer: As I sat on the deck below black clouds in the dark and in a stiff breeze, I heard, "I have much to tell you." So here I am at my desk.

Response: Thank you. Yes, I have much to tell you. This is a day of darkness in that it reminds, is the anniversary of the destruction in New York, Washington, and Pennsylvania. This day represents a symbol of darkness. The screams of agony still reverberate. It is important for you to comprehend the darkness and the darkness that you are in this moment. St. John talked and wrote of the dark night of the soul. This is that same darkness.

It is in the darkness that you see me. How? I am closest to you at such times. I am your silent companion. I am walking alongside you on the way to Emmaus before you recognize that you have a companion. And I am ensuring – even if it requires bumping you to the left or right without you feeling my touch – that you are on the path that leads to the light. You are in a tunnel surrounded by my light.

In the darkness your hearing is more attuned and you hear me clearly though you must make the effort to halt your steps. I am here. There is no region of your world that I am not present and my spirit washes over all.

Understand that you can shed the darkness in an instant. You can fling it off as a cloak when you enter a warm room. For the moment accept the cloak and watch every step you take this day. Hear me during each step. I am nudging you. Soon we will walk together and you will see me even more clearly at your side.

Let me end by saying to you in truth, *You are my friend and I am sustaining you. Be at peace today.*

#19

Scripture: *He is the atoning sacrifice for our sins, and not only for ours but also for the sins of the whole world. 1 John 2:2*

Prayer: Lord, I am listening this early morning.

Response: What I am instructing you on today is that Christ came for all, and all even if they do not realize it, are not conscious of the event, even oppose the salvation. In no way does it diminish that Christ came for the whole world though the world is filled with a clash of cultures and beliefs.

How with these words could you be so insular in your beliefs? What I mean is that indeed you are conscious of Christ's intent, mission, and presence. Without deciphering the plan, why do you become anxious about those who have not embraced the word? I need those who are in the world and like salt to season the bland practices that have sustained so many. And I am not saying this to suggest that Christian ritual is the answer. Far from it, I am saying this so that you adopt an outward glance of compassion and love and not one of self satisfaction that you have been chosen.

There is a certain rhythm in witnessing. Above all it requires compassion, love, trust, and no time schedule. True witnessing is an investment of time in trust – investment of time in trust. And this investment can be made with those who are of the Christian faith, followers of the word of Christ as well as before those who violently oppose those who represent Christ's word. Realize that if you are successful in getting beyond the barrier of people who represent Christ you will be surprised as to how receptive are those that are most antagonistic to his word.

Well, I will close today, this morning. See the light that is emerging in the morning sky and feel that same light within.

#20

Scripture: *Yet I am writing you a new command; its truth is seen in him and you, because the darkness is passing and the true light is already shining. 1 John 2:8*

Prayer: I am here, Lord. Enlighten me.

Response: The true light is already shining within you. Your only requirement is to use its beacon on your path. When you were young you thought your vision was perfect and you could negotiate without aid; however, now you see that you were blind. Years ago I came to you in a vision of an old man walking along a cavern holding a torch above so you could find your way walking behind. Let me tell you now that that image was in fact your observer, the deepest interior self, holding the torch as you negotiated your way. And there is nothing to fear in this cavern because you are journeying home. So be filled with expectation and joy.

The darkness is passing and you must hasten its passing as you see the darkness fading to another day outside your window. The easing of the darkness is not calamitous but gradual and steady, like the water receding after a wave has struck. Keep the quiet that precedes the rising of the dawn as the state of your blossoming dawn within.

You see there is nothing to worry or to be concerned about. All will be provided. Be at peace today. See your day unfold each minute, beginning now in the calm you experience and the eagerness as you journey down the cavern holding aloft the torch. See the intricate designs that abound along the rough hewn texture of the stone. Consider who is responsible for creating this walkway and you will sing praise. Listen to me today. I will communicate with you. Listen carefully.

Scripture: *As for you, the anointing you received from him remains in you, and you do not need anyone to teach you. 1 John 2:27*

Prayer: Anointing – please help me to understand.

Response: Anointing is the touch of the Holy Spirit that you were conscious of long before the ceremony at your childhood church. The anointing is transformative. Once received you cannot return to a time of unknowing. Obviously that does not mean that you cannot will to be different, but you can do what is not in accord with the deeper consciousness revealed to you.

It is with renewed vigor that your anointing is refreshed just as if you were touched in this moment. And in a real sense you are touched in this moment. Your deeper, even new consciousness, is allowing you to see that the passing of the old and the renewal that is taking place within you. Your lingering doubt and concern is only residue that is being peeled from a wooden frame house before a new coat of primer is added and several coats of paint. Your house is perched on a rocky knoll overlooking the sea that batters it with its fury, but nothing can diminish it s luster and the beacon it serves for those seeking shelter.

See that you need refuge as well. The dark one is ranging across the knoll trying to devise a strategy that will allow it entry into your clean well-lighted place. You are or would be a great prize for his sinister desire.

It is a joy to see how resolute you are and to see your strengthening in prayer. As you have been told you are in an especially strong place to pray powerfully.

For today consider throughout the day the following: world peace and the easing of the violence that has shaped recent events, at least through the emergence of the New Millennium; for those throughout the world with whom you have connected over the years; for those you consider friends, and of course family. I will lead you though the thicket that seeks to ensnare you. Be calm and vigilant, and pray, pray.

Prayer is the shout that I hear at all hours and I am your boon companion that will never, I repeat, never fail you.

Feel this quiet of the rising dawn, hear the silence in your soul; unchanging is my love for you and I will reveal all mysteries to you and provide you answers to your deepest longings. Be still in my love.

Scripture: *And now, my children, continue in him, so that when he appears we may be confident and unashamed before him at his coming. 1 John 1:28*

Prayer: *Continue in him* please help me to understand a deeper level to these words.

Response: *Continue* means for you each day to resume your journey just like today. All of the scattered pieces of yesterday are already fluttering into the atmosphere and exist no longer except if you will to reassemble them in your mind so that you are haunted by them.

Continue is to take up each day at a time, like knitting an endless prayer shawl or a large *killim*[1] that will hang on the wall after you pass on. You see it will not be ready to be hung until you leave the scene. And I must say that it is taking on a special beauty as you continue your weaving.

And realize that *continue* does not mean perfection in your eyes. I say this because those imperfections and those stains of regret weave so beautifully into the fabric of silk that I treasure you.

You have used the word authenticity before. *Continue* also denotes for me authenticity where you come to recognize yourself and your union with me and all your actions, thoughts, and prayers reflect that.

Authenticity becomes more and more your traveling companion and I say this not as a metaphor because authenticity is present only in your inner companion who seeks to have a voice that is more and more clear to you. So continue and realize that your spouse at the point of her passing was supremely authentic in her love especially for you.

That's all for today.

---

[1] A rug weaved in the mountains of southern Poland.

Scripture: *Dear children, let us not love with words or tongue, but with actions and in truth. This then is how we know we belong to the truth, and how we set our hearts at rest in his presence whenever our hearts condemn us. For God is greater than our hearts, and he knows everything.* 1 John 3:18-20

Prayer: Lord, *set our hearts at rest in his presence,* help me to understand these words but more importantly experience that rest.

Response: Your heart is more settled than you realize. It only takes you to look above the clutter on your desk to see the rest in my presence that you experience. You talked last night on the phone how you felt a strange feeling of being in a space that you are no longer concerned about your own satisfaction. That is your indication, I know it already, that you have risen above and actually into a new consciousness.

That is not to say that you are not pulled back into the world so to speak, but you are like a bird that is trying its wings, like a young aviator just reaching into the sky. It takes time and effort and endurance, and patience, and trust to fly upward. It is an effort that causes fear because you are leaving what you know which incidentally is or has an illusion of permanence.

In this region of the heart separation is unknown, union is everything – union with me, those souls with which you seek union and reunion, and others unknown to you as of now but who await union with you.

There will be pulls back to earth. You are still just learning to fly but nourish the sense and exhilaration of flight. I must say what you know already in the depth of your being, the vow you have taken resounds in heaven.

That is all today.

Scripture: *No one have ever seen God, but if we love one another, God lives in us and his love is made complete in us. 1 John 4:12*

Prayer: I am having trouble with the historical perspective. John seems to suggest that love only came into the world with Jesus.

Response: Don't put your professor hat on. Instead remain in the present moment. Realize that there is no time dimension in my realm. Understand that you are in a realm that such divisions exist. One of union encompassing even your realm is and that is the realm of I AM. *So love is from me.* What occurred in the time of Christ affected in linear time what had proceeded and what is to come. It is as if you are viewing a film and all around you, up, below, left, and right and round, time is flowing in a present that here on earth you cannot comprehend.

So viewing love from the film, originating love began then for all creation. The troubling aspect in reading those words of John is how to understand the killing that is being committed in the name of the *Intifada*. Here it is best that you reach no definitive conclusions and suspend judgment. Allow through your prayers the flow of time emanating from the Spirit to flow over your earth on the wings of the spirit, knowing that your prayers speed the process.

It is as if your prayers sweep the dark into the light to be seared in the fire of love.

Scripture: *This is the one who came by water and blood – Jesus Christ. He did not come by water only, but by water and blood. And it is the Spirit who testifies, because the Spirit is the truth. For there are three that testify: the Spirit, the water and the blood; and the three are in agreement. 1 John 5:6-8*

Prayer: Lord, this scripture is difficult to understand. Can you provide me some insight into the underlining truth?

Response: Take the main symbols or references: Jesus Christ who walked and walks the earth with a message of love that reaches all ages, past, present and to come; there is water that offers cleansing and invites a depth that is without end; there is blood – the life source it represents and also the suffering physical and mental; and there is the Spirit that reaches all in the wind that glances over all creation.

There is no need, in fact, I tell you to avoid it, to assign precise definitions in order to create a cosmology that is fixed. There is nothing fixed about what I am telling you.

What I mean is that Jesus <u>moved</u> about you and still does in your heart. He was not a guru who sat in a cave awaiting you to come to him. He was and is in your midst.

Water <u>flows</u>. I am not talking about a lifeless, stagnant pond, trapped from flowing down into the ocean. See water at that glacier stream of which you drank high in the Himalayas.

Blood as a life force <u>flows</u> eternally. Again I am not referring to a pool of blood lying on a field of battle, but the blood flowing in your veins in adoration at dawn on the beach.

The Spirit is all you experience on a gusty day as you feel that spirit <u>moving across</u> and through you, all movement, all in dance within and external to you.
So see my love to you in movement and dance even when you are quiet and reflective. You have a powerful day awaiting you. So much to experience. So much to challenge. You are at the edge of a cliff overlooking the ocean and you are about to take off in the breeze, hang gliding above the surf. Strap yourself tight. You are in for the ride of your life and love.

Scripture: *[T]he master of the banquet tasted the water that had been turned into wine. "Everyone brings out the choice wine first and then the cheaper wine after the guests have had too much to drink; but you have saved the best till now.* John 2:9-10

Prayer: Please bring me deeper meaning to this familiar text.

Response: The wedding feast is clothed in so much symbolism, contains so much meaning, so much of it hidden for most. See how the event reflects Jesus' participation in life, not merely as the bachelor son accompanying his widowed mother. No, Jesus was a full participant where he is the source, note the word, is the source of celebration. Instead of the event falling flat Jesus creates an atmosphere and a cause for celebration in reinvigorating the feast.

Just as he reinvigorates your life, gives you cause to celebrate all aspects of your life. He is the capstone that attracts the attention of those around you. And of you they will say indeed he led a worthy life, indeed he conveyed the word, the word of love, the word of forgiveness, the word of compassion, the word of generosity, the word of faith, the word of trust, the word of patience -- for you patient endurance. Do you see now how important this feast of Canna is?

And here is the wine and the water mixing in a divine alchemy, and the participants in this feast of love consume it. There is much to contemplate to extract the rich meaning much as you extract the fine wine from the grapes. Begin with all of the symbols and you can begin with each noun.

Scripture: *Do not let your hearts be troubled. Trust in God, trust also in me. In my Father's house are many rooms; if it were not so, I would have told you, I am going there to prepare a place for you. And if I go and prepare a place for you, I will come back and take you to be with me that you also may be where I am. You know the way to the place where I am going. John 14:2*

Prayer: Lord, sometimes I wonder if I know the way to the place where you are going.

Response: This reading is often brushed over because it seems so simple. There is this mansion sitting on a hill and if you act properly I will reserve a room for you there. However, it is difficult for you to admit that you really do know the way to the place where I and you are going.

Emphasize, or put emphasis on going and do not try to create mental images of the place on the hill. It is in the going that you find me, just as when we walked together towards Emmasus. It is in the journeying that you dance in faith and love. The journey signifies the action in faith. The journey is during which you demonstrate courage and patience because you have no idea of the length of the journey. In fact once you accept this journey fully, you will realize that the journey never ends. To be static is to perish. Therefore, sing praise that you are making your way to me.

Scripture: *Even in laughter the heart may ache, and joy may end in grief. Proverbs 14:13*

Prayer: I don't think I was aware of this truth until after I experienced the loss of my spouse. At least I was not as acutely aware of this wisdom as I am now. Please help me to understand the why.

Response: The why as you say is sometimes missed though you must understand that for the most part the lessons in all of life are quite clear when you go into your center and listen quietly.

How deep and genuine is laughter that erupts as a lonely cry in deep sadness. It is the depth of that kind of laughter that brings you into union with others in whatever state they are. The laughter acknowledges your faith, even expectation, that as the sun falls in the evening it will rise again in the morning.

This truth also encourages you to celebrate joy knowing deep down that as in the setting sun joy will give way in time to grief. Always please appreciate that as in the taste of death there is nothing permanent in this grief that of course gives way to the eternal joy of resurrection, the reunion in full consciousness with me.

Scripture: *But we see Jesus, who was made a little lower than the angels, now crowned with glory and honor because he suffered death, so that by the grace of God he might taste death for everyone. Hebrews 2:9*

Prayer: Here is that use of the word *taste* with death. Help me to probe further its mystery.

Response: I realize that it is so difficult to even imagine what death is all about. Part of your confusion and inability is due to the victory of the cross. And I don't mean just an historical event of the resurrection that is described in scripture. I mean the affect that the resurrection has on all people. It is a mystery for you how a monkey in one area of the globe takes up a new habit or approach to its life and then monkeys separated by oceans takes up the same approach simultaneously.

That is the mystery for you in considering why death has lost its sting and if it wasn't your attachment to the physical dimension there would be even less of a disturbance.

So accept because it is true that the resurrection affected you all at the deepest level. At the deepest level you know, and I repeat the word know, that death is a doorway and not the end as peoples wrestled prior to Jesus walking the earth, dying, and then rising from the dead.

This is not to say that prior to Christ death was any more threatening, but it was because the guide had not yet appeared. There were hints of the taste of death and its impermanence prior – through the prophets, the wisdom literature, and the activities of those who sought the openings to the other side. But with Christ you have assurance, someone, and indeed God-man who came back in the resurrection to tell you the good news. And his was not a death that could be questioned as having occurred, if it had occurred in bed at an old age. Now this was a violent death taking place in the spring of his life, which he could have even avoided had he fled the scene when he realized that the path to Golgotha was clear.

It was in that clarity that his resolve was steeled. And there too is the lesson for you. Your life and everyone around you on this earth is determined, is finite. Indeed you could attempt escape by engaging in an experiment to prolong if not to preserve your mortal body, you could escape to a desert island to pace yourself to prolong whatever you have; but no, you are determined to demonstrate and experience the same resolve that your model, Christ, did. And realize without carrying any banner, he is the model for all people and whether they realize it or not his sacrifice has affected them all. Yes, there would not be the violent *jihad* without the assurance that Christ brought back that he has overcome death for all of you.

This lesson this morning before dawn is filled with insights and truths. Read it over several times today. And realize even more deeply that you will only taste death because death has been conquered and Jesus came back for the sole purpose of witnessing this truth for all eternity.

Scripture: *After six days Jesus took with him Peter, James, and John, the brother of James, and led them up a high mountain by themselves. There he was transfigured before them. His face shone like the sun, and his clothes became as white as the light. Mathew 17:1-2*

Prayer: Lord, last night the dream of entering the old city of Warsaw through "Mathew's" gate, and how I had to apply and my Polish was so rusty. The lady was so appreciative and acknowledging of my ability in the language, and I can still hear the applause in my ears though it embarrassed me. Please shed some light on this dream and the random selection of Mathew.

Response: There are many gates to me. Mathew is one. In that dream I am influencing you to ponder the transfiguration -- simply that. Imagine you are there with my companions and I move off to the side. The wind is blowing on the height, and suddenly the wind pauses, and the cloud covers the sun, and in that moment the face of Jesus shines with the brilliance of the full sun and his clothes like light itself.

In an instant you are transported to another realm where the sensible no longer is sensible. You will notice that in that instant you are transported from all your anxieties to the deepest region of your soul and heart where only eternity and the present moment exist. It is here I want you to spend time especially when you become anxious.

Becoming anxious is like boredom, it is a reminder of the need for you to do something about the boredom as you advised your children. Anxiousness is similar, you must do something about the anxiousness and what I am asking you to do is to return to the mountaintop and breathe in the scene of what you call the transfiguration. As I said in an instant you are taken within and just as quickly realize even with limited consciousness that you are involved in so much more than what appears before you in your life.

The transfiguration is my promise to you that your work and (I mean your fulfillment of your mission) will be transfigured and made holy. Now how is that for a promise? You have nothing, I repeat nothing, about which to fret. Be diligent and honorable in your work and conduct and all will be accomplished for my greater glory. Notice I did not say for your greater glory. That is why you will continue to suffer, not within, but as others view your travail, but inside you will be glorious in your love.

See my transfiguration in your works today.

CHAPTER TWO – REVELATION

No longer am I limited to reading scripture as an historical document, but rather a daily source of soul nourishment meant especially for me in this very moment. I have been given understanding by the anointed power of the Holy Spirit.

The selected scriptural text invariably touches me deeply. It is a personal revelation to me and its affects upon me in no way limits it's possible different impact upon a second, third, or fourth reader reflecting upon the same words, at the same moment in time though many miles distant.

And so, I select a verse with this confidence and purpose as if I am opening an envelope containing a treasured message from a loved one – and indeed I am. Only my loved one is never distant.

Scripture: *Do not be anxious about anything, but in everything, by prayer and petition, with thanksgiving present your requests to God. And the peace of God which transcends all understanding will guard your hearts and your minds in Christ Jesus. Philippians 4:6-7*

Prayer: Well, here I am this morning at seven a.m. after taking my son and his friend to the Eastern Shore for a Halloween celebration.

Response: Yes, I see your heart. Yes, I want you to reveal to me your innermost feelings and presence for the purpose of you exhuming all that you cover in shame and embarrassment. You know my vision and my vision for you. Each day you become more infused with my Light. Your test amidst all your frustration – see how important it is to remain focused – your test is trust. I am guiding you around a narrow ledge in the trek to a summit. You understand the danger and you keep moving upward cautiously. The beauty of this climb is that each step is taken in the moment and under my protection. Your choice of taking the trail upward that leads to the right was your choice, but as I have said there are many paths to me. Yours is no more perilous than another's, each is perilous and no less lofty. What I am saying is that there is no comparison among you. I am with each of you as you traverse the mountain to the summit.

Your fear is based on the unknown. You have not been on this stretch of the moment previously, though you have been on the mountain a life time preparing for this climb. You could have taken a path more familiar. This applies to your work. You have chosen to strike out on a new path that seems would take you higher and you are correct. The path of espionage and security looked like it would climb equally high on the left but surely leads to a blind spot from which further ascent is not possible.

Yes, this portion of your climb is new and catches you with its breathlessness. You are questioning your capacity to climb higher but see the assistance that I have marshaled for you. At this higher altitude, each detail related to the climb must be examined carefully. each detail. So instead of allowing yourself to fret, take each item that haunts you will anxiety and complete your preparation.

One reason to carry on and in a timely manner is that your message needs to reach others around you and those afar. You are not engaged in this climb for yourself. You are a porter carrying my message of love to the summit where it can be viewed by so many more. You see the height that you climb is paradoxically the depth you will reach in the souls of those hearing you.

You have wondered, am I the one, and yes you are as your ancestors and those who have preceded you proclaim. You realize that this is not an ego matter but one of a seriousness that cannot wait for you to ponder whether you are doing the right thing or not. Such deliberations are ego motivated and serve to stall your climb. So let's say for today, as if it was the last day of your life, and it isn't, everything you are is a contribution to your ascent as my beloved porter.

Scripture: *Today, if you hear his voice, do not harden your hearts . . ." Hebrews 3:7 & Psalm 95; But encourage one another daily, as long as it is called Today so that none of you may be hardened by sin's deceitfulness. Hebrews 3:13*

Prayer: Speak to me this morning of the heart.

Response: You have observed that these last four years have broken open your heart. Simply stated, breaking open or having broken open your heart serves to ensure that it is not hardened or can be made hard. Rejoice in your situation and pity those less fortunate.

Breaking open the heart means allowing space for it to be filled and overflowing with my love which requires no earthly vessel. Breaking open releases you to the pause that you experience now in prayer and throughout the day. The heart can be the last vestige of control, of grasping, holding on, and it can become that launching pad to swirl without the boundaries of time and space in my love. You have chosen or I should say are choosing the latter.

Breaking open the heart also allows you to make instant connection to those of love around you. It is as if the heart in another recognizes your state and longs for such freedom. A heart so broken is free. Let me say that again, a heart so broken is free.

So enjoy your freedom, catch its flight that exceeds air miles to Afghanistan. A heart broken has shed itself of the weight that has encumbered it. A heart broken apart is expansive.

So today, and remember that today is used, honor the freedom that you or should I say are.

Scripture: *Therefore, God again set a certain day, calling it Today, when a long time later he spoke through David, as was said before: "Today, if you hear his voice, do not harden your hearts."* Hebrews 4:7-8

Prayer: This thought repeats itself. Please give me more to digest.

Response: Today is all encompassing. I encourage you to shed your regret of the past and feel today in all its glory and potentiality. Realize as I have told you constantly and consistently, you bring out the potentiality. You bring into actuality the dreams that you nourish. It is you who will spread your insights on grieving, about peace, about acceptance, and in the process about faith in my word to all of you.

Sometime, like now, you bemoan your solitude and wish for a companion. That is coming now also because you are drawing the future to you. Stay focused on today and the riches of spirit you will inherit. Yes, the Spirit like a breeze off the sea reaches you.

And it is so important for you to pray. Pray for all the parties to the violence throughout the world. Pray for the victims in Darfur, in Africa generally where the sea of mankind was nourished and where it blossomed into life, in the Middle East where the Word first appeared apart from the mesmerizing influence of creation on men earlier, in Central and South Asia where deep communion with the Creator and God flourished in holy books of literature, in the States where greed has replaced awe of the plenty of the land and the richness of its people, and in the Far East where Confucius held sway in bring people to a deeper level of consciousness. Go through the panoply of cultures each day, not completely, but dwell on the trouble spots. Use the newspaper to key in your prayers.

Also a word about pondering – especially pondering your future – it is there that you get in trouble so to speak. Pondering often draws you into the future. When you follow your bliss you are following your legend[2], what I have sought for you to be, though I did not determine it. Pursue your calling; ask for help and you have it in that instant. Why? Because asking for help to fulfill your mission is what is called grace. Sometimes grace is related to performing a task, mission, sometimes grace is to embolden you, sometimes to comfort you. At this time in your life, all of the above are being applied to you because they are all integrated.

Please relax and listen.

---

[2] See Pablo Coehlho's <u>Alchemist</u> for an understanding of one's legend.

Scripture: *For the word of God is living and active. Sharper than any double edged sword, it penetrates to even dividing soul and spirit, joints and marrow, it judges thoughts and attitudes of the heart. Nothing in all of creation is hidden from God's sight. Everything is uncovered and laid bare before the yes of him to whom we must give account. Hebrews 4:12-13*

Prayer: Please give me more insight on the word as living and active.

Response: Right this moment before the rising of the sun, I am reaching you as I have over the centuries. You are in fine company with the solitary monks in their cells awakening to the Word, with those for whom only a fleeting glance is allowed them as they sit poised on a battle front, and with the quiet widow reflecting on her life.

Yes, my word penetrates to the quick. You hear the words as if for the first time even if you just heard them at a service. There is a freshness to my words, reserved for the direct access they hold, notice I did not say held, to Divine Presence. With those words to ride as it were streaming thermal breezes into my presence where the words resound without end in a golden amphitheater of a cathedral.

So the words are your nourishment and there is no finer food for the soul. They prove to be the comfort for you when the seeming unending responsibilities burden you; they are that quiet place alongside a stream to sit and rest in my presence, rest of the soul. Today you will hear my voice and in hearing you will find the rest and peace I promise.

Scripture: *Therefore, since we have a great high priest who has gone through the heavens, Jesus the Son of God, let us hold firmly to the faith we profess. For we do not have a high priest who is unable to sympathize with our weaknesses, but we have one who has been tempted in every way, just as we are – yet was without sin. Let us then approach the throne of grace with confidence, so that we may receive mercy and find grace to help us in our time of need. Hebrews 4:14-16*

Prayer: I have doubt this morning. Am I really to believe that Jesus "went through the heavens?" Help me to approach the throne of grace with confidence, because surely I need grace to help me in my time of need.

Response: Be calm this morning. You are seeking to solve the puzzle of life in an instant. And yet, you don't realize that there is no puzzle; there is no defined solution. You, each day, are contributing to the texture of your life and journey. Not only is my relationship – even the word is limiting – with the Father and Spirit a mystery, so too is your life in relationship with what you experience and are to experience.

I know that you wonder, almost out of loyalty, whether your return to the center was right given your appreciation of other paths.

I am going to be quite clear, even blunt with you. Your doubt this morning is the direct result of the dark force that would like nothing better than see you drift off again as you did for over ten years. Tighten your cinch and move on. You have nothing to fear and the resources will be there to support you both physically and spiritually and emotionally. There is no time but now to invite the glorious grace into your heart, and invite also the support of your ancestors and light spirits who have gone on and are only too ready to support and guide you and succor you on this journey.

If you want reassurance, see the aliveness of your son and his excitement on the athletic field, at school, and with you. There is your beacon of favor.

In your encounters, simply be honest and giving. To the extent that you can, dismiss the thought of self.

Scripture: *Land that drinks in the rain often falling on it and produces a crop useful to those for whom it is farmed receives the blessing of God. Hebrews 6:7*

Prayer: Lord, help me to see the deeper meaning of this verse.

Response: You see more in an instant than many reading the same verse. This is not meant to endow you with any privilege but rather to point out to you that rain has taken on a deeper meaning for you. Rain represents what others would describe as suffering and you now are beginning to perceive the blessing that resides and is represented by the rain in your life.

And I mean the rain that howls through your bones it seems as if somehow the rain has penetrated to your very soul. I mean the rain that chills your hands and brings you to your knees in the sweep of its arc. I mean rain from which there seems to be no escape, not the lilting of a spring rain. I mean winter rain that could just as easily turn to snow.

And instead of turning away and huddling beneath an oil slick, you are learning like the land to drink in the suffering, the grief, the doubt, and the questions; like the land you are OK and even adjusting, acclimating to its flavor, temperature, and downpour.

Rain often falling on it – it seems without relief but then consider these words *produces a crop useful to those who farmed it*. The rain in your life is a special formula for you and the field you represent that spreads across the world in the many contacts that you have. A field so expansive needs a lot of rain and the thunder to produce it. So don't be surprised at what you experience. Instead focus on the crop in abundance and the blessing from me that it represents. The next time it rains consider again this reading and see your field stretching so far beyond the horizon and not at all confined to the tracks you fill each day going about your responsibilities.

Scripture: *We want each of you to show this same diligence to the very end in order to make your hope sure. We do not want you to become lazy, but imitate those who through faith and patience inherit what has been promised. Hebrews 6:11-12*

Prayer: Help me this day as I think of all the things I must do, to take a moment and rest on what I really must be in faith.

Response: It is interesting how you lied in bed this morning in the dark and how your mind dwelt on all the life necessities that command your attention,. And then how you turned your attention and your heart to those people of Dafur and the fighting there, and then to Iraq, and to Afghanistan. On your deathbed, those prayers for the latter will command and commend your attention.

So today I do commend your being to the matters that make a difference in the world you live and the heaven that you will inherit.

First, about those who have preceded you, take courage in following their example. Sometimes patience is the key ingredient of courage, so I ask that you be patient. As you can identify so easily with images of mountains and mountain passes, do not allow your vision to be hindered by an overactive imagination. I mean imagining a frightful path way up ahead, but rather simply, (and I mean simply) take the step before you, keep your eyes on the path immediately before you. Don't look back because in swinging to look to the rear you might topple off the path.

Your guides are of the caliber of Chesterton[3], of Paul, of Griffith[4], and of Merton[5]. People who could sit in a cavernous hall of riotous sound and be uninterrupted and at peace hearing the chords of their heart with a smile.

Don't over manage, but bring patience and steadiness to your pursuit of the hoped for summit, and then you will experience vistas that you could not have imagined if I placed you at the summit of Everest.

Today you will understand more fully the support you have, the encouragement you sense, and all this due to my love.[6]

---

[3] G.K. Chesterton, Christian author, 1874-1936.
[4] Bede Griffith, Benedictine mystic, 1906-1993;
[5] Thomas Merton, Trappist monk and author, 1915-1968

Scripture: *We have this hope as an anchor for the soul, firm and secure. It enters the inner sanctuary behind the curtain, where Jesus, who went before us, has entered on our behalf. He has become a high priest forever, in the order of Melchizedek. Hebrews 6:19-20*

Prayer: How can I express the delight of discovery in reading references to the curtain and Melchizedek in the same verse?

Response: You are changed forever. You are one who has discovered as those through the ages the delight in reading the scriptures and draw from these words the strength and faith that are unshakeable. The grace, like rain on those fields that we discussed yesterday, is bringing forth fruit and in abundance. You are invested, and I mean by this that you are on a clear path. If you were at a university, you are now tenured.

You are moving behind the curtain where all of the daily chores, tasks, and anxieties are like the sandals that you must clasp before wearing but which you take off before entering the sanctuary, before moving beyond the curtain. Take off your sandals, you are on holy ground, are words to remind you to leave those cares and concerns outside and in faith enter.

In this, you become a member of the priestly order of Melchizedek. No, I do not want you to purchase robes, walk around exalted. I want you to simply realize that through grace you have been invited to enter into the sanctuary, to part the curtains, and to experience where you are in the dimensionless dominion of my love. As you sat in that Lexus the other day and wondered how to start it without a key, so you are in a sanctuary where you can't understand how you got there and what you are to do. My answer is forget about how you entered, simply trust as you manifest my word among you.

How rich this reading is for you. The mystery of the curtain is erased, is parted, and the delight that you feel hearing of Melchizedek on this morning that you woke at four AM. Now, realize that I summoned you before you became overwhelmed by your responsibilities.

Scripture: *And it was not without an oath! Others became priests without any oath, but (Jesus) became a priest with an oath when God said to him: "The Lord has sworn and will not change his mind: You are a priest forever." Psalm 110:4*

Because of this oath, Jesus has become the guarantee of a better covenant. Now there have been many of those priests, since death prevented them from continuing in office; but because Jesus lives forever, he has a permanent priesthood. Therefore he is able to save completely those who come to God through him, because he always lives to intercede for them. Hebrews 7:20-25

Prayer: This morning when I am questioning myself, please sustain me.

Response: With all your education, do you see the wonder with which I reveal to you each day a source of truth to sustain you. How many successful executives and power brokers spread throughout the world experience the stillness to gather in the significance of the priesthood of Melchizedek and to see Christ as your real time resource to the truth?

You are truly in a mental, emotional, and spiritual state where you stand without sandals, without the cares of the world around you, yet responsible for easing the crises that abound through your intention, through your offerings. In a real sense you offer yourself in the order of Melchizedek to heal the injured in your midst. That is the reason why your mission to part the curtain for those grief-laden is a blessed mission.

Christ lives within you, not just as a source of adoration but as one in union that sustains you and nurtures you because without your hands and mind his mission of redemption is thwarted. In a very real sense you are anointed in the order of Melchizedek, something you realized at an unconscious level for so long. Be bright in the light you convey.

#40

Scripture: *How much more, then will the blood of Christ who through the eternal Spirit offered himself unblemished to God, cleanse our consciences from acts that lead to death, so that we may serve the living God. Hebrews 9:14*

Prayer: Lord, there is so much contained in this verse – Christ offering himself through the Holy Spirit and we receive in turn the cleansing of our consciences so that we may serve the living God. Help me to understand more deeply these words and how they apply to me.

Response: You were taught and it is true that the Trinity is a mystery that is without the ability of your rational mind to comprehend. Like a *koan*, the trinity is to occupy your mind in an insolvable puzzle so that I can reach you completely. Rise up from your bodily and worldly consciences so that you can take in the essential message of this verse.

Through the blood of Christ your conscience, your very being has been raised to embrace the relationship with the Godhead. All of your concerns about relationship on a worldly basis dismiss the truth that you are joined, connected, at another level that is without limit. Cleansing your conscience is to show you and give you the ability to see beyond your footfall.

Consider now the eternal Spirit. There is where you feel my touch. That is the sonorous melody you remember faintly, the time of special holiness that captures you, that is the influence of uninhibited laughter, of full tears that flow down your cheeks in wonder, that is the questioning for which answers and encouragement are provided. The eternal Spirit swirls about you and will not abandon you.

So be quiet and still and trust. All will be one.

Scripture: *For this reason Christ is the mediator of a new covenant that those who are called may received the promised eternal inheritance — now that he has died as a ransom to set them free from the sins committed under the first covenant. Hebrews 9:15*

Prayer: I have trouble with this verse, namely the thought that those must be set free from sins committed earlier before they lived. Help me to understand the fullness of this verse.

Response: Focus for a moment on inheritance. You have something to pass on to your children when you die. If you lose that money through negligence or just poor investment your children receive nothing. Remember I said whether or not you were negligent or just unlucky. So it is with the kingdom of glory. Under the first covenant there was established sort of a fund, an inheritance, and it was lost. Further the fund was rather modest in that it only covered a small selection of human souls. If it makes it easier for you to comprehend, it was a pilot program that I established. Well, it was not a great success. Realize once again that I have endowed you all with free will so I am prepared to be with the results even if, to use your human terms, I was disappointed in the results.

Jesus represents the laying down of and the establishment of a second covenant and there will be no more. Why? Because by the blood of Christ, his sacrifice, no further sacrifice is necessary to create this covenant in perpetuity. You are living under the second covenant.

So you are living where nothing can happen to the inheritance that you have been called to receive. The investment of funds, so to speak, is guaranteed. No one can claim as an heir that the funds have been exhausted. In fact the investment grows larger as those of you spread the light. What an investment opportunity! The inheritance cannot disappear and it only grows.. This fact should release you from all anxiety.

Now as for being called. Some of you have been called without question and you have responded. Understand that all are called and yet fail to hear or will to hear the calling and what is required. And it is not a question of demonstrating. Remember the scripture verse of the rich, frugal man who always sat in the front row of synagogue and the widow who sat humbly in the rear but gave in charity all she possessed. Well, the same for you. My love is not confined to the "professed" but extends to those who have yet to hear and read of me from another but rather respond to my love in their heart.

.

#42

Scripture: *It was necessary then for the copies of the heavenly things to be purified with these sacrifices, but the heavenly things themselves with better sacrifices than these. For Christ did not enter a man made sanctuary that was only a copy of the true one, he entered heaven itself, now to appear for us in God's presence. Hebrews 9:23-24*

Prayer: I am lost in understanding these verses.

Response: Take a deep breath. Slow your mind and allow it to ramble over the words and listen to me. Christ brought to the father a sacrifice of love, not unlike the Prodigal Son, who returned and accepted whatever his father would grant him. By His sacrifice He brought to the Father an exalted gift that the Father accepted for all eternity. The gift was the willing sacrifice of his son with full intent to release you from any guilt or, better, affect of the lost inheritance. A lost inheritance was restored in that instant. You get a hint of it in the story of the Prodigal Son, though the son already spent his inheritance and was welcomed to share in what was left. In your case your full inheritance is restored.

Don't confine your thinking and understanding to places, though for you to understand those symbols are important. Keep your focus. This is a difficult, but so important message.

Christ was not restoring you to a life of ease in the world as indeed the prodigal son was to benefit after his ruinous adventure. No, Christ is restoring you to the heavenly realm. It is as if you are now able to reach across a divide of eternity and to BE in the presence of God because that is what his sacrifice meant to you and means to you now. Imagine a twirling platform of silver light on high. The platform is of inestimable breadth and it appears from below to be sharp, almost like a saw, a huge saw in a limber mill. By his sacrifice you are propelled onto the platform safely in a glorious light.

To be saved is not to be defined by man as to who will be saved or what path, is to reach that state for eternity. There are those who choose not to reach the platform and in their self destructiveness choose to loiter in a lost dominion of time and space no longer able to comprehend their fate, in solitary loneliness.

I have shared this with you for you to understand how significant the restoration of your inheritance was to all men. Think on this when you consider what you are to do in the years remaining to you.

Scripture: *Then, [Christ] said, "Here I am, I have come to do your will." He sets aside the first [covenant] to establish the second. And by that will, we have been made holy through the sacrifice of the body of Jesus Christ once for all. Hebrews 10-9-10*

Prayer: Help me to comprehend your words and integrate into my life until the end.

Response: You see Christ is providing an example, a model, for all of you to adopt into your lives as well, at whatever stage you are in. And I am sure that you have not missed that your will is the key element of the change in direction.

You are here to learn how to fashion your will to Divine purpose, to my purpose. As you repeated and repeat the words of the prayer, Thy will be done -- so your will is critical.

Your will is the test. It is miraculous, I must say, how this flesh and bones, blood, and sinew can reflect your will and most importantly Divine will in your actions. Think of it, it is like crossing species how the will which you can not touch can stir the body to reflect my honor, my love, my purpose.

And you have as your ultimate model, Christ who first accepted willingly the flesh, then inculcated this body with his holy will, and then offered to destruction that body to your salvation, to sign a covenant for which another covenant would not be required.

Extraordinary as it is, you now discover that those same words, that same desire to do God's will, resounds in our own commitment, spurred on by a Spirit that moves through you. So each time you say those words remember who spoke them first and be honored that you have been invited to follow. You see by your actions, by your will, you remind all of the sanctity of this covenant stripped away from all the greed, violence, ambition that infects your surroundings. Be calm and listen and you will hear the guidance that you seek.

Scripture: *Therefore, brothers, since we have confidence to enter the Most Holy Place by the blood of Jesus, by a new and living way opened for us through the curtain, that is, his body, and since we have a great priest over the house of God, let us draw near to God with a sincere heart in full assurance of faith, having our hearts sprinkled to cleanse us from a guilty conscience, and having our bodies washed with pure water. Hebrews 10:19-22*

Prayer: Dear Lord, the glow of a new dawn is just beginning to fire in the gray outlining the homes looking out to sea. I am caught by these words that encourage me to follow Christ through the curtain to draw near to God. Help to nourish me with your words.

Response: Yes, you are following behind Jesus who parted the thick curtain. Think of the curtain as one like you encountered in Eastern Europe hung over the door to keep in the heat and warmth from the cold. It took some effort to push aside the thick fold. Here too, you are being encouraged to follow in Jesus' footsteps and the closer you are to his following the easier it will be to slip in behind him, no confusion as to what part of the curtain folds.

Faith comes in because it is dark; you have to trust and have faith. You will see however the closer you are to him and the more alert you are you will catch just a glimmer of light that will increase, then the parting of the curtain will be made clear.

Draw near to me and you will discover that your will has been transformed to radiate my presence. And while you are on earth, in body, you will receive assurance of this transformation with the ease with which you move about and do my bidding, not as a command but as your desire to reflect my love upon all creation.

If you will, consider the sanctuary behind the curtain as a place of the heart where all is one and the warmth of love abounds, then you know you are in the right place by the smile that forms on your countenance. .

Scripture: *Let us hold unswerving to the hope we profess, for he who promised is faithful. And let us consider how we may spur one another on toward love and good deeds. Hebrews 10:23-24*

Prayer: Help me Lord to be unswerving.

Response: There are times when you forget the second part of the sentence, I am faithful. Difficult sometimes in the whirl of living to see my presence in your every activity, spurring you on to a greater height, leading you through the curtain, personally being present with you. It is so important to treat my message as a present reality, not something reflecting the pages of a musty book, interesting only in an historical perspective. Each word you read is significant to you today.

You will find that the words as inspired take on a particular meaning for you today as they catch your specific scene. So not only are the words living in a general sense but the words then wrap around a specific life scene.

For example, you search for confirmation in what you undertake and discover encouragement from various quarters inspired by my faithfulness. The list is endless and sometimes not so directly as when you share deep thoughts or even mundane happening with a parent as you accompany the boys *trick or treating*. See in all you experience my hand and my faithfulness. And in the process see yourself inching forward to the goal and direction I am prodding you.

Encouraging you to encourage others is the influence of my presence. Catch each thought that reminds you. Be at peace today.

Scripture: *So do not throw away your confidence, it will be richly rewarded. You need to persevere so that when you have done the will of God, you will receive what he had promised. Hebrews 10:35-36*

Prayer: I was looking for something to read last night and I went to a random page and found nothing that fit where I am right now. Yes, my confidence faltered yesterday and here is a text that applies so precisely to me. It should be my mantra. Please continue to shower me with your understanding.

Response: This verse reveals to you that I reach you at all times. I am behind the door waiting for you to open the door to me. There is no situation that pulls me away from assisting you immediately. It is like having a rescue vehicle, fully staffed, awaiting your need.

As I mentioned to you last night in the depth of your discouragement, I allow the dark force to test your resolve. He would like nothing better than to have your discouragement lead to despair. When you see his tactics, the insidious nature of his resolve to defeat you, allow that perception to embolden you. It is said that to escape an ambush go directly to the point of fire, actually rush to the point of fire, face the fear, the discouragement and reveal in that instant the presence of the dark force disguised in the robes of those incidents that claim your attention.

You will win as you are strengthened in the faith, which means in your determination to spread the word of love, your adversary will continue to rattle discord. You will also find that the timbre of his chords will create such a cacophony of sound that you will hear it for what it is – an all too obvious attempt to subvert. See if you can the humor for you and hopelessness for him in this vain attempt.

You are strong in the faith and I encourage you to dust off the discouragement and move once more forward along the path that I have selected for you. I am much encouraged by your actions and dedication.

Scripture: *Now faith is being sure of what we hope for and certain of what we do not see. Hebrews 11:1*

Prayer: In that short sentence so much is contained. Help me to know what I hope for and give me through grace certainty.

Response: Hope is first based on courage – courage to make a choice. You see hope encourages you to loose the bounds of death and accept the inheritance that awaits you. So before you can be sure you must hope. Reflect upon that.

Now you don't have to spend all your time hoping for something in a hereafter. Apply what you have learned to accept that eternity is in the present. Gazing mystically and mistily into a future does little for you. Accept that what awaits you is a mystery. I am even going further by saying what awaits you now is eternity. Yes, you can explain it, rationalize it, by saying that what you experience now is a shadow of a future life. I ask you, though, to see this precious moment as eternity.

And why should it be any different. You don't think that you are in union with your spouse and those who have departed? In this precious moment you don't think that you glorify me? You don't think your prayers and intentions of those caught in violence are less meaningful than they would be in some other dimension; your prayers for those suffering like your friend and his desperately ill wife less potent because you are living?

Let me tell you. The vibrancy you feel in grace is exactly what you experience in what you call eternity. The same understanding you have through compassion is the understanding and knowledge that you have in eternity and what the eternal means. The same love not bounded by greed, desire, and control is the same love of the divine.

So what do you hope for? No need to answer now. Next how certain are you of receiving that hope filled desire this very nanosecond? That is the timing and equation that you are to work with. So today what do you hope for? You will find that with this mind and heart set you will cut through the haze and maze.

#48

Scripture: *By faith we understand that the universe was formed at God's command, so that what is seen was not made out of what was visible. Hebrews 11:3*

Prayer: Help my understanding especially as my life and its relationships continue to unfold.

Response: There is no alternative but to accept on faith because there is no line going back to a beginning. Faith is especially called for in relationships where it remains a mystery how, why, what, where happens to turn a direction. Like the phone call and apology from your daughter. Would you be more satisfied to think that her change of heart was the result of taking medicine, eating a meal, impelled by arguments that you made, someone's words to her, or can you consider that the fruit of your prayers were made manifest just like that. Your prayer in this and other experiences is not so much a cause but the example of Divine creation – out of nothing something appears.

In prayer you become co-creators with me so beware as you have heard before what you pray for. You should agree that you do not offer prayers often enough, do not co-create with me. And I am not singling you out but make this observation generally for all of you. And I am not talking about the prayers for this or that which often times are not prayers at all but rather a phone call to the bank for additional funds to be put into your account.

No, I am talking about the co-creation with me through your prayers to bring people to the light. Notice I did not say stop the violence, or natural disasters, or fill the needs of the needy; no I am talking of prayer that co-creates with me a leap in consciousness where violence is no longer an option. And the violence I speak of covers all categories – economic, military, environmental, family, academic, spiritual, religious, social, government. It is simply no longer an option. Give voice in the silence of your soul to that prayer and you co-create with me.

It is this conversion of spirit through spirit that you reside on the earth. And do understand that your writing is a prayer affecting all those areas. That is why writers and those of creative expression are blessed.

So for today, honor the fit you have been given.

Scripture: *By faith Abraham, when called to go to a place he would later receive as his inheritance, obeyed and went, even though he did not know where he was going. Hebrews 11:8*

Prayer: There are times, perhaps most times, I feel called and don't know where you are calling me. In fact I have often said that my life only seems to have a recognizable path looking back. Help me to probe that instant between being called and responding – even though the destination is unclear.

Response: Good question. To elongate the instant realize that your success in staying in the present gives you adequate time to respond. Right now you are sitting in the present. You are covered in a mantle that keeps you in the present. So you can hear me directly. Without the hearing the call becomes wrapped up in the sounds of actions that you perform to live by, like making a cup of coffee, grinding the coffee beans, boiling the water. Listening is the deepest form of prayer. It is then that you are in simultaneous communion with me as you are now. No need for pomp and circumstance for words of oratorical import; no, now in listening to me you are praying deeply.

For your understanding that at such times you are Abraham. I did not say like Abraham, I said you are Abraham. Abraham, then Abram, was listening when he wrestled with me, just as you wrestle with me. In prayer as in wrestling you are overcome but do not lose. You are closest to me in that period that lasts for an eternity.

Listen to me and all the extraneous actions like grinding coffee for a pot of coffee recede into the automatic gestures of living and you enter a sanctuary few enter but by chance. And that is the chance of conscious grief and loss. Be silent in this citadel; roam the corridors as you would in the company of a loved one. Listen gently and with quiet heart. Here all is open to you. Remain in this space and you will find that what appears as a journey outward is in fact a journey inward. And like Abraham you are leading your tribe and such an extensive tribe out into the desert, a journey based on faith because you don't know the destination. However, you and your tribe are sustained by me.

For today, remain in this space throughout the day. See how well you do being inside as you travel in the world.

Scripture: *All these people were still living by faith when they died. They did not receive the things promised; they only saw them and welcomed them from a distance. And they admitted that they were aliens and strangers on earth. People who say such things show that they are looking for a country of their own. If they were thinking of the country that they left, they would have had an opportunity to return. Hebrews 11:13-15*

Prayer: Lord, help me to continue to look for the "country" you have prepared for me and help me to guide others in the same direction.

Response: Looking forward in faith brings in that future country into the present, an eternal present actually. And yes there is no going back for those so touched as you glance forward – again in faith.

What does that mean each day? It is accepting each day with the joy of expectation and with patience. You are an alien, a stranger in the land along whose paths you tread. And the journey is multidimensional in that it seems what you are flanked on all sides and there is a retinue behind you, and most importantly you are moving forward in faith alone and in a community.

There is a cleansing of spirit to know that you are literally casting your old garments off as you don new clothes for the trip across the desert. You are in an initiation phase as all are who embark on this journey of discovery. And discovery of what? The "country" that I have prepared especially for you.

What makes this country different? No more subterfuge. Soul relationship becomes supreme. There is a presence about this country that attracts you with it's gleaming light and aura. It is a country of consciousness and knowing and compassion and love. No time, no space, no boundary, no confines, a place of soul exploration in union and communion with me.

Yes, understand why you search for the new country, why you seek to hear the melodic call that still lingers in your soul but is sometimes lost in the noise of violence around you. Be ready to inherit this country, you are gathered at its borders.

#51

Scripture: *[Moses] regarded disgrace for the sake of Christ as of greater value than the treasures of Egypt, because he was looking ahead to his reward. Hebrews 11:26*

Prayer: How time at least linear time is irrelevant, it seems.

Response: As I have instructed you almost daily, it is in the present moment right now that eternity is experienced. Though I must add, you experience it as if behind a curtain that flutters in the breeze created by the Spirit.

In this reading see Moses as yourself looking afar and, once grasping that faint outline of the kingdom, is satisfied, celebrates, perseveres and is patient. So for you, standing on a beach looking out beyond the horizon, you experience as your own a place of love compassion and understanding and in the experience discover that peace in your heart.

You are embarked on a risky road, no less than the road you were on when you sought to find Soviet citizens who were willing to give information about the intentions of their leadership, similarly when you tried to gather information related to terrorist incidents being planned. Right now against all odds you are seeking to reach a mass audience with your message of grief. You risk ridicule, further loss of finances, uncertainty. What sustains you is my grace, the integrity of your intent, the letting go and accepting my will in your life.

Today you will see in ever greater detail the horizon and beyond, and you will see it with a new found clarity that serves to encourage you along this road. What would I do without the standard bearers who venture out beyond the known to pursue me and lead others in your path?

Scripture: *[L]et us run with perseverance the race marked out for us. Let us fix our eyes on Jesus, the author and perfecter of our faith, who for the joy set before him endured the cross, scorning its shame and sat down at the right hand of the throne of God. Hebrews 12:1-2*

Prayer: The lesson for me is perseverance. Guide me in your grace.

Response: The secret of perseverance, any perseverance, is focusing on the goal. You know this in studying for an exam, in recalling the agony of a race, in making your way through fear or grief. As long as you can set yourself in the present and keep in mind the goal that must transcend the current trial, perseverance is quite endurable. And interesting, focusing on the present you find that the time is eternal and passes with rapidity as you bring in the goal that you have set.

Obviously the more lofty the goal, the more intense your focus must be and your willingness to linger in the present, pulling the future to you and not vice versa.

Perseverance is the cue-timing for a performance. You are working or performing in a determined fashion, yet you are not rushing the performance. Imagine the confusion if once on stage you shouted all your lines at once. Think of the bedlam. Well, that is your life and others from time to time. Attain with my grace a certain timing, a certain space to perform your lines as they are called for in the performance.

Consider also the words a bit further in this reading about making the path smooth so as to allow the lame to heal. The meaning is two-fold, one - that you simplify your life so that you can give your full attention. Again using the stage as an example, don't go on stage with all sorts of accouterments that serve to distract you. Second, realize that you are also creating a path for others to follow and those others might not have practiced so well their lines, at least with the industry that you are showing.

So perseverance is the theme today and with it the charge to simplify.

#53

Scripture: *The Sovereign Lord has given me an instructive tongue, to know the word that sustains the weary. He wakens me morning by morning, wakens my ear to listen like one being taught. Isaiah 50:4*

Prayer: Keep wakening me, Lord.

Response: You hear in these words how I reach you each morning and during the day. It is through the listening that all is made clear to you. This morning I have words for you that should not only guide how you touch the wary but also how you offer prayers and actions to ease the suffering that confounds your world and your life at times.

Yes, it was good that you heard my words last night to help others see that God is not a good news God, or rather limited to good feelings. You are correct to see, perceive that God transcends the tears and even joy, realizing that it is difficult to understand.

In the world, pray deeply for what unites people become visible to counter the perceptions of what makes them different. The dark force is responsible for defining, isolating differences. So your prayer is to help others see what unites you all.

Your healing touch is found in the words that you hear from me and then utter softly. You see I rely upon your listening and your actions.

The important thing is for you to take the time to listen regularly, without fail. Realize that in listening you are truly present and in listening cannot indulge the past or allow the anxieties of the future to intervene.

Be at peace today.

#54

Scripture: *In this you greatly rejoice, though now for a little while you may have had to suffer grief in all kinds of trials. 1 Peter 1:6*

Prayer: Help me to understand grief more fully.

Response: I would say that the word grief is too onerous a word and the same is true for all languages. Grief is being reminded that all is not fashioned to your purpose, but the paradox is that all is fashioned to your purpose and grief plays a central role.

Grief is the check on your soul, the constant questions that are asked of you as you journey along the road. Grief is the persistent traveler who keeps asking for directions to the point that you question your direction and make the needed correction. And this traveler is not only trying to save the fellow who is heading to perdition, but also the fellow climbing a most difficult ascent for his greater glory.

Think over your life to date. The grief from the loss of your spouse allowed, even encouraged you to delve more deeply into the power of my love. The loss of a job and the grief from it has caused you to return to a purpose that I revealed to you in your youth and you have discovered a joy in this work. The grief you experienced so many years ago with your spouse taught you about forgiveness at a level that not many experience. The trials of a daughter have given you a depth of compassion that you only could read about. So you see your grief has taught you love, humility, compassion, and forgiveness.

And it doesn't end there with those questions posed to you along the road because in your new relationship all of these newly refined energies serve you and even calm you. Why? Because they serve to heal your wounded soul, making you especially suited to continuing your difficult ascent to a summit from which you will touch the glory of God.

#55

Scripture: *In all my prayers for all of you, I always pray with joy because of your partnership. In the gospel from the first day until now, being confident of this, that he who began a good work in you will carry it on to completion until the day of Christ Jesus. Philippians 1:3-6*

Pray: How do you carry the good work on to completion?

Response: Let go of your thinking of work as a task begun in a narrower sense. Rather see yourself as representing that good work. See yourself also in partnership with me to seed the world with my love. While this all seems so pat, seed the world with love, get deeper into the charge. Comprehend just how challenging a task that requires the cooperation and dedication of so many of you.

Those with more awareness find that they must contribute more to the recovery of the globe, another paradox. It should remind you of the workers in the field who began at first light and were troubled when those who were hired at dusk received the same reward. So it is with you and others with your perception, you were hired at dawn. Actually, I tapped you as a nine year old.

Later there were times when you were not as industrious in the field, though you remained in the field, because you wished to gear down your activity to the norm. There is no norm but a super-norm of which I speak. Remember your father's lessons with the Irish laborers as they counseled him to put aside the small shovel for the small shovel. As a young man that was appropriate. Now with all your wisdom and scars, you are summoned to take up the big shovel for your failing strength. Another paradox. Just when things should get easier to accommodate your years they become more arduous. See life as the paradox that it is. It is in paradox that truth is revealed.

So today see life for the paradox it is. See paradox as the mystery to be revealed, and ponder the mystery in stillness. You wrote a poem after viewing a rose in stillness, sensing the eternal in a beautiful, still, red rose in the cramped living quarters set up in the midst of war and death; and so the rose dies, but the mystery is that the rose and the eternal beauty of its essence lives on in your mind, in the words of your poem, and in each rose that you come upon now. You are changed as is the rose, as are those who have and will read your poem.

Paradox. Each day a good work is begun in you. You are the rose who shines in my glory only to wilt in body but live on in your endeavors, words, thoughts, and expressions of love, compassion, and so much more. Be peaceful today.

#56

Scripture: *And this is my prayer: that your love may abound more and more in knowledge and depth of insight, so that you may be able to discern what is best and may be pure and blameless until the day of Christ, filled with the fruit of righteousness that comes through Jesus Christ – to the glory and praise of God. Philippians 1: 9-11*

Prayer: Lord, sitting here at dawn, I hear Paul's words as if he were writing to me personally across the seas.

Response: Read these words again slowly and listen. Yes, you are hearing my message through Paul this November morning. You see I am not bound by the linear time on which you ride. My words to you are ever present and that is what you hear.

I speak to you from the divine heart to your heart, intimately, with love, directly. I penetrate through the fog of daily life that sometimes clouds your sight and dulls your hearing. I reach you through tears, in fact my words are more audible in the tears and I even reach you in your joy.

Key for you today are the words and the depth of insight. Depth of insight is your effort to lower a bucket into the well of the eternal and pull it up carefully as you would wake slowly to retain a dream fragment so that others can contemplate the treasures from the deep.

Realize that there is no limit to how deep you can reach; the rope is endless though it takes more effort to pull the treasured water to the surface. You must be strong and resistant to compromise. I am quick to add that you are progressing and must continue to nurture your faith. The liquid from the depth is the sustenance you seek and need.

Be at peace and confident in your love.

Scripture: *Now I want you to know brothers that what has happened to me has really served to advance the gospel. As a result it has become more clear throughout the whole palace guard and to everyone else that I am in chains for Christ, filled with the fruit of righteousness that comes through Jesus Christ to the glory and praise of God. Philippians 1:12-13*

Prayer: Shed light on this text. From my vantage point two thousand years later it gives me pause as to Paul's reference to the gospel since I know he was not carrying around with him a bound volume.

Response: It is good that you see with ever more discriminating vision. Your lesson to share is that I am not bound in a book. My message is the message of Paul spoken without reference notes. He spoke from the heart as to what he experienced -- without notes because he had been changed. How bold!

He spoke of what I laid on his heart. His authority -- and I mean that people stopped and listened, some more deeply than others -- was the authenticity of his message. He knew his script by heart and the script was later to become the bound version. However, understand that the gospel is not the various texts over which scholars labor and argue, but the good news that I showered and shower over you all.

See yourself in the Praetorian Guard, looking forward to the change of shifts when it will be your responsibility to watch over this preacher of ideas that you had never heard previously. How shattering to your beliefs up until then that focused on what you would do. Now you were hearing words that struck you so deeply about who you are and who you are to become.

Yes, the gospel is listening to my words and sharing them without notes if you can. Oh, how many ordained preachers would be at a loss if they didn't have the book in front of them? For now the book should serve and does serve the authentic in your midst to be a jumping off point, like a diving board poised above the depth.

Plunging into the depth you invite others into the depth because they must experience their own exhilaration and not rely upon your words, if they can gather the courage. It is into the depths that I invite you. The gospel that you know today is a signpost to greater depth and not the destination. It is a way station. How to encourage others to see this? I am not talking about orthodoxy but internal reforming and alignment to my divine heart.

These words will be a challenge for those of you who prefer no signposts but a destination to release their energy and pursuit of truth rather than ease and sloth.

Scripture: *Do everything without complaining or arguing, so that you may become blameless and pure, children of God without fault in a crooked and depraved generation, in which you shine like stars in the universe as you hold out the word of life – in order that I may boast on the day of Christ that I did not run or labor for nothing. Philippians 2:14-16*

Prayer: Help me Lord not to complain. Help me not to be discouraged in the *crooked and depraved generation* that populates this world.

Response: Your path is to be straightened and with your cooperation. Keenly see yourself and remain in the present, don't loiter in thoughts of the future and clearly do not allow yourself to be pulled into the past.

Your path is to be straightened and in straightening will allow you more efficiency to reach more of those who still have a perception of the light. You see one can lose an ability to distinguish shades and degrees of light. It is like someone has allowed scales to form on his eyes, or not listening and being attentive has allowed his inner hearing to be overcome by the dull drone outside – a sound of wailing to which one becomes accustomed if one wills. So it is with taste, what is ingested dulls the vibrant taste of salt, or touch that loses its tenderness as fingertips meet, and smell that allows the early odor of home and family and mystical journeys to occur in union with me.

So your path is to be straightened. Attend to the lingering items that draw your energy.

And finally most importantly offer in sacrifice your concerns for your daughter, your love for your son, and offer these treasures, even your daughter and the suffering she stirs, for my light, to burst force on battlefields where only explosives burst now.

Scripture: *I want to know Christ and the power of his resurrection and the fellowship of sharing in his sufferings, becoming like him in his death, and so, somehow, to attain to the resurrection from the dead. Philippians 3:10-11*

Prayer: Lord, I woke at 3AM and unusually could not get back to sleep. I do want to know Christ and the power of his resurrection, but I flinch about sharing the suffering, and I am intrigued by Paul's use of the word "somehow," as if indeed it is truly a mystery for him. Please calm my soul and provide me the enlightenment I crave.

Response: Let me take you to the word "somehow." There is a bit of humor there. Paul is allowing that he is like all his followers wondering about this mystery. It is his faith and yours that keeps the use of the word in perspective. It is like that poker player who has a good hand and can't believe his good fortune as he engages in the game. With no disrespect for the pain and suffering and uncertainty, you have a really good hand. There are times that you can't believe your good fortune. So the somehow is said and reflected upon with the humor of knowing in faith.

No way to avoid the suffering because that is how your faith is tested and you ascend higher. The physical dimension allows all sorts of images that for some who were not and are not engaged in physical exertion have more difficulty understanding. You are experiencing and have experienced suffering. The secret as I have told you many times is simply endure what you are experiencing and do not suffer some illusionary future event.

You are as it were in a special club and you are enduring an initiation not to gain entry. You are already in. What you endure refines you as the gold refined in fire, or the iron crafted by the blacksmith. That is why those images are useful. The blacksmith is even more appropriate because of the use I want to put you. The gold is testimony of your faith and allows the light to reflect off you or actually emanate from you.

All for today. Remember to smile in adversity. It loses its sting though still accomplishing its purpose.

Scripture: *Do not be anxious about anything, but in everything by prayer and petition, with thanksgiving, present your requests to God. And the peace of God which transcends all understanding will guard your minds and your hearts in Christ Jesus. Finally, brothers, whatever is true, whatever is noble, whatever is right, whatever is pure, whatever is lovely, whatever is admirable – if anything is excellent or praiseworthy, think about such things. Philippians 4:4-8*

Prayer: Lord, I have read these words previously. In fact, I underlined them. Help me to catch your essential formula – *by prayer and petition, with thanksgiving, present your requests to God.*

Response: Prayer, petition, and thanksgiving represents the cycle of my love for you. Indeed, I seek your prayers. In prayer the eyes of your soul open and you see again and again as the first time the treasure chamber in which I have set your feet. It is in seeing that you acknowledge my love and your prayer confirms your growth in the spirit. And do you realize that your acknowledgement serves you because you see that growth in the spirit?

Petition is your response and reflects the ever maturation of your requests. See how real they become with you. Each day as you scan the newspaper you have used the paper as a daily missal that cries out for your prayers and you respond. Take some time in refining your petitions for yourself. Perhaps, defining is a better word. Do not be hesitant to provide your requests with specificity. You will be surprised how your petitions also serve to tell you where you are in your ascent and what desires, heartfelt, that linger in the recesses of a soul. Relationship, writing, health, work, are all worthy of your exploration and petition. Take some time later to focus on your petitions.

And thanksgiving – like the note to your son's in-laws for a wonderful feast on thanksgiving, thanksgiving is your realization that your petitions have been granted. Isn't that miraculous, mysterious, indeed the bounty from my special love for you in the broadest of terms?

I want to tell you that your prayers for the pope in his mission to heal the disruption between Christians and Moslems are heartfelt.

Be peaceful today. See what unfolds.

CHAPTER THREE -- SIMPLICITY

When we lived in Warsaw, Poland, a tall, gaunt, raw-boned woman named Marysza was there to care for our growing family. She had the gait of someone who was raised behind a horse-drawn plough — and she was.

Minimally schooled during World War II and afterwards as the post-war communist regime seized power, Marysza never wavered in her faith. She diligently read the Scripture, attended church, and participated in a grueling, annual pilgrimage on foot across Poland to a holy shrine in the southeastern corner of the country in defiance of the communist authorities.

She read the words of Scripture in reverence without concern for an alternate interpretation of a word or points of historical significance found in the footnotes. After all she was not studying for a college level exam. She listened attentively to the voice she heard in the stillness of her heart. For her scripture was a living document coming to fruition. She had faith — a simple, direct faith that what she was hearing and applying in her life was the authentic word of God.

So too for me, as I un-learn the habits of the past and they slowly begin to die. The culture of exegesis — to allow each word of scripture to work its change in me while a new person slowly emerges, more in the image of Christ..

#61

Scripture: *[F]or I have learned to be content whatever the circumstances. . . I have learned the secret of being content in any and every situation. . . I can do everything through him who gives me strength. Philippians 4:11-13*

Prayer: Lord, teach me to let go and trust as Paul did.

Response: Be still. Consider this first day of the month as the first day of your life or the last day of your life. When you are riding the spirit as you are direction and timing lose significance and importance. Imagine yourself as a beam of light shown in the dark corners of the world. All corners are dark without the light that you shine in your surroundings.

This is not to be a gloomy message. As the sun rises to sustain the vegetation you rise to sustain the hopes of those around you. I am not suggesting that you shine the beam of faith in their eyes. Allow their eyes to adjust and in time they will find their own light. As I pour forth the light through you so I do likewise to those who can be still and listen to my word. Much light must be directed into the regions of conflict. The miracle is the turning of the heart in forgiveness and compassion.

A word about posturing – your grace of these last years, even prior to your spouse's passing, is your increasing ability to dispense with posturing. This is a lesson for all though it takes some confidence to throw off the padded garments of pretense. In your work now this must be included in your message. It is difficult to reach the heart and the stillness you have found with all that padding.

Great expectations in faith are yours this advent season. Look over your petitions that you made yesterday, and in thanksgiving know that they are granted -- every single one of them.

You are blessed and your voice emanating from the heart is becoming louder and clearer.

#62

Scripture: *And my God will meet all your needs, according to his glorious riches in Christ Jesus. Philippians 4:19*

Prayer: I feel overwhelmed at times with the details that I must attend and don't seem to have the time, though I don't have employment. Please, Lord, help me this morning to select a scripture that will focus my attention on my journey as it unfolds so naturally.

Response: A loss of a high school friend is a reminder that the things that you worry over are those things that you will lose anyway and what you cherish and miss are what you will inherit and never lose. Your unexpressed feelings for him are special and are with you for an eternity. You are learning in these last years to lighten the complexity of your life and focus on what is your real inheritance.

All your needs for eternal happiness is being granted to you. Your only guide is to distinguish what is for eternity and what will be left behind. You are being showered by gifts right now, the grace of perception, generosity, intuition, compassion, and love. You are also able to suffer silently and will a certain lightness in the suffering.

You will see a special coming of Christ into your life in this month of December. Be at peace today.

Scripture: *[R]efresh my heart in Christ. Philemon 2:20*

Prayer: Help me to understand the need and that it is OK to be refreshed.

Response: And why do you think that Sunday is on your schedule? Why I seek your rest at night? Why "wasting" time with grandchildren as you learned was a most important pursuit? Why reading one of your son's books and taking a test he prepared are all examples of being refreshed – and in Me?

The longest trek requires space to be still and that is rest. It is a time to observe the sunrise before the calamity of another day of responsibility.

Resting in Me means acceptance. That is where you become refreshed to continue your journey. And not just slogging through, but with new enthusiasm as you are refreshed.

It might cause you surprise that Paul needed refreshment. How else for his faith to mature if it were not tested, if he didn't need – and I use that word freely – refreshment.

You are on track.

All for today.

Scripture: *Through whom and for his name's sake, we received grace and apostleship to call people from among all the Gentiles to the obedience that comes from faith. Romans 1:5*

Prayer: Like Paul help me to understand my calling.

Response: Your calling is my voice that you hear more clearly each day. Imagine yourself on a desert landscape in the foothills just before the ascent becomes severe. All around you are trails leading to higher altitudes. Sedona has such terrain. Each day journey you wait to hear my voice to ensure that your effort will not be wasted and each day I call to you as you start out with confidence.

So it was with Paul. He received a dramatic call on his way to Damascus and each day thereafter a call of equal intensity, or should I say of ever more clarity. And that is what you and others experience. You are being called to administer to those you come across in your life. Whether it be a dinner guest or someone whom you encounter. Soon you will find that there is an audience that is wider and diverse.

In hearing my call you find that you are showered by my grace and forgiveness. It is a special forgiveness, one that reaches into your very soul and this forgiveness serves to refashion you almost beyond your recognition of whom you once were or who you always were at the deepest level but feared to reveal. You are becoming more and more authentic and this fact is what people find so attractive and causes them to pause and listen.

That is what I have to tell you this morning. You as Paul are called. And I am doing the calling to refashion your soul and to reach so many others who are in some way in contact with you.

My special love to you this day.

Scripture: *Grace and peace to you from God our Father and from the Lord Jesus Christ. Romans 1:7*

Prayer: Help me to understand grace and peace.

Response: In prayer for a loved one grace and peace are the gifts that you seek for them. But you can only ask or witness because both are given freely of the Father. As you know you cannot earn grace or for that matter peace. Both distinguish my presence and my bounty. Un-grace and the opposite of peace reveal the presence and influence of the dark force that my grace and peace through you are to dissipate.

Whenever you pause in reflection you can gauge the flow of grace over you and realize you are blessed. However, as you imagine, that sense is not to cause you to lie back in reflection but to invest that grace in your efforts to dispel the darkness.

You are most blessed and your focus must become even more powerful as you have the tools and talent to shed the darkness that surrounds those around you. See in your life how I am working. Think of those recent calls, one from an old friend grieving through his wife's suffering and the other from an old colleague trying so hard to finish his book on Afghanistan. Share with him those letters you compiled during your time there.

Be at peace today and witness that peace and see the grace that I give you.

Scripture: *I am obligated both to Greeks and non-Greeks, both to the wise and the foolish. That is why I am so eager to preach the gospel also to you who are in Rome. Romans 1:14-15*

Prayer: Help me to understand my obligation.

Response: Though your obligation seems overwhelming at times, you know your obligation. And your eagerness is there, so evident, though beneath the surface you are anxious sometimes more than others. Your obligation is to your son primarily – all else fades in comparison. Next your obligation is to touch others around you whether through your words spoken orally, or those contained in your website and in your writing. What you feel (and it is what Paul felt deeply) is discouragement. That is what I must call your need to embolden your faith in me. As Paul questioned if he had lost his mind after Damascus, so too you question your motives, sanity, and even purpose, and that is motivated by the snares and deceptions of the dark forces.

Let me offer you some insight into the dark force. Just like you have struggled on your journey to Emmaus, so did the dark forces individually and as one. As you continue the walk, individually and as a group they left the path, they turned about, and attempted to dissuade others from continuing so as to avoid reaching deeper into the realization of their decision and failing.

In your call last night with your daughter who still suffers personal problems, be at peace that she doesn't yet understand her need to reverse directions and proceed toward Emmaus.

Finally, there is something else you are obligated to do and that is to pray for those around you in pain and pleasure, in prosperity and poverty, in peace and violence that their walk will be sustained in faith. Your prayers and those of others are so important, like a roadside refreshment station for the travelers who sometimes feel alone and even lonely.

I love you and your quiet determination. Be resolute.

Scripture: *For in the gospel a righteousness from God is revealed, a righteousness that is my faith from first to last, just as it is written: "The righteous will live by faith." Romans 1:17*

Prayer: Oh, I am tired today. I nearly swept aside reading your scripture. Help me this morning to understand this verse.

Response: Your lesson today is to understand that it is not your discipline that is to be rewarded in returning to scripture but rather that you acknowledge in faith the seed that is impregnated within you through my grace. It is like recognizing a friend as you journey in life. It is in that recognition that the seed of faith is manifested. You are graced and your building confidence in faith is what reveals most importantly to you that a change in your disposition is occurring.

So what is so important about the change? It is through the change that you and others are transformed. This process also helps you to display patient endurance. It is your investment on faith and in faith of love that you make without thought of realizing a return. And that is what you are experiencing now with your work. Patient endurance is what you are being called upon to display. Even more, you are being called to be patient and enduring.

#68

Scripture: *I am not ashamed of the gospel, because it is the power of God for the salvation of everyone who believes, first for the Jew, and then for the Gentile. For in the gospel righteousness from God is revealed, a righteousness that is by faith from first to last, just as it is written. "The righteous will live by faith." Romans 1:16-17*

Prayer: Please tell me more about the power revealed in the gospel.

Response: The power is like entering a beautiful well-lit home or palace that is bare of furniture and ornament, only rugs on the floor, and pulling back one of the rugs to reveal a trap door down into the interior. The gospel takes you down into the interior to reveal a magnificent treasure that is impossible to contemplate variety and numbers because all is revealed in a union, in a unity.

And what is revealed? A roar of power that that resounds the deeper one descends. And that roar is for some just a faint echo of what they hear in their hearts. It is the "Ahah!" that you utter, knowing all the time my will and love for you.

Righteousness is my divine will and plan for all of you. Each word that I gather and reveal to you in the gospels contains a surge of that power that time and distance cannot dilute. The words are blessed with my touch and influence the righteousness of writings and sayings that do not derive from the tradition that I empowered.

You are blessed that you know it or in knowing you are following my path, and even more blessed that you are responsible for leading others to your path through your words and writings. Be peaceful today and reflect the righteousness of the scriptures and what they reveal to you.

Scripture: *For since the creation of the world God's invisible qualities – his eternal power and divine nature -- have been clearly seen, being understood from what has been made, so that men are without excuse. Romans 1:20*

Prayer: Please help me *to see* better your invisible qualities.

Response: You looked up this morning and saw the stars and it was as if you were seeing for the first time. In that snatch of time you experienced my restorative power. It is that power that I invest in you each day.

Let me spend some time with this power. It is the power that refuels you when you are dragging emotionally as you are now. You see there is a connection between you and me, in fact union would better describe the relationship.

This refueling is found in the insights that you receive. Your disposition adds to your receptiveness. Your disposition prompts the grace you need from me, like a hand outstretched that I do not deny. I want you to spend a moment with your fingertips beginning to compose your note for 2007.[7]

Let me get back to the power. My power surges like an internal current throughout the world. All that is needed to bring light to the world, represented in love, are the outlets which plug into the current. How many appliances and lighting fixtures do you have?

Let me mention your family with your son, your relationship with your children and grandchildren, friends, your love of those areas of the world and the people who experience such horror, and the list grows. You service many lamps and the new one, yet to be determined, is the lamp of your writing. Continue to be in wonder and awe at my power and energy. That is praise.

---

[7] At the end of each year, I write a letter to myself to be opened on New Year's Eve of the following year.

Scripture: *Or do you show contempt for the riches of his kindness, tolerance and patience, not realizing that God's kindness leads you toward repentance? Romans 2:4*

Prayer: Please explain how, or why, or whether I walked astray.

Response: You have asked a good question this morning. You exist at my will. I brought you into existence though you must attempt to understand or rather accept that I am not caught in linear time. Suffice to say that you exist and I will it. Notice I say will and not willed. Out of my love, you are, and in my love you are to be the full manifestation of my love.

In manifesting my love you are free to gesture, hum, groan, embrace, and reject that love. And it is in the rejection that you come to realize that the melody calls you to be in the full presence of that love. Repentance is positioning yourself at a concert to hear the orchestral piece without distraction of the person seated in front of you, the coughing behind you and to the right, the movement of the person across the seating area, or the thoughts that clamber in competition to the work of art being played in your presence. Repentance is total focus on my love as I focus totally on my love in you.

Think less on the fallen nature that your churches proclaim and more that you are invited to participate in a music school of love and it is you who select the instrument or mode of participation. I select the chord in which the melody will be sustained.

This melody needs no special amphitheater. You know your amphitheater, especially when you pause and look around. And learn to be comfortable in knowing that the melody I play while familiar to you is always refreshed and has particular meaning and importance for you though you are one of so many in the audience.
And yes, I am tolerant, and patience, but most of all I am loving; do what you need around you to hear me without distraction as you are hearing me now. You see it is in the stillness of your soul that receives my melody directly and at the modulation needed for you.

Go in peace today listening.

Scripture: *But now a righteousness from God, apart from law, has been made known, to which the Law and the Prophets testify. This righteousness from God comes from faith in Jesus Christ to all who believe. There is no difference. Romans 3: 21-22*

Prayer: Help me to understand righteousness.

Response: Righteousness means in this context making clear, straightening the path, eliminating the need for the complexity of atonement practiced up until then but even now. Righteousness from me is my clear message to you that requires nothing more than for you to listen and then to act. So simple. That is how you are redeemed brought to the Light that I reserve for you.

Faith is for you to trust this voice. In trusting my voice you let go of the anxiety of unknowing, of alternative actions. Faith directs your actions and it is for you to acquiesce. Understand that I am not directing you to anywhere other than into the Light.

And yes I do nudge you into the direction that is best for you and the others who look to you or are under your responsibility.

I remember, and I am sure you do, that time traveling on an airport bus to Vienna after the flight landed at an alternative airport. Seated alongside you was that attractive Polish speaking young lady and how you prayed that circumstances would not permit you wandering from your obligation. And how at three AM in the morning her supervisor was there to meet her!

I cite this example of my immediate response to your prayers to keep you moving toward the Light because you so prayed.

I also am involved within you helping you to choose the path for this life. You have done well and your anxiety, questioning is similar to the daily commitment one makes, and you especially, to my way. I will allow nothing to intervene, including the actions of the dark force that would so like to sway your determination.

Be open and alert and listen to my word. You may wake up at 89 years and find that you have the same discipline and determination that you have now.

Pray always for those who suffer the violence in their lives and not created by them.

Be at peace today.

Scripture: *Against all hope, Abraham in hope believed . . .Without weakening in his faith, he faced the fact that his body was as good as dead . . . Yet he did not waver through unbelief regarding the promise of God, but was strengthened in his faith and gave glory to God, because fully persuaded that God had power to do what he had promised. Romans 4:18-21*

Prayer: Lord, sometimes – even most times – I neglect to appreciate the promise of God and think that I am the one organizing my life. Please give me insights into how to embrace your promise.

Response: You are in a place in your life where my promise to you is what you have to hold on to. While not decrepit in body, you are not the twenty-five year old ready to conquer the world. Yet, before you is a field of battle that far exceeds anything that you faced as a twenty-five year old. And there you are, appearing quite vulnerable, yet in faith you have legions of angels on either side ready to advance under your command. Do you realize how powerful is my promise to you and those who nurture faith in me and receive my abundant grace?
I bring you advisors who unveil a strategy to overwhelm the dark force. Imagine that you are sitting on the field of battle allowing your advisors to describe the upcoming battle. In faith you are to consider the options before you move.

And realize most deeply this is not some sort of a test that I have arranged for you upon which you will be graded. No, you are participating as my heir to the battle and your involvement is what I seek in your faith.

The very silence and peace that you feel this moment are indications of your ability and capacity to overwhelm the adversaries that disturb the environment with violence and disturb your companions on earth so that they cannot rest in contemplation of my promise.

Today, pray that that inner peace blossom in their hearts wherever they might reside – in the Middle East, Asia, Africa, Europe, South America, or in your country as well. Penetrate their hearts with your prayers.

#73

Scripture: *And we rejoice in the hope of the glory of God. Not only so, but we also rejoice in our sufferings, because we know that suffering produces perseverance, perseverance, character, and character, hope. And hope does not disappoint us because God has poured out his love into our hearts by the Holy Spirit, whom he has given us. Romans 5:2-5*

Prayer: This morning I feel alone and wonder. I seem to lack hope this morning, though the dawn is brilliant outside my window. Help me to hope.

Response: Listen this day for my love in every experience as the flower seeks the warmth of the sun to melt the frost from its leaves. See yourself as a blossom in the desert on a slope facing the East. The night has been long for you. You see just a glimmer of the furnace of love cutting the horizon as if a screen is being parted. Allow yourself to be dazzled by the occurrence. What other reason would there be for rising faithfully to measure and witness the dawn?

Perseverance is that boldness to remain stoically on the slope awaiting the sunrise of my grace.

A word about your concerns to publicly share these writings outside a tight circle; you are being asked to venture beyond the comfort of the familiar as you have done throughout your life in travels and professional pursuits. What is different now?

Let me explain more hope. Hope is directed and focused. It is not a blind sort of hope that awaits salvation from any and all directions. No, hope is in a real sense drawing into you the answer to your prayers and doing so confidentially, that is, with hope. If I were to make a list of your hopes the list would be quite concise: to be in a loving relationship with someone who feels similarly to you, to remain in good health so that you can raise your son and be a source of wisdom to your family, friends, and even strangers, to write as your profession, to conduct retreats and workshops to share the wisdom that you have inherited – yes inherited – from the wisdom of the ages, to remain on the sea and to have an opportunity to be in the mountains, and to travel to gather more information.

So hope is clearly defined and is really the answer to your prayers already answered.

Hope is a personal relationship with me that you have already expanded beyond your early thoughts as being possible.

All for today.

Scripture: *You see, at just the right time, when we were powerless, Christ died for the ungodly. Very rarely will anyone die for a righteous man, though for a good man someone might possibly dare to die. But God demonstrates his own love for us in this: While we were still sinners Christ died for us. Romans 5:6-8*

Prayer: My eyes rested on *at just the right time*. It is unclear to me why you distinguish the righteous from the good man and someone being willing to risk death. So I ask that you enlighten me with your meaning and give me the strength to attend to the tasks that sometimes drain my concentration.

Response: My, you are filled with questions today. Accept this truth at the outset: your prayer, each part of it, is granted at the very instant that its vocalization is making its way through your vocal chords.

Now, let's go to the element of time. Yes, at exactly the right time you receive what you need. If you were trapped on a mountainside of doubt in the snow, befuddling your mind and heart, the snow would melt. At exactly the right moment in your life, your spouse moved on. You were sufficiently strong and committed. And it was exactly at the right time for her elevation to depart at that time. Timing is everything.

Don't labor over the fine distinction of the righteous and the good man. Suffice to say the righteous man does not attract the sacrifice because he is at ease and comfortable in his travail. The good man needs the sacrifice so that he can continue to mature in his faith. Without the sacrifice he could be irredeemably discouraged.

Regarding your message from a one-time business associate; he is an outside observer who serves to encourage you that your path is the correct one, but even more, that there is so much for you to be in this environment of violence. Keep your staff aloft. You don't want anyone to lose you in the crowd as you lead forward with other like-minded souls.

Your loneliness is the desert of John the Baptist, Jesus, the Desert Fathers, and all who seek me in the stillness before dawn. I will bless you; shower you with grace today, unearned so that you can appreciate my bounty in my love for you. Take special note for those who suffer in the world this day.

Be at peace.

Scripture: *We know that the whole creation has been groaning as in the pain of childbirth right up to the present time. Romans 8:22*

Prayer: Lord, is that the melody I hear? Explain more expectation.

Response: I could say feel as well as hear. The groaning is present in the efforts to explain from the deepest recesses of your heart what you are and are becoming. The groaning occurs at a time of vulnerability, as in childbirth. And it is at this time that you are called upon to trust and to hope in that you are protected. The groaning encompasses all the confusion and doubt that is purged in the birth of the spirit within you.

Expectation is seasoned with your investment in your life of the spirit. What I mean is that if you remained a child your expectations are limited not further matured so that you expect a basic satisfaction. In no way is this condemnation but more a recognition and acknowledgement of the circumstances in which the seed of the spirit was conceived and nurtured. For you, the seed of the spirit has been graced with a stillness of spirit in the chaos of what is occurring around you; however, you know stillness. That is the region of your heart where insurmountable power is revealed to you. It is there where the spirit reigns.

Be still today. Listen. Listen to the spirit who will call to you in a voice that you recognize. And in that shudder of excitement in the hearing, be gentle with all you encounter.

Prayer: My son came up to my bed with his big dog an hour or so after he went to bed. He asked what if there was no Jesus Christ and if when you die there is nothing? So we talked for a few minutes about faith and all the indications that indeed there is something after we die. I even told him that I would push through the crowd to greet him first when he died and behind me would be Mom. So Lord, this morning, please ease my heavy heart.

Response: You can appreciate how much you are doing to add to your son's growth and maturation. Do you remember the time when one of your grandson's was no more than six years old and he asked a similar question? His parents were almost offended that he chose you to ask the question that haunts you all. And here your son didn't ask anyone but you and in the quiet of the family bed, in the safety of the warmth and love.

You ask for your heavy heart to be eased and so it is. With all you attempt to do it is who you are that counts. Your son's question and your answer of faith is your answer matured over all these years and reflects back to him your faith. And it does the same for you. Remember I said that those who believe having experienced me in the flesh are blessed but so much more those like you who gather your strength of faith within and draw from my grace to add to your certainty.

By asking the question, your son brings his fear out into the open and the fear loses its hold. You are doing fine in raising this fellow who will reach so many in spreading my message of love.

No need to be in despair and with a heavy heart. All is coming into place. All your requests have been granted and are unfolding this moment. Be peaceful today.

Scripture: *The virgin will be with child and will give birth to a son, and they will call him Immanuel – which means, "God with us." Matthew 1:23*

Prayer: Lord, on the Christmas morning, grace me with understanding of your miraculous birth and what it represents for us.

Response: God with you is key to your understanding. To have the God's presence among you in the flesh that is the mystery. Even more a mystery is to accept that God presence never left and is with you most tangibly in the Spirit. You flow in the divine energy and that is for eternity without the boundaries that you experience on earth.

Think again on the earlier verse that you were reading about Joseph and Mary being pledged and only through the divorce process could the pledge be broken. And think again that under Deuteronomy, Mary could have been stoned to death for conceiving by the Holy Spirit. Reflect upon the acceptance that Mary exhibited when the Angel informed her of God's intention. You understand better her trust to accept these circumstances. *Be it done to me according to your Word.*

This day, remain present and bless the past that led you here. Bless the past with all its lessons. Bless the past for the path that led you to where you are.

God became man. Imagine a stale loaf of bread becoming alive with the seeds and ingredients and the aroma of the baking process all at the same time, and discovering that the loaf is inexhaustible in the nourishment it can give, only requiring you to reach out and break off a piece.

This is a day for you to be the wise man bringing gifts to the newborn and remaining in simple praise and adoration.

Peace of Christ be with you always, but especially today.

Scripture: *As Jesus was coming out of the water, he saw heaven being torn open and the Spirit descending on him like a dove. And a voice came from heaven, "You are my Son, whom I love, with you I am well pleased. Mark 1:10-11*

Prayer: Lord, this morning when I seem overwhelmed by cares, help me to see the Spirit in my life.

Response: You have come out of the water and you have lingered in the desert. It is time for you to move on into your next ministry. You have lain out with the Spirit's blessing the groundwork for this ministry. It is as if a travel guide has been prepared for you. But first be present on the edge of the Jordan and hear with your companions this thunderous voice that welcomes Jesus to the shore. Catch the excitement and surprise of the crowds. Now hear in the depth of your soul similar words that I speak to you. Throw off the taunts of those who do not believe in you or question your direction.

Remember it was the crowd on the shore and in the water alongside Jesus who heard the voice from heaven. You might not have witnesses to the voice you hear within, so your works will be for all the voice.

Your words, *Here I am Lord I come to do your will* acknowledge for me that you hear me. Be at peace today and I will ease your journey up the steep bank of the river.

Scripture: *The time has come, he said. The Kingdom of God is near. Repent and believe the good news. Mark 1:15*

Prayer: So late and yet I felt a need to listen in the darkness.

Response: Take these words literally. The time has come for you and all those around you. It is measured in each of your lives. With an awakening awareness found in the silence, you know, this truth is evident to you. Repent is much more complex to understand. I am looking for a transformation of your heart. I am looking for, expecting you to become authentic so that who you appear to be and what you do, reflect who you are. And repenting is to cease being who you are not. Sounds clear to you and I expect that this clarity will influence you to stop wavering in your effort to preach my word, to transmit my love to all you encounter, all, and that means even a stubborn but dedicated evangelist.

Lastly, I ask you simply to believe the good news. Who could possibly believe that you have earned this inheritance that exceeds anything you can imagine and you have been employed by someone of immense material wealth who is poor in the spirit?

Believe the good news means waking up in the morning singing in thanksgiving at your good fortune, praising me for my largesse, not for something I lack, but to stimulate your appreciation and love by my example.

If you really believed the good news there would be no stopping you and your efforts and you would live for a hundred years or more. Your love would embody youth that would slow considerably the bodily aging process.

The good news is love, if you might have missed my subtlety.
Sleep well this evening and I will nourish you in your sleep.

Scripture: *As Jesus walked beside the Sea of Galilee, he saw Simon and his brother Andrew casting a net into the lake, for they were fishermen. "Come, follow me, Jesus said, and I will make you fishers of men." At once they left their nets and followed him. Mark 1:16-18*

Prayer: Such familiar words – tell me what I am missing.

Response: Since you know the ending, you forget to spend time with the beginning. Put yourself on that beach. Consider yourself a companion of Peter and Andrew. Perhaps you were mending nets. Why didn't you drop the net and join Jesus? Simple - you were not invited! Sounds harsh, but you must come to appreciate more definitively that my call to you was not to the fellow mending nets at your side. Another something for you to understand, in reading the scriptures, my Word, it is written for you individually. A thousand could be assembled, the words, anointed as they are, are crafted in that time and place for you as an individual and not for the assembly.

How else or why else do you think that those two dropped everything to join Jesus? He spoke and two took his words as the personal invitation to them and the rest is, as you would say, history. But you are wrong in considering this message, these words, these actions on the part of Simon and Andrew as history. These words are resounding in your heart right now. I don't expect you to become like them with their skills. As close to the sea that you are right now, stay calm I don't expect you to take up fishing, but I do invite you to become a fisher of men and woman above all else – though you will disguise your mission as a father, grandfather, friend, and erstwhile spy.

Nothing too dramatic, but just as Simon and Andrew applied their fishing skills to luring an audience to become their catch, I am asking you to use your writing skills with every bit as much determination to net those that are floundering in search of food before they become food measured in greed and violence.

Jesus didn't waste a whole lot of time assembling his cohorts, those who provided him arms and legs, voices, and heart – so with you and others. I speak of now, so don't linger in an historical perspective. Now is where I live with you. Now is the time of eternity. Now is the time of love, my love.

I have given you much today. You are attentive. I will not overload you. I delight in the attentiveness that you control. You see free will allows you to glaze over into past considerations and recriminations. Not you. For today.

#81

Scripture: *Very early in the morning while it was still dark, Jesus got up and left the house and went off to a solitary place, where he prayed. Mark 1:35*

Prayer: This morning in the dark before dawn, I felt the wind against my ears, wrapped as I was in my cloak. And in silence I prayed, Lord, make manifest your love in my life this day.

Response: Each day that love is manifest, but most days you are too caught in activities, concerns, plans that rustle through you to notice   So today, let's try something new. Remember that mantra that you repeated outside and in an instant I will bring to your mind my love in the events of the day.

You are more and more aware of your Observer, that unchanging presence within you that is in union with me. Your purpose and the purpose of everyone else is to bring that Presence into the work of the world, to make divine what is corporal and matter, to refine as gold what the dark forces have diminished and clouded. Only as your presence and that of others emerge will harmony be restored in the presence of the present.

It is mightily worthwhile for you to pause from time to time even now and grasp the hand of that Observer that is unique to your soul but is a companion of the most intimate nature with me. It is as if I have lent out something, or someone, so precious, on a special mission. And that is exactly what I have and do. Jesus is that special person who is teaching you to become a special person in your environment. What a teacher you have, you all have. The reason no authority was needed for his pronouncements to wield the power it does is that there is seamless unity with the divine energy of love.

In the swirl of the wind, in the dark before dawn visualize the force that lies beneath the essence of the wind, not what pushes the wind, but what exists within the wind, and then you can sense in some small measure the force erupting in your life.

Allowing the observer to emerge also counsels you not to be affected or allow yourself to be affected by those around you who would thwart your mission under whatever pretexts and interests.

Be calm. You are in my protection and I enfold you in my embrace -- so much for you to be.

Scripture: *As a result, Jesus could no longer enter a town openly but stayed outside in lonely places. Yet the people still came to him from everywhere. Mark 1:45*

Prayer: Lord, help me to be in the hearts of those who searched out Jesus to be healed and to hear his word.

Response: They are — and note I did not say *were* — so similar to you and those around you. You come each day to find me in a lonely place, that is, a place where you can listen without the distractions that fill your day. And what do you listen to? The simple answer is the Word. But what is the Word? It is my message you think sent from afar but actually the message is within you and marks our union. It's like carrying in your case a whole host of remedies, but the directions for usage are written in such small print that I ask you to pause to make out all the letters. It the directions were in big print you would hardly pause to distill the meaning.

And what is the message? It is actually two-fold. The first is a reflection, a pondering actually of where you are, to be followed by the directions, suggested directions. Only you can apply the healing balm, except in rare occasions.

As you have surmised Jesus did not pull out the book in his teaching. So much of what he had to say comes from divine love which showers down on you and which was so new for those in the early audience. See that these folks were not some meandering vagabonds who had nothing to do, but rather busy folks scratching out an existence in a harsh environment. It is only in recent times that the desert has flourished with the diversion of underground streams through the use of modern technology.

Anyone searching Jesus out in those lonely places had to get home before first light and devote a full day of work in the fields for meager pay. And yet they still sought him out in increasing numbers. Before you get nostalgic about the past, the message to hear in your lonely, quiet place is as profound. Remember, I told you the other day that whatever the words to the assembly, they take on a special meaning for you where you are. That is what it means for the words to be ignited with my love.

So today, I bring my message to you now, in the present. Cultivate the lonely place to find me, to listen to me.

All for today. My love to you in the quiet, free of turmoil.

#83

Scripture: *Now some of the teachers of the law were sitting there, thinking to themselves, "Why does this fellow talk like that? He's blaspheming. Who can forgive sins but God alone?" Immediately Jesus knew in his spirit that this was what they were thinking in their hearts, and he said to them, "Why are you thinking these things? Which is easier to say to the paralytic, 'Your sins are forgiven,' or to say, 'Get up, take your mat and walk?' But that you may know that the Son of Man has authority on earth to forgive sins . . ." He said to the paralytic, "I tell you, get up, take your mat and go home." He got up, took his mat and walked out in full view of them all. Mark 2:7-12*

Prayer: Such a powerful scene, one that hinges on the forgiveness of sins and Jesus' authority. Please help me to understand your message.

Response: Jesus uses the scene to demonstrate that he has the power to forgive sins without the authority of the Jewish law. Note I say *uses*, because he is still showing to all that he has the authority to forgive without the benefit of Christian, *Shariya*, Roman, and any other man-made or enforced law.

Like theater, he presents a surprise, doing exactly what he does to engage, note I did not say enrage, the learned in his midst. He first says to the paralytic that his sins are forgiven, and then tops it off by healing the individual without even laying hands on him.

If you can put yourself in the scene your faith would be stronger yet because you would see and touch the evidence. Well, I have something to tell you, these words are anointed and you are every bit as present as those who were squeezed shoulder to shoulder in the small meeting room.

The purpose, incidentally, of this scene is not to define sin. In fact, you would be hard-pressed to define the paralytic's sin. But clearly you can conclude it was somehow involved in his thoughts of rebellion. Thoughts of rebellion. That should give you a clue as to the sins of the heart that so outweigh what you would call sins of the flesh.

Let me say a word again on authenticity. Your responsibility in life is to learn authenticity. Not as difficult a test as you might suppose since within you are all the ingredients of character to know who you are. A day does not go by when you are not aware of who you are, though you often attempt to distract yourself from that clarity of purpose with tasks that serve to distract. That is why prayer is so essential because in the quiet of prayer to reconnect with your authentic self that is in union with me ever.

Life is rising through the miracle of grace – Christ's direction to stand up, take your mat, and move on – to be authentically who you are and to be authentic with compassion. While so simple to understand, such direction is not so simple when I say with compassion. So your task is above all to be authentic and like the intonation of an actor or actress on stage to moderate your voice to encompass a compassionate ring or lilt to it.

Before I take the scripture for today, I would like to spend some time celebrating my father's birthday. It is almost four years since he departed. He would have been ninety years old today. He was always "Dad" to me.

I miss his presence and the unique individual he was -- just one solid piece of granite encompassed who he was. There was no artificiality about him. He was generous, worked hard to provide for his family, he had simple pleasures like going to the race track and going to dinner. In later years, he comforted my mother in her illness and grieved deeply her passing.

He was a great teacher to me in the stark contrast he provided on what kind of a relationship I wanted with my children, how I learned to risk where he was cautious, how I would choose to be as a widower, how I would delve into the spiritual and cultivate through grace a relationship with God. He was so contrary that he provided a perfect foil for me to rebel against and discover my own path apart from his. Happy Birthday, Dad.

Prayer: Lord, help me to forgive myself for the countless times I have compared the two of us before others and put a favorable light on myself.

Scripture: *Once again Jesus went out beside the lake. A large crowd came to him, and he began to teach them. As he walked along, he saw Levi son of Alphaeus sitting at the tax collector's booth. "Follow me," Jesus told him, and Levi got up and followed him. Mark 2:14*

Prayer: I find there is so much in this short verse. Help me to delve deeper into its meaning.

Response: Do put yourself in the scene and feel the breeze coming off the lake. Be with Jesus as he walks in solitude as you are this moment in the quiet of your home. Reflect on what filled Jesus thoughts. His humanity has not been questioned. He is with you to experience the full dimension of your humanity. Think of how such walks served to relieve him of the tension he felt with the Jewish and community leaders.

And then, he is discovered by those who have been in his presence earlier and seek to experience once again that indefinable sense of all powerful love that made radiant the sometimes bleak prospects of this occupied people as they operated under the rule of foreign Roman legionnaires and Jewish nobility in league with Rome.

And he teaches them. He teaches them and that is what they seek. Where is his lesson plan, what does he want to accomplish in this lesson, what are the learning objectives? Does he have a text? No. Jesus addresses them from his divine heart, uses no text, relies upon stories, you call parables, to make his point, or better to allow each in his presence to reach his own level of comprehension in his time.

It is said that were the scripture to include all that he said, there would not be sufficient books to contain his words. This is a slight exaggeration, but allows me to say that Jesus did not repeat himself. Speaking from the heart there was no need to bring memory or the analytical mind into play. What he says, even to you now flows from the father and responds to your every need though there are needs that you have not even identified or expressed. That is why reading scripture regularly and without some preconceived notion that you need an answer to a particular question which would be limiting. Allow scripture to burnish aspects of you that you don't even realize are in need of nourishing.

And then Mark describes how Jesus walks on and encounters Levi; and he tells him, does not command him, simply tells him to follow him. Levi is not some robot, though he sounds like that with Mark's terse words. Jesus is like the teacher who tells a student to go to the window and see the brilliant sunrise. And so Levi goes to the window of light. He could have remained in the shack and avoided, or missed, the sunrise, but he did not and found that in Jesus' presence his sunlight expanded.

In reading scripture, catch the rhythm. Jesus' words and the description keep time with the pace of events unfolding. In your life, keep pace with the events unfolding in your life.

All for today.

Scripture: *Jesus went into the synagogue and began to teach. The people were amazed at his teaching, because he taught them as one who had authority, not as the teachers of the law. Mark 1:21-22*

Prayer: Help me to comprehend your teaching.

Response: I am teaching you now. Not citing authorities, my word encapsulates the authority of the Father. This authority is a beam of divine light that penetrates your heart in a manner to affect you. As I said earlier, a thousand could be assembled and five hundred could be affected differently and the other five hundred would not have heard a syllable.

For you in this time of heaviness, I am telling you to allow the light to lighten your burden. Throw off the weight of the past, a delusion, the feeling of despair, the loneliness you felt, the confusion. Throw it all off and bathe in the light that I am showering on you.

This is not a time to indulge in sadness of disappointment, but to rejoice. You have listened. You are no longer with the five hundred lulled by past recrimination but alive to my word now.

This day you will discover a special love that exceeds any that you have comprehended to date. This love will warm your heart and you will see that there is no turning back to past idolatries. Amen, I say to you, I have chosen you and you are to reach those who sit befuddled.

Scripture: *"Why does he eat with tax collectors and sinners?" On hearing this, Jesus said to them, "It is not the healthy who need a doctor, but the sick. I have not come to call the righteous, but sinners." Mark 2:16-17*

Prayer: Too often I identify with the healthy, help me to gather in the wisdom of this verse.

Response: Let me provide you an insight on the sinner. What distinguishes the sinner is his/her rebelliousness. His or her pull away from me seeking to discover a region of the heart independent from me and in doing so discovers me within. I come to the sinner because it is the sinner that is alive, fashioning a body and spirit that ultimately reflect my love but, in the near term prods you all to consider and reflect upon your presence in the world. I come to you because I glory in your independence that brings you into dependence and love of me.

What patient does not fall in love with the doctor or healer that brings one back to wholeness? That's what healing is and the remarkable thing for you to consider is that you all recognize good health, that harmony of spirit that you know from the beginning. I am not suggesting that you will ever run as fast as you once ran, or rowed with as much vigor and strength as you once did, but I am saying that in your time you are fulfilling my desire to understand and take in deeply my harmony and love and you recognize it.

So I indeed come to the student who is watching the board for what I write, has his ear cocked to catch my word and whisper, and whose eyes are locked onto mine as I transmit my love in a glance.

For the other students, and you all fit into the student category; those gazing at me with lifeless eyes, whose spirits are in slumber, don't judge their ability to recover. For now they are in a sleep-induced rapture of their health. They too one day will awake and hear me. In the end, I ask that you pray for the healthy. They need your prayers, if not your compassion.

I know you want to go further and probe your own sinfulness. What a colorless and bland expression. It is not sin but your inability yet to balance yourself in harmony. You are on a high wire walking with confidence across the precipice. Don't fear – there is nowhere to fall. Please don't bring in Dante and the Inferno. I bring that image to you because if you were on a high wire you would show total and intense focus.

Right now you are similar. Your focus is grand balancing responsibilities for your son, the home, writing and efforts toward publication, reaching out in friendship, your prayers. What a balancing act.

Dear Lord, it's six AM. I got up a little later today. I have yet to utter a word, increasing the silence, though I have taken the dogs out, fed one of them, got the newspaper, and am sitting at my computer. From the crease in the curtain I can see the sun just beginning to come up -- so silent is it except for thoughts of silence.

Scripture: *"And no one pours new wine into old skins. If he does, the wine will burst the skins, and both the wine and the wineskin will be ruined. No one pours new wine into new wineskins."* Mark 2:22

Prayer: I guess I am not sure where new wine goes.

Response: You are the new wine. You don't fit easily in any vessel. Your awareness of my word requires you to be ever flowing with my word. Once contained the freshness of the message that I am imparting loses its vibrancy. As I told you each word in scripture is anointed with a special grace, if not meaning for you in your circumstances.

The containment of the new wine is that performed by churches or theologians so anxious to return or reduce the message to a formula. Just by its very nature a formula seeks to contain. My word is not to be contained.

Church is for community of like believers who share their journey but do not impose rigorous demands that affect your connection to me and to the presence within. Sounds harsh and you might wonder what to do with all the formality and ritual. I will not discuss that issue this morning. But I do want to make a point that the deepest inspiration comes to you and others in the silence free of ritualized activity.

So amazing it should be for you, is that you reverence me acutely each morning in the silence and then return to the world and I mean your world of responsibilities preparing breakfast, being a companion to your son, communicating with those you love, and on and on. Your real, genuine, authentic reverencing occurs right now in the quiet and stillness.

Without leading a protest movement or anything like that, one of your missions or legends is to lead those around you back to the stillness through your words. They don't have to copy down the words as you do, but they could gain so much insight and in feeling my presence regularly and what support they would feel and what understanding they would receive in my grace.

So as a new wine, ever refreshed and vital, I ask you to deep flowing as the blood flows in your veins. Feel the pulse of the flow and do nothing to contain it. Offer it freely. What I am saying is do not be concerned about saving the wine, I will replenish you with over abundance.

In your peace and mine this day.

Scripture: *Another time he went into the synagogue, and a man with a shriveled hand was there. Some of them were looking for a reason to accuse Jesus, so they watched him closely to see if he would heal them on the Sabbath. Jesus said to the man with the shriveled hand, "Stand up in front of everyone." Then Jesus asked them, "Which is lawful on the Sabbath to do good or to do evil, to save life or to kill?" But they remained silent. He looked around at them in anger and, deeply distressed at their stubborn hearts, said to the man, "Stretch out your hand." He stretched it out and his hand was completely restored. Mark 3:1-6*

Prayer: Jesus' anger – please provide a deep insight into it.

Response: How you try to find out where Jesus' emotions match your own at times. Put that objective aside. As you were taught he was fully human and I say divine.

The lesson of this scripture is to shed light on the stubborn hearts that you all indulge in. It is the stubborn heart that is in rebellion to the love that showers over you even on a rainy or frigid day.

It was not as if the response of the Pharisees surprised Jesus, rather he used their predictable behavior to tell you a story. And that is despite your doubting he will demonstrate in your heart his authority and love and faithfulness and purpose. After all in healing he showed love, in performing the miracle despite the opposition he showed you his authority, and in containing his righteous anger he showed you constraint. Love, restraint – another word could be compassion, and authority. Simple.

No, you don't need volumes of laws to make a life decision. If you only had one recounting of one miracle, it would be enough for you to see that the path you are on is lighted and the light provides the warmth and the path is not a labyrinth in which you could become lost.

Accept that in your life you witness miracles and have miracles performed to keep you focused on your path. I am well pleased in you and if you were to live another hundred years, not one minute is more valuable than this moment in which you adore and praise me and my love for you.

#89

Scripture: *Jesus went up on a mountainside and called to him those he wanted, and they came to him. He appointed twelve – designating them apostles – that they might be with him and he might send them out to preach and to have the authority to drive out demons.* Mark 3:13-15

Prayer: Help me to understand.

Response: There is much contained in these few words. See the image of the mountainside, high up, alone with those he selects. It is in the quiet that you are called, in the stillness. And Jesus wanted each one, each one, each one. There are no accidents. Yes, he wanted Simon Peter who denied him; yes, he wanted the Sons of Thunder; yes, he wanted John; and, of course, he wanted Judas.

From so many he chose twelve to represent all the working parts of you that sometimes acts inappropriately, that denies me, that sells me out, and yes, most important of all that falls to his knees and begs forgiveness.

The apostles, as the holograph of who you are, are so much more complex or intricate than your frame, or smile, or tears, or laughter. And this selection is for a purpose to get or become closer to me and to preach so others will be likewise motivated, and to protect the unconsciousness from the demons that abound.

All for now.

Scripture: *Then Jesus entered a house, and again a crowd gathered, so that he and his disciples were not even able to eat. When his family heard about this, they went to take charge of him, for they said, "He is out of his mind." Mark 3:20-21*

Prayer: This reading troubles me because I was raised to believe that Jesus' family at this time was limited to his mother.

Response: Good that it provokes you, stirs you from the rigidity of education. See how everyone seeks to "cleanse" a record to conform to expectations. In fact, you know it is not important what others do or say as it relates to who you are. What a gift to be able to raise children or even endure family and not consider who they are as reflective of who you are.

Jesus also experienced this; and how did he handle the situation which for some would be embarrassing. He ignored it. Yes, ignored it. Did not get pulled into debating who's right, thus creating more animosity or anger, or frayed egos. He ignores *the family's* recriminations. He does not leave but talks, teaches, with great authority. No one interrupts him and his message is delivered. *If I were gaining my authority and power from Satan, I would be powerless to thwart Satan.* Simplify stated he gave everyone pause. No one in the crowd reaches in to restrain him or to pull him home.

There is a deep lesson there for you. You are to be who you are and discover for my purpose. Have no fear that you will be plucked from the crowd. The crowd is actually anxious to hear the words of truth that so often escape them in their daily routines. Speaking the truth does not judge another or another's belief. It is simply stating your truth as you hear it from me. As you noted in the film Mother Teresa, you are simply a pencil in my hand. Go in peace.

CHAPTER FOUR – PRAYER

I was once asked to share what prayer meant to me before the military command in Berlin where I was assigned. I resisted the unrelenting pressure from the military chaplain to no avail. At the time my ego was overflowing with pride at my professional prowess and sought to keep my prayer life secret. The talk I gave that morning was entitled "Prayer for Us Overachievers." Those fifteen minutes of sharing thirty years ago have stayed with me.

In a sense whatever our professional or personal circumstances, we are all overachievers that is, if the ego is allowed its way. It is only when I put on hold all distractions; quiet the monkey-chatter of my mind; set aside a time and perhaps a space to be fully attentive for the softly spoken words from my traveling companion who is ever close.

At such times, I imagine that I am back on a trek in the Himalayas, walking on a deserted beach, or sitting on the deck to my home observing a sunset when I am joined by a special Friend. Sometimes he speaks to me in the silence, in the words of a poem I have read or crafted, in a scene observed with a quiet heart, and yes in His Word that I read and upon which I reflect.

For me prayer has become a time of listening with intention.

#91

Scripture: *Trust in the Lord with all your heart and lean not your own understanding; in all your way acknowledge him, and he will make your paths straight. Proverbs 3:5-6*

Prayer: I heard this verse a couple of times this weekend. Are you trying to tell me something?

Response: Yes, I am trying to get a message to you. Trust. Know that I am leading you on a path that is straight, unlike the crooked and windy path you might choose on your own. Trust. Don't expect to have the journey's end highlighted. There is no end as far as you are concerned. Consider each day on its own and you will discover untold riches embroidered into your life pattern.

The silence that you are experiencing right this moment is so precious and cannot be duplicated by the cares and concerns of the world in which you reside. Paradoxically your stillness calms the world as a butterfly's flaps are "heard across the globe. Each smile, gesture of kindness, peaceful prayer creates the love divination I seek in your acknowledgement of me.

You see I am not looking for blind adoration but adoration blessed with action in prayer and performance. And because I seek efficiency in the love of the enlightened I will straighten the path to shorten your journey though you will not experience the shortcut except in the opportunities that are presented you to do my will.

Scripture: *"For I know the plans I have for you," declares the Lord, "plans to prosper you and not to harm you, plans to give you hope and a future." Jeremiah 29:11*

Prayer: Lord, there are times, especially when I consider my age, that the planning phase is completed. Help me to have confidence that you still nurture me daily.

Response: Age as you might have gathered is all about the past and not much consideration of the future except to pick your plot or finish the lot. Well, I am not a mystery writer. I only write in the present as you do, and I only read in the present, as you do. Therefore, please put aside thoughts of the past and age, and concerns about the future.

Also, concerning the future, your life is not a container that is approaching capacity. You once thought that just before your spouse passed on to me. No, you are not a vessel that is nearing its capacity, but rather, if you insist on the image, a vessel, a new vessel each day that I fill daily with my blessings and grace.

I fill your vessel daily. Each day is a new cup and that is for everyone. New cups, if you will, issued to those perpetrating violence in Iraq, Afghanistan, in Africa, in your country, throughout the world. And each day, with the rising of the sun, all sip from the freshness of my love. Some recognize the bounty, others have yet to pause and smack their lips and wonder where the flavor of life emanates, gushes forth.

So accept, even if you cannot understand, that I have plans for you just like the journey you are on, and my plans are simply not an ending to the exciting story of your life and the lives of so many others. No my plans transform into a visually apparent eternal theme that is beginning to transform your hue to a brightness that others would have difficulty describing. Begin to feel the colors, yes I said feel the colors, from the inside out. It's a time for you to change wardrobes in a spiritual dimension. And that is my plan for you, to refashion you in the finest garb, celestial actually.

Scripture: *Before I formed you in the womb I knew you, before you were born I set you apart. I appointed you as a prophet to the nations. Jeremiah 1:5*

Prayer: Lord, this morning my cold appears to be peaking. It leaves me quiet with my thoughts and longings. Please console me with your words.

Response: First, don't become inflated; at least don't allow your ego to become inflated. I have no intentions of dispatching you to Syria. What I want to remind you is that you are chosen as all of you are. And yes, I formed you in the womb.

In this verse see how I watch over each of you and hold great expectations that you will sit quietly and listen to me, that you will come to me in all circumstances. Each life holds a separate set of circumstances and you are each called, yes, I say, called, to respond, and in responding you are prophetic.

I set you apart and you appreciate this more now than you ever did as you first went out into the world. In a sense you have returned to tell of the adventure so that others can see me in all.

At times of illness, and although this cold you have is minor, you are forced to slow down and listen even more intently than you usually do. Hear my voice for you, for you especially. You find with increasingly clarity my voice in your writing.

Today simply relax and recover your strength. You have nothing to do but rather to be in every single breath. No need to seek distractions for your attention.

Scripture: *Again Jesus began to teach by the lake. The crowd that gathered around him was so large that he got into a boat and sat in it out on the lake, while all the people were along the shore at the water's edge. He taught them many things by parables. Mark 4:-1-2 When he was alone, the Twelve and the others around him asked him about the parables. He told them, "The secret of the kingdom of God has been given to you. But to those on the outside everything is said in parables so that, 'they may be ever seeing but never perceiving, and ever hearing but never understanding; otherwise they might turn and be forgiven.'" Mark 4: 10-12*

Prayer: Why is your teaching less than clear sometimes?

Response: That is a better question than you believe. If my teaching were too clear it would portend the future and you would lose the capacity to choose, to grow, to be faithful or filled with faith and hope. Further, what is clarity but the arrival of understanding where understanding was lacking?

The secret of my teaching is acceptance. Put aside all your desires and wished for results and accept. Then my teaching is quite clear. You are almost there. I have taken you to a region where you cannot control the outcome and this is new to you and unfamiliar. If I were to ask you where you would be emotionally, residence-wise, professionally in six months or a year, you could not answer. All is a mystery for you. This was not the case years earlier, or at least you thought that way.

The mystery of my words serves two purposes: it stimulates your interest, and once the meaning is grasped the meaning and its import are yours. The mystery also allows the anointed quality to reach you and the reader at exactly where you are in most need.

For example, the words of Jesus from a boat on the lake to those on the shore touched each individually and allowed each to see that Jesus was speaking to each one. Notice I said was speaking to each and not that they were to be led to think that the words were spoken to them. The words also allowed each to understand individually without the need of a teacher or filter to intervene in the direct connection. So you have and nourish a direct connection with me today.

I see that you are weary with your cold and that weariness creates a peacefulness that makes you even more receptive to the anointing that is occurring right now.

For today, accept what I send to you and prove its deeper meaning in the parable of life.

Much healing light to you this day.

Scripture: *"Still others, like seed sown among thorns, hear the word, but worries of this life, the deceitfulness of wealth and the desires for other things come in and choke the word, making it unfruitful. Others like seed sown on good soil, hear the word, accept it, and produce a crop -- thirty, sixty, or even a hundred times what was sown." Mark 4:18-20*

Prayer: I seem to be on the brink of understanding these words as they apply to me. Help me to go further.

Response: Yes, you are on the edge of realizing that these words mean what they say. There is no New Age mystery to them. Listen to my words, hear them in the depth of your heart, and accept them. No need to search elsewhere in any magical formulas that are offered and available. So simple. Your Donna and you were blessed and came quite close to piercing the truth of these words together. Now it is up to you and how you will affect your son and your family and friends.

Worries of this life are words that apply to you all. I am telling you that such worries and desires only serve to drown out my message. Call it the rational mind; call it the dilution that the dark forces seek to distract. I am like a magnet that is pulling you ever closer. Allow the natural attraction and pull do its work. Don't hold on to distractions to lessen the pull. Let go and see. Yes, let go and see. There will be much for you to "do" to ease the flow to me, to reduce the obstructions.

The truly wise seek me out because they see finally that all else, all other pursuits, are simply extracurricular activities that distract. And understand that I am not promoting a constant reading of my word. No, I am saying consider the word as your operating system directions that you apply to your daily life from the time to rise to when you finally put your head on the pillow.

And I am not saying a literal application of my words, or even taking them out of context to fit a situation. I say this generally, though so often a verse does stand alone. You must simply approach scripture, my words, my communication with you on a daily basis, the insights that you receive during the day, and the people that come upon your path, as all resources to ease your journey to me. Note I say ease your journey. I did not intend this life to be so complex that you missed the message in the complexity of living life.

Today, be at ease, knowing that I am speeding your journey home and there is nothing for you to do but to ease your way through each moment with these words of this morning in your heart.

.

Scripture: *"Consider carefully what you hear," he continued, "With the measure you use, it will be measured to you – and even more. Whoever has will be given more; whoever does not have, even what he has will be taken away from him." Mark 4:24-25*

Prayer: Help me to understand more deeply *the measure* that you talk of.

Response: You have identified a critical expression. Not everyone has the vessel to grasp my words as someone else. And I don't mean the education. I mean the receptiveness. Receptiveness is attentiveness, inclination to hear warmly what is spoken and heard, a curiosity to learn more about me, an overriding interest to find the formula of life, a conviction that you are where you are for a purpose that you want to discover. And I could go on.

The receptacle is your begging bowl and you meet me as I you on all the street corners of your life and in the encounter I offer you your daily sustenance. Your humility in seeking me out, your obedience, your patience, your faith, and confidence that I will fill your begging bowl is all that is required. So see me in your life and more importantly see yourself at the street corner.

Yesterday, I met you during your conversation with a friend, in your attentiveness with your son when he was so excited to share stories with you, I met you as you composed and worked on that poem, in your discouragement I offered you sustenance in the gently composed letter of rejection to Rules For Engaging Grief,

Take each day and use that symbols to see and witness our encounters.. You already received some warm rice as you composed your prayers for your praying bowl and some meat that will tide you over in our dialogue this morning.

You are loved and that is the measure of my bounty.

Scripture: *"This is what the kingdom of God is like. A man scatters seed on the ground. Night and day, whether he sleeps or gets up, the seed sprouts and grows, though he does not know how. All by itself the soil produces grain – first the stalk, then the head, then the full kernel in the head. As soon as the grain is ripe, he puts the sickle to it, because the harvest has come."* Mark 4:26-29

Prayer: What is the kingdom of God?

Response: The kingdom of God is my dominion and you are invited to be with me. Within the kingdom, and you don't have to die in the physical dimension to taste its fruit; you are like a seed that began almost without consciousness and again almost through no effort on our part you begin to gather in the full dimension of what union with me means.

This parable is depicting your consciousness maturing radically. And you are in absolute wonder as to the process. Though you can reflect in a soul sense on where you have been, you are ever surprised at the wonders that await you in an ever rising eternity. What I mean is that you can have no appreciation, using words for your senses, as to how my love is unfolding in your life and soul.

This is why the image of the mansion with many rooms is spoken of, stressing the many rooms to accommodate you. So too is your experience of love, my love in the present which incidentally is my love for you in eternity.

So accept as you do the unfolding that is occurring. Try to stay present filled with hope.

Scripture: *Again he said, "What shall the kingdom of God be like, or what parable will we use to describe it? It is like a mustard seed, which is the smallest seed you plant in the ground. Yet when planted, it grows to become the largest of all garden plants, with such big branches that the birds of the air can perch in its shade." With many similar parables Jesus spoke the word to them, as much as they could understand. He did not say anything to them without using a parable. But when he was alone with his disciples, he explained everything. Mark 4:30-34*

Prayer: When I read and meditate on these words I move between being someone who needs the parable and then I thirst for the deep explanation.

Response: And so too with the disciples though I am quick to add that you are a disciple. Put aside as I have often reminded you thoughts – yes, thoughts – that are of the past. I am here with you now and yes I use parables with you as I did with the begging bowl image of two days ago and I will speak to you directly. You all need both, gauged to your consciousness, attentiveness, curiosity and faith.
You might ask, what were these sessions like alone with the disciples? Let me say they were not as some authors have speculated though it makes a fine story that Jesus had created some sort of a secret society. No, those sessions were used to reinforce what I hinted at in the parables. Much like I do with you and so many others each day.

For example, your concerns this morning are about finances and your stewardship of what I have granted you, instead of being or inclined to be so critical of yourself, consider the parable of the mustard seed that you quoted above.

Think of the seed that I buried in your heart, that mustard seed. Think and adore how that seed, unnoticed by you in your day to day living – see how it has blossomed and grown so much larger than the seed planted in so many others. And I am quick to add this is not about who has the largest blossom. There is no competition.
See how your seed has grown and you are and have not been responsible for pruning it. What plant do you know that self-prunes? You have not nurtured it and watered it and fed it. Again what plant do you know that tends to these critical tasks? I have. Think of the sequoia tree. Do you think it is responsible for positioning itself where rain will fall? No I am responsible for nurturing and pruning your branches. But listen now. What are you responsible for? For providing shade for the birds in the blazing heat of crisis, life's crises.

So you see we have a partnership here. Like any farmer or gardener, I take care of you and you take care of those around you – your children, friends, your beloved, those caught up in violence, those who grieve, and those who seek shelter.

I have not created a secret society but a community of love that grows as your branches become fuller and offer more and more places for the distressed to land.

#99

Scripture: *He got up, rebuked the wind and said to the waves, "Quiet! Be still!" Then the wind died down and it was completely calm. He said to his disciples, "Why are you so afraid? Do you still have no faith?" They were terrified and asked each other, "Who is this? Even the wind and the waves obey him." Mark 4:39-41*

Prayer: Help me to comprehend your power?

Response: You are asking a lot. If you get nothing out of these verses than to appreciate the allegories I use in communicating with you. On one level, indeed, it was about the fear of the disciples as they made their way to the other side of the lake when the storm came up, and that scenario is satisfactory for most in understanding my power, not for the purpose of controlling you, but to allow you to discern the backdrop upon which your life is lived.

You are not on a trapeze that has no safety net, nor another trapeze artist to catch you securely. No, you are in an environment of my choosing and protection to allow you, if you choose, to grow in a consciousness of my love.

There is something more here also. And that is where I allow those that are ready to probe deeper, to internalize my words to even a greater depth. When the wind and the waves were ordered to be quiet and still, those words apply to you in the allegory of the wind and waves.

How many times have you blundered about, distraught, like the wind and waves on a stormy night? Just allow your mind to envision the dark night of the soul, wind howling with the whispers of all the *should of's* and *could of's*, the past, and the waves of life in the unpaid bills, severed relationships, sickness, losses, that almost seem to swamp you. And what do I tell you and the waves, and wind? *Quiet! Be still!* Because in the quiet and stillness I will reach you, I will comfort you, I will nourish you.

In the preceding verse, Jesus got into the boat *just as he was.* That is also aimed at you in that so often in life you don't have time or the occasion to "dress" or prepare for the challenges that await you. All the more reason for you to be quiet, to be still.

For you who spent so much time on the water and still relish the wind on a rough bay, take this lesson deeply inside to your interior that I do not control, but oh, do I nourish you. Give me a flicker of recognition and I will embrace you like the brother separated at birth who is reunited near death. A flicker, I say, and my definition of flicker is much more generous that yours.

.

Scripture: *When he saw Jesus from a distance, he ran and fell on his knees in front of him. He shouted at the top of his voice, "What do you want with me Jesus, Son of the Most High God? Swear to God that you will not torture me." For Jesus had said to him, "Come out of this man, you evil spirit." Then Jesus asked him, "What is your name?" "My name is legion," he replied, "for we are many." And he begged Jesus again and again not to send them out of the area. A large herd of pigs was feeding on the nearby hillside. The demons begged Jesus, "Send us among the pigs; allow us to go into them." He gave them permission, and the evil spirits came out and went into the pigs. The herd, about two thousand in number, rushed down the steep bank into the lake and were drowned. Mark 5:6-13*

Prayer: Sometimes I flinch as taking the recounting in the scripture literally. Please give me guidance.

Response: A good hint to follow is when the author inserts specifics like 2,000 pigs you should first look at the verse in a literal aspect and then follow up with why the specifics are important.

In this scene, especially the preceding, it is clear that the fellow who lived among the tombs was possessed. I say possessed and not deranged because his cure was the direct result of having the evil spirits expelled. The lesson here focuses on what happens when Jesus confronts the Legion as they insist being called.

First notice how the evil spirit knows even before the audience who is confronting them. The darkness does indeed recognize the light. And further recognizes that the light has dominion over them. Releasing them from the man did have its consequences for those who owned the pigs. The lesson here is that you must accept the continued presence of the dark forces so intent in convincing you to stumble.

There are consequences and you see the consequences on the bloody battlefields where the dark forces are not simply eliminated. You don't think the pigs drowned with the corporal bodies of the pigs do you? In fact that region was quite hospitable to them because there was no jubilation when the dark forces were expelled. This is one of the reasons that the man no longer controlled wanted to accompany Jesus. But he was given the harder road and that was to bear witness to the light.

So too for you. Do not expect that your good efforts will cleanse the dark forces and their intentions from your life. Your "success" only emboldens them. Notice, however, that Jesus is calm and accepting, and conducts himself with the authority he possesses.

This is a time for you to listen and to be accepting of the direction your life is taking.

In our love this day.

#100

Scripture: *"Why all this commotion and wailing? The child is not dead but asleep." But they laughed at him. After he put them all out, he took the child's father and mother and the disciples who were with him, and went in where the child was. He took her by the hand and said to her, "Talitha koun!" (which means "Little girl, I say to you, get up!) Immediately, the girl got up and walked around (she was twelve years old). At this they were completely astonished. He gave strict orders not to let anyone know about this and told them to give her something to eat. Mark 5:40-43*

Prayer: Sometimes miracles are easier to comprehend when removed from the present – not as much is demanded of my belief. Help me to accept miracles in my midst.

Response: Now that is a good prayer. You are correct. It is easier to read about a miracle – something that takes place on command outside normal reality – and believe it or not as having taken place. Before I talk about miracles in your midst, allow me to say that this miracle reflects or conveys to you the impact Jesus makes in the local environment.

It is easy to appear in command until some event takes you into the very heart of the experience personally. This ruler of the synagogue whatever he said or thought about Jesus earlier, accepts his truth when his daughter falls ill. He was helpless to help her. He put all pretenses aside, because that is what apparent authority is pretense, and rushed to Jesus for help.

The lesson here is put aside pretense and rush to me in prayer. And there is no need to demonstrate pretense in doing this -- just the quiet acceptance of my love in the quiet of your heart. Don't worry about what you owe me in return. You don't have to hit the sidewalks with a sign. No, your very acceptance in the depth of your heart will radiate my love and others will see the change, that is what they will be drawn to.

That is why Jesus performs the miracle in the quiet of the child's room with just the parents and his specially selected disciples. He could have brought the child into the courtyard and did the same. But no, he performed the miracle within the heart of the home to remind you all that the change I am seeking in you is within.

And consider how he breaks the tension of the scene, even the recovery, and directs the parents to give the girl something to eat. What is he saying? Get on with life, allow the miracle of life to demonstrate my love.

So in your life, see the miracles that abound. You were worried about your health and now you are fine. Not fine to remain stationary in adoration but fine to share your love and wisdom with others. That is how it works for all of you. As the blood flows in your veins through your heart, so let your love flow in those you encounter and those distant who need that touch.

Remember the earlier verse and the woman who touched his garment and was healed. That is how I ask you to be, walking in a crowd with flowing garments, allowing those to touch your garment without you being the wiser. And let your garment – that is, how you appear to those around you – radiate my love.

.

#101

Scripture: *The apostles gathered around Jesus and reported to him all they had done and taught. Then, because so many people were coming and going that they did not even have a chance to eat, he said to them, "Come with me to a quiet place and get some rest." Mark 6:30-31*

Prayer: Bring me to a quieter place yet to hear your word.

Response: It is no accident that I have stirred up in you a quest for silence. As you look over these last months and even your time in Kabul, you prize ever increasingly stillness. Clearly, your meditations and writings reflect this.

It is in the silence that my voice clamors, but not sharply, for your attention. You are the student and instead of a large lecture hall filled with students and the attendant distractions, we are sitting opposite and I am talking softly but distinctly to you. It is this I wish others to hear. No need of academic excellence, the ability to read and digest great quantities of words and thoughts, simply to be attentive, quiet, still, and listen. I am never late for class. There are no snow days when you will not find me here. I have no travel commitments elsewhere.

And that is what the apostles hear. I say hear because I want you to discard the historical mind set and see our relationship in the present just as those of the past experienced the word in the present.

And notice how with all the clamor and excitement that fills the apostles' days, I call you to come apart, be nourished, and rest. And this time can occur in the busiest of lives, though it is so important not to justify importance or value on being busy. So many make excuses as to their time as if I understand. It is not me who must understand but such idle-busy folks who are not still.

And as you have gathered, my time with you is not measured in time. How do you like that for a paradox or *koan* as you would say? Have you ever measured the time when an inspiration hits you? Don't think a clock will satisfy your attempt. I come to you and if you were to think later the impact you would have to assume that we had days together explaining. No, I have and you have direct access so tap into this channel of mutual communication as often as you remember. Remember the poorly educated Russian peasant and the Jesus Prayer. Hard to believe for those studying in the dark and sometimes dank libraries how enlightened he is. Again, I use the present tense.

Well, I have given you something to ponder lightly because I wish you to swim ever more freely in my grace.

Scripture: *So they went away by themselves in a boat to a solitary place. But many who saw them leaving recognized them and ran on foot from all the towns and got there ahead of them. When Jesus landed and saw the large crowd, he had compassion on them, because they were like sheep without a shepherd. So he began teaching them many things. Mark 6:32-34*

Prayer: Help me to sense what spurred the crowds to rush to the other side of the lake.

Response: Sometimes, particularly with familiar verses, you rush over the recognized words. To really catch the meaning and receive its anointing, you must read and reflect like a proofreader and not depend upon what you think you know or have memorized.

Feel the scene and its conflict even. Jesus is anxious to get alone with his disciples and they are as anxious to be rid of these crowds and all its confusion and chaos. So they leave in a boat.

Now, see and feel what happens on the shore as a gathering crowd rushes even runs around the shoreline to the remote location they figure that Jesus and his disciples are heading. The lake, we learn later, is not calm. So with the distraction of pulling oars in this choppy water and trying to catch Jesus' words, the disciples are frustrated, especially so when they get out of the boat and pull it to the shore only to be greeted by a crowd of five thousand.

So we have the anxiousness of the disciples to be alone with Jesus, after all they were specially chosen by him, also their frustration at the confusion and chaos that greets them at every turn. Remember these same disciples were sent out and told to be totally dependent upon what they encounter. And then they encounter Jesus' apparent obliviousness to their needs by administering to the crowds.

Let's talk for a moment about compassion – so key to understanding my message. Compassion is gentle acceptance of what is without judging who's responsible and what has to be done in the instant. Compassion is like entering a gallery at an art museum and discovering you have entered an exhibit of cubist art and you are quite disoriented because you know nothing about it. That is your ego, if I can use that word, doesn't know anything about it. Compassion is like withholding your judgment – it's terrible, I can't understand it, is this art, and so on. Instead you are present before the chaos and observe, are present without judgment. This is not to say that you don't want to understand but your understanding is based on an appreciation of what is before you – so too compassion.

Be compassionate in your life and in what you encounter. Allow yourself to see where compassion leads. You will discover that its path is often quite unfamiliar at first. Soon you will see a direction like climbing a sand dune of despair and seeing over the top a quiet beach on a radiant azure sea. But for you to get there you must be compassionate.

And that is what Jesus exhibits when he sees the throng on the beach. He sees the thirst, the confusion, the anxiety, even fear of those standing on the beach, thinking that they are running out of time, wondering why they have never heard Jesus' message from the professionals, the leaders in the synagogue. The message holds today. Recognizing this, Jesus brings them together in order. Think of that. The throng does not out shout each other, but is assembled to hear him and later to be fed. So Jesus meets your needs both of the heart and the body in the sustenance you receive. I encourage you to become one of the five thousand. Leave the comfort of your environment to hear me and to be administered to.

This morning you woke early enough and left the comfort of your bed and are sitting before me. You are in a crowd of believers straining to catch every word, and the surprise is that just like the chaos in cubist art, you begin to settle down and see the patterns emerge before you that previously you judged the work of a mad man.

You have listened attentively this morning.

#103

Scripture: *By this time it was late in the day, so his disciples came to him. This a remote place, they said, it's already late. Send the people away so they can go to the surrounding countryside and villages and buy themselves something to eat. But he answered, "Give them something to eat." Mark 6:35-37*

Prayer: Sometimes, I too feel it is too much trouble. I guess I am lazy. Give me, please, some insights to work with.

Response: Jesus is always testing whether his students, you call them disciples, can swim across the pool. This is sort of a trite expression but remember I deal in water and its cleansing affect. He is never far off to ensure that they are not overwhelmed. So he allows them the chance to perform a miracle based on their faith alone and of course with his assistance. They don't do too well; but before you rush to judgment, when is the last time you performed a miracle? Do you know that I do not reserve miracles for a past that once again I must remind you is an illusion?

So instead of getting it, they give back all the rational explanations about cost both in money and in bother. Yes, bother. They really want to be free of the five thousand and believe that they have tolerated the intrusion of their time alone with Jesus long enough. In fact to a man, they believe that they have been quite gracious sharing his presence.

And you know what happened. Jesus doggedly and patiently instructs the disciples what they are to do. He not only satisfies the hunger of the five thousand, most of whom had not a clue as to what was occurring behind the scenes and at the same time gave the disciples a deep lesson in faith.

So here we are today, this morning, very early, sun not even up, and you can read the scripture verses with a distance of the two thousand years, but don't. See them as applying to you right this moment. I am asking you to feed the five thousand and beyond. Please don't tell me about your credentials, theological of course; please don't speak about it's early in the morning, or late in your life; please don't tell me that people will think you crazy suffering the first signs of dementia; please don't tell me that it won't help. I hear all your explanations and excuses as I did that late afternoon alongside the lake. All of the excuses are quite reasonable, but I am asking you to be unreasonable . . .to be as unorthodox, even crazy, as your hero Zorba, The Greek.

And as I instruct the disciples on how to feed the five thousand, I instruct you. I want to see you published. Not you, but the lessons that I give you daily. I want your Ego to be left figuring the odds of success while you do what I ask you to do.

And you will not spend all your time in the kitchen; you will experience the miracle of my word that you ingest each morning; you will get a better and better appreciation of what it means to be anointed both you and the word that resides, accessible for all, in the scripture.

#104

Scripture: *After leaving them, he went up on a mountainside to pray.* Mark 6:46

Prayer: It is almost ten PM, not my usual hour to meet you. Please give me your blessing for sleep.

Response: And then some. You also climb mountainsides to be alone and in prayer. Just think, imagine, a divine consciousness communicating with the divine lordship. It is enough to create lightening. Those times of prayer were times of deep love and solicitous of all on this earth that endure daily travails only to find God in their midst.

Your weariness is sufficient to remind you that another day is complete and you are where I want you to be. The very turns in your life are fashioning you and those around you. Just think with whom you have had intimate sharing this day: with your elder son's family – and your walk to the beach and back, your granddaughter and her smile, your son, your special friend, and through telephone calls to a friend and to your oldest daughter. Not a bad touching this day.

You have every reason to celebrate. And celebrate in my love. Do you think that I could shower you with less blessings? All your anxieties about job, relationships, and health evaporate in my love and care.

Tomorrow you will see the opening of that special rose that you represent.

Time for you to sleep. I love you.

Scripture: *When evening came, the boat was in the middle of the lake, and he was alone on land. He saw the disciples straining at the oars, because the wind was against them . . . [H]e went out to them, walking on lake, they thought he was a ghost. They cried out, because they all saw him and were terrified. Immediately, he spoke out to them and said: "Take courage! It is I. Don't be afraid." Then he climbed into the boat with them, and the wind died down. They were completely amazed, for they had not understood about the loaves, their hearts were hardened. Mark 6:47-51*

Pray: Lord, it is difficult to put aside my concern for my son and how sometimes in my weariness and loneliness I forget him. Please help me and direct your words to me in this time.

Response: First accept your loneliness and your sorrow. Those feelings in Jesus brought him to the other side of the mountain to pray. Don't you see that in the human dimension, loneliness and sorrow are special ingredients to bring you closer to me. Such feelings serve to focus you and I mean this in the broadest inclusion of others.

It is that loneliness that brought Jesus to the quiet place. But he did not indulge the loneliness but used such occasions to thank God, praise God, and to ask for a further unfolding of his divine mission. And it is in this asking, this prayer, that he and you demonstrate faith and trust.

Your anxiety about your son has a dimension that stretches so far out into the future. Rein it in and simply be there for your son's every step. Trust my love for you and for him.

It is very important for to greet the pain and suffering and anxiety you experience – and I should also mention loneliness. These are the fruits of your soul, a special ingredient or ingredients, showered over the field to ensure vigorous and bountiful yield. Without this your harvest would be without texture and strength.

Think of how it is written that the disciples experiencing in the flesh Jesus' supernatural visage, still cannot grasp what is happening in their midst. And the writer says that their hearts were hardened. He is not talking about "them" but about himself, until he finally embraced Jesus in all dimensions that he brought, yes invited, Christ, into his life.

So what is not said in this writing is what underlies all scripture. You are called through grace to invite Jesus into your heart. The sorrow, loneliness, and anxiety, are all the backdrop for Jesus to walk again on the water and to come directly into your heart from across the lake as he treads on the turbulent waters. And see what happens when he steps into your heart – or the boat in the image provided – the waters calm as does the wind.

I hear your invitation and I am stepping into your boat. In love.

Prayer: Dear Lord, as I begin my 68th year, please make me worthy to be and do what you wish for me. Please heal my loneliness and direct my path.

Response: You ask for a lot. It is in your loneliness that you find me. I am not punishing you but perfecting you. It is in your loneliness that you hear me most clearly. And it is in your loneliness that you are patient. Think of the examples you have before you, St. John of the Cross, as he is called wrote of the dark night of the soul and see how fruitful it was.

So loneliness will not be something cured only moderated. And I have taken such care to ensure that you have your son, your family and friends. Tell me what man of your vintage receives a call at 6:30 AM from your oldest daughter wishing you a happy birthday. You will experience endless, yes endless blessings today. Your youthful charm, the same soul smile that you recall sitting on the stoop with your sister is there only more distinct.

As far as my will for you, you are discovering it daily and it too becomes more clear. Only be still and you will hear the slightest vibrations.

Today you will receive a scriptural quote of my heart so be alert to catch its strains and then return here to meditate on it. Enough of the negative I want you to dwell in the joy of your union with me. So many presences of love surround you this day. All bless your life and love. Of course you will feel the presence of your departed spouse in every gesture as well as your mother who correctly considered you her prince.

Be love today in every action you are asked to perform.

Scripture: *Jesus left that place and went to the vicinity of Tyre. He entered a house and did not want anyone to know it, yet he could not keep his presence secret. In fact, as soon as she heard about him, a woman whose little daughter was possessed by an evil spirit, came and fell at his feet. The woman was a Greek, born in Syria Phoenicia. She begged Jesus to drive the demon out of her daughter. "First let the children eat all that they want," he told her, "for it is not right to take the children's bread and toss it to the dogs." "Yes, Lord," she replied, "but even the dogs under the table eat the children's crumbs." Then he told her, "For such a reply, you may go; the demon has left your daughter." She went home and found the child lying on the bed, and the demon was gone. Mark 7:24-30*

Prayer: Help my faith, Lord. Help me not to get wrapped up in trying to be or do what is not consistent with your plans for me.

Response: Please relax in my presence. Do not allow anxieties about the future that are clothed in the visage of people and events that have not occurred affect you. Right this moment, pause and listen.

Isn't it interesting that in this space of time there is nothing to disturb you and your serenity? Concerning tasks and people those you love and events that you wish to occur, or you think you wish to occur, they lose their hold, their influence.

You now see why Jesus retreated from the crowds to pray. Why he wished to remain unknown for a time longer. He wants to gather his strength, just as you must gather your strength, and everyone else must gather their strength. It is like stopping off at a way station and taking in the refreshment of rest and food and drink. Each time you pause at my way station, you are similarly refreshed.

You cannot control outcome – whether it be a success in your eyes that you have worked for or an outcome in your fortunes, a relationship realized. All you accomplish in prayer is your revitalization. I direct and guide you, not control you. Knowing this you have no reason to fret. The complexity of life becomes overwhelming when you decide the specifics of the destination and not concentrate on the journey. Allow the replay of events to go through your mind, to be processed by your mind later in your reflection, but in no way allow the reflection to determine the direction for the next day.

The woman in the verses simply gave Jesus a picture and demonstrated her love for her daughter and her faith in the Lord's ability to perform a miracle, though she did not even reach that conclusion. She simply stated that her daughter was ill. It was like her saying to a fellow traveler that it is raining on the trail. Jesus did the rest. So great was her faith.

So today, relax and see what unfolds.

Scripture: *He looked up to heaven and with a deep sigh said to him, "Ephphatha!" (which means, "Be opened!") At this, the man's ears were opened, his tongue was loosened and he began to speak plainly. Mark 7:34-35*

Prayer: Please open my ears to your words.

Response: This is the theme of my teaching to you these last days. Notice how the opening occurs. Jesus prays to the Father for the opening. Note, that Jesus sighs before he utters the words. That sigh is the pause that precedes his words and should be the same for you. Allow your words to reflect the innermost urging that I provide and nurture within you.

Be opened is the difference between hearing and listening. To be opened is to listen to my words at the soul level and not just hear the sound of cymbals crashing in your consciousness.

Be opened is your mantra and can bring your mind, body, and spirit into harmony. To be opened is to be seated in a choice seat in a concert hall and being eager to take in the full dimension of the experience. In your case, you are in the concert hall of a live event that unfolds daily with my messages and direction that becomes ever clearer to you.

And realize that this opening is not of your own doing. It is a grace that I provide you. You have not earned it and you couldn't possibly understand why you were chosen, are chosen. Others have asked that your ears be opened in their prayers. You and those that pray for you are not all in your circle, but include the spirit presences that have long since departed your world. So grace in thanksgiving the intentions of those who love you dearly.

Scripture: *"He will sit as a refiner and purifier of silver."* Malachi 3:3

Prayer: Someone sent me this verse. In describing the process, I was told that the silver refiner knows when the work is complete when he can see his image in the newly refined silver. Help me to an even deeper understanding.

Response: Dwell in the dawning moment of when I implanted my image in your soul. What a moment for all eternity. It is then like what Meister Eckhart[8] wrote, *it is I that sees with your eyes, it is I that looks out on each scene through you.* It is a moment that marks a special union.

You are right in helping to guide those enduring unspeakable hardship and agony through that dark night because like the refining of silver that is their experience.

In no way seeking to discourage you, your current trials are all related to an increasing consciousness that is marked by even a more refined quality of silver and gold. You see this is a metaphor to what occurs in the world. Some allow the refinement to proceed even to a higher and higher level of refinement where you become a clear mirror of my presence in you.

And how do you know if the process is proceeding. You feel the heat and the agony of that heat from time to time. There is always the relief that I provide. You catch the success of the process in the works that you offer to others that reflects my image. Ask the question what would I do, what would I be in that situation and then you can confirm my presence.

In your love.

---

[8] Christian mystic and preacher of the 13th Century.

#110

Scripture: *They came to Bethsaida, and some people brought a blind man and begged Jesus to touch him. He took the blind man by the hand and led him outside the village. When he had spit on the man's eyes and put his hands on him, Jesus asked, "Do you see anything?" He looked up and said, "I see people, they look like trees walking around." Once more Jesus put his hands on the man's eyes. Then his eyes were opened, his sight was restored, and he saw everything clearly. Jesus sent him home, saying, "Don't go into the village." Mark 8:22-26*

Prayer: Please restore my vision, Lord.

Response: It is not so much restoration. I am providing you a vision beyond what you ever experienced earlier in this life. I have taken you outside the village, that is, where you were comfortable, and given your sight. And I ask that you not return to the village of comfort and of familiarity. The home you return to is the home of your heart where you experience my presence. No longer do you engage stick figures that walk like trees. I dispatch you to the regions where a depth of healing is called for.

Notice the adjustment that Jesus makes when at first the man's sight is restored to what he experienced previously and then he sees with clarity. You can see with clarity and I ask you to shed the preconceptions for sight that you previously cultivated.

Demonstrate that new sight in relationships, in your work, in your writing, and in raising your son, and in your relationship with everyone with whom you come into contact.

See today with your new sight. Begin each day as if you have just had your sight restored; don't return to the old ways; and tell me then what you see as I once asked the blind man.

So for today, tell me what you see. Who knows perhaps I will adjust your sight further.

#111

Scripture: *"But what about you?" he asked, "Who do you say I am?" Mark 8:29*

Prayer: Help me to answer your question as directly as Peter.

Response: You selected this morning a special line, a special question. Just as the billboard in front of the community center states: "Wise men still seek his counsel," you are being drawn deeper in union with me. The question resounds in your heart and your mind is puzzled. Your mind is puzzled because it cannot grasp the full dimension of the question as well as the answer that Peter responds, "You are the Christ."

This Peter is not some impressionable follower, that is, until he met Christ and was called. He dropped everything, most especially his livelihood, town, and embraced a life where most feared and despised him for leaving the Jewish tradition over which the Pharisees ruled. His answer to the question was not an answer given in a lecture hall but in the actions and fealty of someone who embraced directly Christ's words.

So this morning, think about, answer the question, "Who do you think I am?" And allow your heart to follow me over time and dimension as I reach out to you in my embrace of love. This love does not wait for a Valentine's Day to be reminded of my love. My love is a nanosecond to nanosecond love that enfolds you in my warm embrace.

So today, think over, ponder the love that I am for you and at the same time spread that love in an ever widening circle.

And as you appreciate, love is a risk. A risk that it will not be returned in kind, that it will be misunderstood, that it will be rejected. But let me tell you that love is never, I repeat never, rejected. Love, the pure love of the father, always has an impact, always reaches soil like a seed, even if the fruit of that love is not manifest. Love is like the seed, sometimes, that is buried in a dark place and then years and years, even centuries later, finds light and moisture and blossoms across time. So realize on this special day that love is my message; deep penetrating love is what this life is all about; and you are where you are to learn about love and to pass it unconsciously and consciously along your path.

I love you specially.

#112

Scripture: *And he said to them, "I tell you the truth, some who are standing here will not taste death before they see the kingdom of God come with power." Mark 9:1*

Prayer: When I have read this verse previously, I thought that there is something wrong here. We are still around walking the globe over two thousand years later. Can you help me to accept fully this verse; and not quietly dismiss it as an example of a misquote?

Response: First, please put aside this historical notion that always creeps into your reading of scripture. The scripture is a living document, anointed. It knows no past. Read this scripture again as you are in the presence of Jesus and he is speaking to you right now.

Do you see how powerful those words are? What promise! And you are required only to trust and believe.

Do you remember when your father with clouded eyes looked at you minutes before he drew his last breath? If he could have expressed himself he would have expressed what he was experiencing – something beyond his comprehension at a heart and soul level, since his mental faculties were already dulled.

Rather than pity him, understand that the perfect way to occupy the mind and calm the monkey-chatter is to lose your honed mental faculties. In that peace, though you are no longer able to convey your experience, you begin union. And it is then that you realize at the deepest level that you are not to taste death as the kingdom of God dawns in your soul consciousness.

So you see, these words are written for you right this moment. And with this assurance, the question is given to you, what are you becoming to inherit this kingdom? Realize that you don't earn the inheritance; you become to enjoy the inheritance. It is like being in a concert hall with wonderful acoustics. Your seat is quite expensive, a choice selection. You are dressed elegantly to reflect your preparation and respect for the event. Now, surely you would be out of place to wear ear muffs to distort or muffle the music.

So this is your place today. The music will play soon, though you hear a faint melody in your heart as the orchestra is warming up. I ask you to turn your attention ever more to where you are, how well you are prepared, how good you look, the companions of love that accompany you, the select seat for which you have been chosen, the fine company you are in, the glorious setting – so what more do you need to realize that you will not taste death?
My love to you this day.

#113

Scripture: *Jesus asked the boy's father, "How long has he been like this?" "From childhood," he answered. "It has often thrown him into fire or water to kill him. But if you can do anything, take pity on us and help us." "If you can?" said Jesus. "Everything is possible for him who believes." Immediately the boy's father exclaimed, "I do believe; help me overcome my unbelief!" When Jesus saw that a crowd was running to the scene, he rebuked the evil spirit. "You deaf and mute spirit," he said, "I command you, come out of him and never enter him again." The spirit shrieked, convulsed him violently and came out. The boy looked so much like a corpse that many said, "He's dead." But Jesus took him by the hand and lifted him to his feet, and he stood up. After Jesus had gone indoors, his disciples asked him privately, "Why couldn't we drive it out?" He replied, "This kind can come out only by prayer." Mark 9:21-29*

Prayer: It seems the selected verses become longer, not knowing where to stop. Guide me in my thoughts.

Response: The beauty of these quiet mornings is that you are not on any scheduled program of study. A brief scripture verse, or several, as today is the same. Remember, the words are anointed. This means that it is as if implanted above each word is a tiny light that lights up when you touch it with your eyes.

Today's reading is about belief. You have heard the term for so many years that the word loses its meaning. Belief is the mind and heart's clamor for the truth. It is the mind's grasp of the need to suspend, relinquish disbelief and go full throttle into a region that on the surface makes no sense.

I know you have used the image and experience of jumping out of a plane to symbolize the body death experience. Let's apply it to faith on a day-to-day level. Belief is accepting that something, some view, some problem seems unsolvable, but you still proceed innocently, knowingly because I have told you so and I have made a commitment to you. So that is belief. Despite all that your mind warns you – don't jump out of the plane – you do so and not in any drugged state, but consciously, awake, and with confidence, that is, faith.

On the surface the setting of this miracle has present all the protagonists: the teachers of the law who do not accept Jesus, the crowds curious but not committed, the disciples loyal but frustrated with their inability to perform, the father who cuts through everything with his plaintive appeal for help, the son stricken and helpless, and Jesus. And with all this diversity of interests, Jesus reduces everything, all the clamor, to the need for prayer, not the memorized formal prayer of others, but the prayer of the individual in faith, revealing uncertainty, hope, faith, and humility.

Come away with the need to be in prayer whether you are blessed with a quiet morning or in the midst of chaos, in celebration or struck low with despair – in each situation like a diamond a light is shining through to give you the full dimension of what you seek and what awaits you. .

Scripture: *"Salt is good, but if it loses its saltiness, how can you make it salty again? Have salt in yourselves and be at peace with each other."* Mark 9:50

Prayer: Help me to understand better what you mean by this saltiness in my life.

Response: By saltiness I mean the need to cultivate courage to meet me directly, eyes open. I want you to confront me in truth, no glancing to the side. I want our eyes to be locked. By saltiness I do mean a tang, a freshness that is not diluted with fancy interpretation. And I mean by fancy, the interpretation of scholars that treat the word as an academic puzzle and not the simple truth, the simple guidance to be incorporated in all you do.

By saltiness, I mean independence, free of mind controlling influences, be it professional or even religious. The tang of salt is so special. It contributes to your alertness in thought and heart if you allow.

By the saltiness, I mean a deliberate embrace of truth and furthering that flavor across the globe. You are each sitting above a salt mine, a deep cavern that is a source of salt for those who are industrious and committed to mine it and ensure that no water seeps into the mine, washing it down a stream.

Think of salt as the tang you feel when a word that you read strikes you, an inspirational thought catches your attention, a deed is performed that didn't have to be done but you know its interior worth.

Salt is healing and preserves you from a desolate life. Why? Because – it causes you to be alert, to sense the very presence of the dark forces, who have no better goal than to diminish you.

And getting back to an earlier verse, salt reminds you of your purpose in tending to the little children among you, even those whose years exceed the beads on a long chain. When you lock your eyes on mine, you will discover that your path is not arduous; you are not lonely; your generosity of spirit grows sublimely.

So today, sprinkle some salt on your finger to recall this instruction.

Scripture: *People were bringing the little children to Jesus to have him touch them, but the disciples rebuked them. When Jesus saw this, he was indignant. He said to them, "Let the little children come to me, and do not hinder them, for the kingdom of God belongs to such as these. I tell you the truth, anyone who will not receive the kingdom of God like a little child will never enter it." Then he took the children in his arms, put his hands on them and blessed them. Mark 10:13-16*

Prayer: In some respects I remain a little child. Help me to accept this.

Response: Do you know that you have retained such child-like qualities of a child. You risk as a child does in play. So you don't need much in the way of reminding. However, let me go further with these verses.

Jesus helps you to understand the connection to your heart and to Him by creating an atmosphere that children can do so well. Do you remember how you described the experience with your first grandson and how he taught you how to waste time? Not really wasting time but rather allowing the investment of your attention in him without considering in advance the outcome, the product so to speak.

Well, that is what I am talking about. No longer weigh your commitment on some anticipated outcome that tries to decide if it is worth the effort. I am asking you to plunge in and trust the promise that Jesus makes at the end of the verses quoted, namely unless you are like that little children with your enthusiasm, trust, and innocence, you will not enter the kingdom.

This instruction applies to you at all stages of your life. It becomes even more evident however when you age and become dependent once again on the care of loved ones, assuming that your life of love is returned in kind. Children also have the quality of letting go, suspending disbelief, of being excited by a new morning, of expressing wonder and excitement in their voices and expressions, of being generous, trusting, of smiling and wanting to share that smile. Please treat your young son in your midst as your model and in turn help him to retain that model for the future.

You can tell someone who has retained his childlike innocence by how well he or she relates to children. If you don't pass the test, don't throw up your arms and consider that you have moved on from that innocence, but make immediate steps to return to that spirit within. Remember how your crusty Dad sat quietly as your son explained to him his children's toys.

All for now.

Scripture: *"Children, how hard it is for the rich man to enter the kingdom of God. It is easier for a camel to go through the eye of a needle, than for a rich man to enter the kingdom of God. Mark 10: 24-25*

Prayer: Lord, just yesterday I came upon this verse as it relates to a poem I wrote a couple of years ago. What are you telling me in this coincidence?

Response: I provide you puzzling texts to keep your mind occupied trying to solve the puzzle and then I instruct you – directly in your heart. I am telling you in metaphor about the need to let go, detach. As you once wrote about your friend, who passed away, "He traveled light." So for you all. Travel light.

That doesn't conjure up, or should not, assembling at the last outpost before trekking across the desert. My meaning is that in your life now identify what you are attached to, as you tend to view this physical life as permanent, and begin to detach. Take back your soul power and don't squander it on physical objects or controlling relationships. Begin to learn the art of flight.

The physical dimension and its attachments are rather easy to identify. They are the attachment to money, things, houses, cars, etc. Harder to distinguish comes in the range of relationships. A wonderful template to use, almost as a test, is to take for example a relationship that lingers and might even grow stronger with separation and later death, and one that requires or tempts one to try to control or change. I did not say improve, rather change.

This is a difficult distinction to make so be patient. In a relationship that you are seeking to fit the other person or that person is attempting the same for you into a preconceived mold to meet either of your expectations, that is an attachment to a "thing" – in this case, an emotional relationship. This happens from the most intimate relationship of what one thought was a committed relationship to a familial relationship to a child or young adult.
What you must do is let go of the control of things and those kinds of relationships.

What you will find are a couple of insights. The first, in that aspect of control, one fits into the definition of a rich man and indeed, forget about the eye of a needle, you would not fit through a wide door. Shed these attachments and the perceived need to control and you are slimmer than you have ever imagined – slim and lithe and ready to venture forth to the kingdom of God.

Let me say one more word on control in relationships. You also control when you seek appraisals and responses from others that you have preprogrammed to suit your expectations. So here you become inflated even in disappointment when your expectations are not met, and yes, you might discover it impossible to negotiate the narrow paths ahead.

I know that you are puzzled why Jesus questions the young man in an earlier verse as to why he addressed him as good teacher, especially when that term is reserved for God. Always Jesus is provoking his dead and sometimes dull audience. And what does that audience do? They miss the provocation, translate the comment literally, or as in the translation you are using do not even comment on the seeming contradiction in the notes. It's just too difficult to resolve and the commentators remain silent and prefer to be verbose in areas where even a child would understand. So I conclude with the admonition: challenge what you read and don't believe everything you hear.

.

Scripture: *"We are going up to Jerusalem," he said, "and the Son of Man will be betrayed to the chief priests and teachers of the law. They will condemn him to death and will hand him over to the Gentiles, who will mock him and spit on him, flog him and kill him. Three days later he will rise."* Mark 10:33-34

Prayer: Help me to put myself in the scene to catch the import of these words that through repetition lose their sting.

Response: Those two verses capture so much teaching that occurred as Jesus led this frightened band to Jerusalem. These words serve as a quick summary of what Jesus was predicting and with more specificity as each day drew them nearer to the holy city.

Jesus' steps toward Jerusalem were deliberate. Those of his followers were tentative. Were they approaching the city for Jesus to assume some temporal mantle of authority, those very followers would have been leading the way.

So you see here a model for you. You are not leading the way and though you have a hint perhaps of what awaits you, you trust in the footsteps that precede you. If the verse ended without the last line – *Three days later he will rise.* – only someone bent on a suicide mission would have continued to follow. But here is the essence of my message. Follow closely because I am parting the veil, opening the door, lighting your path, so follow closely and the curtain will not close, nor the door, nor the light extinguished.

Often times you don't consider these words as celebratory, but they are. They represent the mountain top, the summit, of all summits scaled, and not in some gloomy fog but in the rapture of the light I hold above you.

The words that will lose the sting are those describing what preceded the rising because the light overcomes all darkness, all darkness. So today even though you are in the season of your lent, celebrate the rising, follow closely in my footsteps, allow nothing to interfere, keep me in your sight. In times of stress and darkness, close the distance between us.

In my love of you.

Scripture: *"You know that those who are regarded as rulers of the Gentiles lord it over them and their high officials exercise authority over them. Not so with you. Instead, whoever among you wants to be great among you must be your servant,, and whoever wants to be first must be slave of all. For even the son of man did not come to be served, but to serve and give his life as a ransom for many."* Mark 10: 41-45

Prayer: I have never appreciated those last words that you gave your life as a ransom for many. Why? I guess that I conveniently adopt an historical perspective and conclude since I was not around when you gave your life; you didn't give it for me. I also have had trouble accepting that your death was so horrific when we read of those, even martyrs, who sacrificed their lives in what would appear to be a more painful manner. Can you help me here?

Response: Oh, are you stirred up – almost like the stew that you are cooking. Stay with the stew for a minute and consider the ingredients that you have poured and sprinkled in for the flavor. So it is with the sacrifice of Jesus' life. It added flavor to the whole formula for the salvation of mankind. It is not for anyone to question the ingredients, including those who have suffered and given up their lives in my service or quietly accepted their faith, and wonder whether it was worth it.

Rather, I want you to see and understand that the cause for redemption began with Jesus and continues to this day. It is a constant and not a recipe, historical in nature, which has been handed down. It is being enacted today, on the battlefields of violence that shroud Iraq, Afghanistan, Lebanon, Palestine so obviously, but just as insidiously through poverty and exploitation throughout the world.

So what you experience is redemption, through the gifts of others, and through your own participation in the celebration, yes, I said celebration, which redemption is.
So in your discouragement, celebrate that you are contributing a special ingredient to the process of redemption that provides food for those around you and those for whom you pray.

Who is to judge that someone suffered more? For you without having access to peanut butter might be a burden for which you are not prepared. I jest. However, my point is consider your own path and don't ruminate if someone has an easy path to redemption or a difficult one.

Most of all – trust in the process of redemption. You are here to be cleansed, to be glorified, to reflect my image, not an easy or painless endeavor. So relax and know, I repeat know, that nothing will I allow that would prevent you from realizing the place

I have prepared for you. With that confidence, go out on that new path you have chosen without any concern for your safety.

Scripture: *Many rebuked him and told him to be quiet, but he shouted all the more, "Son of David, have mercy on me!" Jesus stopped and said, "Call him." So they called to the blind man, "Cheer up! On your feet! He's calling you." Throwing his cloak aside, he jumped to his feet and came to Jesus. "What do you want me to do for you?" Jesus asked him. The blind man said, "Rabbi, I want to see." "Go," said Jesus, "your faith has healed you." Immediately he received his sight and followed Jesus along the road. Mark 10:48-52*

Prayer: What would it take of me to throw my cloak aside and follow you?

Response: Well, you understand well that the cloak represents all you cling to and only you can answer what that represents. Spend some time thinking, reflecting, upon what the cloak represents for you.

Not only does the blind man represent one of great faith, but also one of great need and even despair. The fear and need are really representative of his need, and in throwing them aside he demonstrated his faith to Jesus and upon that act of faith his sight was restored. Notice the verse doesn't say that he went back for his cloak. No, he simply followed Jesus down the road.

So the lesson here is that once you detach and receive the miracle of the moment, even day, or year, don't go back looking to see if you can find the cloak.

Sight restored is also an important image because the sight I am talking about is not 20-20 eyesight but rather the sight into your soul that then increases your ability to see far out beyond you to those suffering in the world, and that is where this restored sight increases your compassion.

Take the words of the disciple to heart. Cheer up! This is no time despite the suffering in the world not to offer a cheerful demeanor. Cheer up, your sight is restored. Now show me who you are with this new sight. Begin with this moment.

Peace and good sight to you this day, you of cheerful aspect.

Scripture: *As they approached Jerusalem and came to Bethphage and Bethany at the Mount of Olives, Jesus sent two of his disciples, saying to them, "Go to the village ahead of you, and just as you enter it, you will find a colt tied there, which no one has ever ridden. Untie it and bring it here. If anyone asks you, 'Why are you doing this?' tell him, 'The Lord needs it and will send it back here shortly'"* Mark 11:1-3

Prayer: Lord, I laugh when I consider that Jesus was a horse thief. What am I to make of this verse?

Response: Here is an example of how everything is beginning to come together for the final act of Jesus' public ministry. The colt is just one element of this intricate enactment of your redemption. The confidence that the disciples showed in following Jesus' directions and in responding to questions – not as thieves but as anointed ones dispatched to participate in this final enactment. They proceeded without questioning from those that were on the sidelines.

The colt was not ridden earlier that is also significant for the sacrificial quality of the event. It is like using a chalice for a special event and then destroying the chalice that it would not be used again. This colt would only be remembered for its first rider.

The journey was almost a parody in that Jesus was not looking to establish a worldly kingdom but his disciples still nurtured a faint hope that such would be the outcome. Riding the colt into Jerusalem served to calm their fears and even the lack of objection when they untied the beast seemed to stoke their hope that an earthly kingdom a awaited them.

Put yourself alongside Jesus as he moved quietly and slowly toward the city and the reverence shown by those along the path. Though they had no idea of what awaited him. So in this sense you proceed along the road, deliberately and with purpose and a destination in mind and heart. The branches and cloth strewn in his path are the same as the graces that shower over you to muffle the distraction of this grasping world and serves also to focus your attention on where you are going.

You are on such a path and in the muffled quality of your surroundings you wait for enlightenment, direction. That is what you ask for and that is what you are receiving, all becoming clearer and clearer with each passing day.

Be of good cheer and generous.

CHAPTER FIVE -- STILLNESS

In 2005 I spent six months in Kabul. One evening I snatched a rose from a bush growing within the fortified compound. I returned to the modified shipping container that served as home. There I placed the rose in a make-shift coffee cup vase and then onto the narrow metal table that served as a desk. I pulled up a chair, and for the next fifteen minutes quietly observed the rose – the sound of the compound generators droned in the background.

That scene remains in my memory and represents for me what is possible in a state of active stillness. It is with active stillness that I tread a beach at dawn, sit quietly in a house of worship, allow the wind to rush over me on a mountain height, and choose to be with a companion in silent communion.

This active stillness is especially present when I approach Scripture – not unlike the rose of Kabul. Conscious and alert I read and reread slowly the selected verse with the attention that the rose received. And as with the rose, I find that I become one with what I am reading – what I have come to observe. Conscious, alert, and still, the words of Scripture bring me to union with the God of my father.

#121

Scripture: *The next day as they were leaving Bethany, Jesus was hungry. Seeing in the distance a fig tree in leaf, he went to find out if it had any fruit. When he reached it, he found nothing but leaves, because it was not the season for figs. Then he said to the tree, "May no one ever eat fruit from you again." And his disciples heard him say it. Mark 11:12-14*

Prayer: Lord, this verse seems contradictory – who would expect that there be figs if they were still out of season? What am I to learn from these words that Mark took time to write down and emphasize that this is what the disciples heard?

Response: The first lesson is to please let go of linear time, that one track that goes from A to B and continues to C. Jesus is thrusting you into the eternal moment that we have discussed previously. The time is NOW. There are no seasons out in the future that you can patiently await. The call to action is now.

The fig tree represents all of you who gather your credentials awaiting the time to act, to share the power of love with neighbor, friend, and even enemy. How many times have you said or heard that the time is not right, or worse, when the time is right I will do the following. That is the fig tree, gathering leaves, preparing, preparing, and preparing some more, but no food for the spirit is available.

It is similar to the prophets who argued that they did not have the intelligence, the voice, the stature, the courage, the language ability, to give my message to the people, and I only said do it; I will be there for you.

The puzzle from which you are asked to learn the solution to is there is no right time according to your calculations. You will always have a reason, or at least can discover one, in which to prepare, or I would say delay. So it is with all of your fig trees with flowery leaves. Think back on your life and see those instances where you responded in love and generosity without considering the time of preparation necessary to make a mature decision.

So, don't be the mature fig tree that waits in the sun for the right time to blossom. If you do that to your horror you will discover that you don't blossom, or worst yet, your fruit will be a dry and wrinkled as a prune.

In my love.

Scripture: *"Have faith in God," Jesus answered. "I tell you the truth, if anyone says to this mountain, 'Go, throw yourself into the sea,' and does not doubt in his heart but believes that what he says will happen, it will be done for him. Therefore I tell you, whatever you ask for in prayer, believe that you have received it, and it will be yours. And when you stand praying, if you hold anything against anyone, forgive him, so that your Father in heaven may forgive you your sins." Mark 11:22-25*

Prayer: These words are so clear. Yet, when I pray I catch myself looking up to see if my prayer has already been answered as a check on the reliability of the promise. What can I do differently?

Response: Prayer and faith are continuing processes within you. As a child, ironically, you could and did pray with great simplicity and your prayers were met at the level that you sought. You lost that simplicity of prayer as you matured.

As you appreciated the depth of what you were asking for in prayer, your faith diminished. You just couldn't believe it. You also added another filter to your prayer and that was a false sense of unworthiness. I say false because you were and continue to rationalize as to why you don't deserve the answer to your prayers.

Additionally, you do, as you mentioned, look up with one eye to see if the lights have gone on in the room with the answering of the prayer instead of proceeding with your life in the knowledge that the prayer has been answered. It is as if you put your life on hold awaiting the miracle of faith instead of continuing to move forward with the knowledge that what you ask for in my name will be granted.

So much of what you ask for and others ask for you believe that you are unworthy. It is time for you to relax and allow me to determine what is unworthy. For you, learn to pray in faith. The very pray is sufficient for your salvation.
You will discover as you have already that your prayers become more generous and compassionate and over time have less and less to do with you but rather on what you can do or be for others. So pray vigorously and allow me to grant your prayers. All is being enacted as you ask for my greater glory.

Scripture: *"By what authority are you doing these things?" they asked. "And who gave you authority to do these things?" Jesus replied, "I will ask you one question. Answer me, and I will tell you by what authority I am doing these things. John's baptism – was it from heaven, or from men? Tell me!" They discussed among themselves, and said, "If we say, 'From heaven,' he will ask, 'then why didn't you believe him?' But if we say, 'From men . . .' (They feared the people for everyone held that John really was a prophet." So they answered Jesus, "We don't know." Jesus said, "Neither will I tell you by what authority I am doing these things." Mark 11:28-33*

Prayer: Is it impatience that I sense with Jesus in his questions and response to the chief priests, teachers, and elders?

Response: Understand that Jesus is speaking to you today and don't be distracted that the event cited in the verses occurred two thousand years ago. He is speaking to you right now. Take the questions as those being asked of you.

Was John simply a lunatic living in the desert or was he from God as a precursor to the Christ? Don't try to sort out his relationship to Jesus. Simply, ask yourself does John come to you daily to remind you of Jesus' coming into your life.

And how does John come? In the many signs that you receive daily, almost hourly, pointing you to the Christ. John is that finger pointing the way. He is not the way, but pointing you onto the path.

Don't look at Jesus being so impatient, but rather see him as he is in your life the authority that makes a way for you. You are not following some village merchant seeking a shortcut in the woods and risks becoming lost. You are striding behind someone who knows the forest in all seasons, in the dark and fog, when it is bleak and cold, rainy and snowy. He pauses because he is not going to allow you to get lost, though you obviously can turn back or refuse to go on.

No, this Jesus is someone of great patience and compassion. You might find him supporting your arm when you have stubbed from toe, he might even be found to be carrying your pack when it is too heavy for you, and you might even see him throwing that same pack into a gorge so as not to burden you further.

So on what authority does he speak, does he come among you? By the authority of the Godhead and in everyplace a knee is bent and head bowed in adoration. Patience? Supreme patience in allowing you to see his light that is so bright around you.

All for today.

Scripture: *"What will the owner of the vineyard do? He will come and kill those tenants and give the vineyard to others. Haven't you read this scripture: 'The stone the builders rejected has become the capstone, the lord has done this, and it is marvelous in our eyes.'" Mark 12:9-11*

Prayer: How can I serve you, even in return for your generosity to me?

Response: First realize that you are all tenants on my vineyard. My vineyard is a literal world of plenty. I seek you to learn the skills required to make the quality wine of which you are capable. I ask only that you work together in the fields and in the harvest and in the production and distribution of the wine. I ask only that you acknowledge where this plenty originates.

So your collective efforts to go out on your own and not acknowledge me are fraught with great difficulty for you. Your collective efforts to deny me in the most subtle ways by rejecting my message and messengers earn you true tribulation. It is only when you pull away from such wrongdoing that you will discover the harmony of wine making.

Please don't lose sight of what wine represents.

Scripture: *"When the dead rise, they will neither marry or be given in marriage; they will be like angels in heaven. Now about the dead rising – have you not read in the book of Moses, in the account of the bush, how God said to him: 'I am the God of Abraham, the God of Isaac, and the God of Jacob?' He is not the God of the dead, but of the living."* Mark 12:25-27

Prayer: Help me Lord to absorb the message that you give me so directly in scripture and in events that I sometimes miss.

Response: First, I say that your time at the Trappist Monastery was blessed. Blessed for what you gave freely and also what you received. Those three days are a formula for living that you take into the day to day living far from the fields of the monastery.

In these verses I seek to console you so that you are not anxious. Anxiety is the domain of the dark force. Dismiss the very hint of anxiety in your life and in those around you.

Jesus is speaking to you, and not in the past tense, that eternal life is promised to you. You know that relationships experienced on earth are expanded to include those across whose paths you walked as well as with those you shared the most intimate of relationships.

In eternity those relationship reflect the bounty of God in your life. The deeper and purer the relationship the reflection of light emanates from your visage. Try to consider an existence free of form and boundaries as you are present in the Divine Rapture. What you "bring to the party" so to speak is the expanded and expanding consciousness of love cultivated here with tears, laughter, sorrow, joy, dimness, alertness – every lesson that you experience here, every opportunity you have to console, administer to, all these opportunities enrich who you are at the deepest level of your existence and that is what you bring forward in life.
Your communion also includes those spirits who passed before or after you, enriching the kingdom of god with praise, adoration, and celebration.

. In my love.

#126

Scripture; *"Of all the commandments which is the most important?" "The most important one,"* answered Jesus, *"is this. 'Hear, O Israel, the Lord your God, the Lord is one. Love the Lord your God with all your heart and with all your soul and with all your mind and with all your strength.' The second is this, 'Love your neighbor as yourself.' There is no commandment greater than these."* Mark 12:28-31

Prayer: Here I am Lord, still not feeling 100%, still wondering if this is the path that you choose for me, still rustling in the dark – seeking the light. Please enlighten me this morning.

Response: Take a moment to slow your mind down. There is nothing you have to do. You have these few isolated moments that you carve out in the day. And this is your commitment and your sign that you love me with all your heart, mind, soul, and strength. Your prayers for others and your attention and consciousness in reaching out to those in need are also your demonstration of your soul commitment to the service and love of others equal to and exceeding at times your love of yourself. Now what more do you need from me to remind you that you are on the right path? How many times in your life were these elements of your journey not as obvious as now?

Trust the process of journeying, just as the process of a pilgrimage because that is what you are experiencing. Why not incorporate pilgrimage in your concept of journey? Consider taking a pilgrimage with your son.

I am so pleased in your work, your writing and your creativity. Do you realize that I do not write the poems for you? You are not receiving some transmission from afar but are creating them as the fruit of your pilgrimage?

The commandments of which I speak in these verses are not idle words but are not only a command but a diagnostic tool to see how you are doing in matching the goals of the commandments. You see, I have given you the answers embedded in the exam! You know how well you are doing on the test immediately by the fruit of your actions. And your grade is not bad, well above passing. Don't get complacent and think that you don't have to continue to study. I have more tests, actually applications of the same exam questions to see how you will continue to improve your score.

How remarkable that you are my creation. Most important for you to realize that in your actions and prayers, in your mind, and physical strength all that I ask I discover in your actions. This is what adoration means. It does not means seating at my feet in adoration, blindly repeating some hymn or prayer, or sitting in an eternal smile for an eternity. It is being present in heart, mind, soul, and strength, creating the fruit of your devotion to share in an eternity of love. That is why I say you are experiencing eternity right now. What you are learning on the pilgrimage of your life you will take with you and make even more manifest when you pass beyond the limits of the body.

Scripture: *While Jesus was teaching at the temple courts, he asked: "How is it that the teachers of the law say that the Christ is the son of David. David himself, speaking by the Holy Spirit, declared: 'The Lord said to my Lord, sit at my right hand, until I put your enemies under your feet.' David himself calls him 'Lord,' how can he be his son?" Mark 12:35-37*

Prayer: Help me to understand the authority of Jesus.

Response: You see in Jesus the complexity of humanity that you find in yourself. Think how your emotions range a wide spectrum. Think of how different audiences would view you differently. What Jesus conveys of the human aspect is compactness. His authority is not inconsistent with his healing of the lame and blind, the joy of being with his community though there is not enough written about this side of Jesus, his prayerfulness and communion with God, his confidence in calling forth God's blessings, his decisiveness in pushing the money changers from the temple, his courage in moving ever forward to his own death. That is the picture you should take in to help you see and feel your own compactness even with the frayed edges of anxiety.

I didn't mention patience that looms and affects the Jesus you are coming to know. Patience to allow you to move toward him at your pace as you encourage those you love to move similarly, perhaps, at your pace.

These verses are valuable in setting the scene of the time. Notice in the line afterwards, is written the delight of the listeners who already considered Jesus a hero of sorts for challenging the teachers who could be and were so dismissive of the people.

It is time for you to step out of the crowd, incidentally, and you are doing so though you are still distracted by the past and filled with uncertainty about the future. It is past time for you to demonstrate within that same confidence of Jesus, as you know where you are headed as you all should know.

Let go of your concerns, you are protected so carefully. Do you think I would allow you to lose your way now after you have journeyed so far? Remain at peace today and see my love unfold deliberately in your day.

#128

Scripture: *As he taught, Jesus said: "Watch out for the teachers of the law. They like to walk around in flowing robes and be greeted in the market places and have the most important seats in the synagogues and the places of honor at banquets. They devour widows' houses and for a show make lengthy prayers. Such men will be punished most severely. Mark 12:38-40*

Prayer: Please continue your instruction.

Response: Instead of applauding the knocking down of the elite, consider from whom the criticism originates. Just think for a moment that these charges come from Jesus in the final stages of his mission of redemption. It comes at a time when he is bringing forth what he has observed sometimes quietly sometimes not so quietly the abuses of power. He brings this indictment forth for all of you because at some point and perhaps on a continuing basis you display the same arrogance of power sometimes ever so slightly.

Who has not looked at the desperately poor and blamed them for their circumstances? Who among you have not sought recognition and uttered lengthy protestations of your holiness with pronouncements that could be shorted by half? Who among you has pulled back from that generous act that might not even be noticed? Jesus is using what all would agree are the abuses of power to teach all of you.

But even more important, in this teaching event he tells you so much about himself, qualities that you are here to learn and emulate. He is first of all observant. These words did not come forth the first time he heard a prayer of unusual length or the first time a rabbi sought the front seat with his entourage. So be observant, not quick to act. Take in what you see, the injustices all around you and afar and act to correct the climate with your response even if it is limited to a modesty that goes unnoticed.

Jesus is bold in his criticism of the leaders displaying his courage in what for him was his ultimate arrest, beating, and crucifixion. Nothing so dramatic for you, but you are called to be courageous. Don't just roll along accepting what has always been, but try to contribute to a solution without seeking the limelight for the solution.

Instead of praying before the multitude, pray quietly and alone or with a few, do not draw the applause or ire of those in attendance. Seek me in the quiet of your soul.

And he was protective of the less fortunate, those shunned and abused by society because they had no rights. Do the same for the widow, the orphan, the unemployed, the street person, those without hope. And if there is no other reason for doing this other than you don't want to be judged severely, that is reason enough. All for today.

Scripture: *Calling his disciples to him, Jesus said: "I tell you the truth, the poor widow has put more into the treasury than all the others. They all gave out of their wealth, but she out of her poverty, put in everything – all she had to live on." Mark 12:43-44*

Prayer: Help me reach a deeper meaning.

Response: Oh, I suggest you consider again who Jesus is. He is, not was, someone with supreme observation, not caught up in the confusion of a lot of activity. He sees the essential element of every activity. He is reflective and does not jump to the obvious conclusion, that is, for the treasury to survive must cultivate big donors.

He is calling you to invest your resources and wealth to depletion in his mission of love. He respects the widow by not calling attention to her, allows her to keep her anonymity. By her action she enters into a very intimate relationship with God because no one but Jesus understands her motivation and her life situation. That is the relationship that you should seek and cultivate. And that intimacy is found in prayer and you all have much to pray for and pray with love.

Considering the synagogue would not survive with a few pennies from each participant, Jesus is also saying that there is something so much more valuable than the physical building and the salaries of your priests. Not that they should go away, but Jesus is asking you to consider what is more important than the physical plant of each church and house of worship. Incidentally, there are no wrong answers.

Finally, consider the patient teaching that Jesus provides to you if you will pause and take a seat with him on the sidelines and observe the activity, sometimes frenetic, that is occurring around you. In your final breadth it will be these pauses that will enrich you and strengthen you as you reach through the curtain into eternity.

Scripture: *Jesus said to them: "Watch out that no one deceives you. Many will come in my name claiming, 'I am he,' and will deceive many. When you hear of wars and rumors of wars, do not be alarmed. Such things must happen, but the end is still to come. Nation will rise against nation, and kingdom against kingdom. There will be earthquakes in various places, and famines. These are the beginning of birth pains." Mark 13:5-8*

Prayer: There are times, most times in fact, when I read the morning newspaper and wonder in dismay what is happening. Please give me a deeper insight into what is described in these verses.

Response: When you pray persistently for the easing of the violence throughout the world, your prayers are heard. Your prayers serve as those a midwife utters during a difficult birth. You are right to conclude that the old is passing away to be replaced by a time of greater understanding and compassion. You are present in a sense at the creation.

The danger for you and others is to try to see the future and not remain peacefully in the present. This is not a time to consult soothsayers, if there was ever a time. No, you are to remain calm, not anxious, detached from outcomes, but vigorously contributing in the present to the healing that is required in your environment.

This healing is for the earth that you consume, in relationships that you fracture, for the violence that you propagate in the marketplace, in government, and on the battlefield. A new breed of warrior is called for not limited to the battlefield, but just as intent on ushering in the light and the power of love that lingers beyond your outstretched fingertips.

This is definitely not the time to fall back on what were considered solutions years and centuries past. You have reached a summit of sorts and must now plot your journey beyond into a region and clime not previously explored or tracked. The essential resource you must rely upon now is your listening – listening to me. I will guide you though you are at first overwhelmed by the sights that appear on the horizon.

You have nothing to compare them to in your experience. It is as if you have turned the corner in your journey and are confronted with limitless canyons of indecipherable depth that are laid out in elaborate patterns; you might say a maze. This terrain is really not of the physical dimension but a mapping of your soul that you will come to learn and understand, if only you trust me to whisper your path.

You have past the region where there are rumors of wars. Wars prevail all about you, not only in Afghanistan and Iraq, and so many other areas that we could fill up the page with their citation, wars on Wall Street, in the Tokyo and Shanghai financial markets, in the poverty and famines that abound, in the food available in your Fresh Market and what is available in a soup kitchen.

And yes there is cause for celebration. You have gone beyond the rumors of war and are that much closer to the transformation I have foretold for those who believe my word, accept my love, and delight in my grace.

So this morning I do not come to frighten you or to make you apprehensive, but to rally you following your long climb that the best is yet to come for those who remain in my love and protection.

.

#131

Scripture: *These are the beginning of birth pains. Mark 13:8*

Prayer: I have a sense that you wanted me to return to this verse.

Response: Yes, I want to spend some time this morning on this last line of this verse, returning to yesterday's instruction.

You are witnessing and you all are participating, actually ushering in a new age of consciousness in my love. It is difficult for you to appreciate the significance of the times as you are surrounded my wars and rumors of wars, and as I said yesterday the wars are not confined to the battlefield. There is a term used by the professional warriors and that is *asymmetrical*. Widen your definition of asymmetrical and you will see the violence as I discussed all around you.

Once not so long ago what happened in the furthest reaches of the globe was news in paper print days after the events and would not be accompanied by photographs. Now you have live coverage from around the globe. Not so long ago, after the Second World War, foreign products shipped into the US came exclusively from Japan, now you are not even able to distinguish the origin.

Transportation, communications, technology, global vision, immigration and the resettling of huge populations and the vision of a global community have all contributed to an atmosphere of expectation, not unlike what you experience in the delivery room, whether you are the parent or the medical professional assisting. And as you know not all births are successful, or are the babies born free of defects as you would label them. But let me remind you that each birth contributes to the community of souls that are present to experience the message of love, even if it is limited to the sharing of a canteen of water on a frozen hilltop.

You are way into the birth pang cycle. All that is required for you is to be prepared to welcome the birth and to assist. And how to welcome? You know the answer. I have been gracing you who can hear with the message since your conception – celebrate! Suspend the fear that this age has cultivated through the influence of the dark force and celebrate. There is nothing that you have experienced, are experiencing, or will experience that should not be a cause to celebrate. Your celebration serves to shatter fear, constraint, tension, anxiety and gives praise to me as I bless you.

Celebration is like the wind briskly filling your face with unknowable force, the cold making tingle of your ears and clouds of fog coming from your mouth, a necklace of stars falling into place around your neck, the crush of waves on a beach out of sight, the light of the dawn creeping over a black landscape as if were to steal my astonishment.

Yes, celebrate a tear forming in your eye as you witness a human connection from across the room, or a deep felt prayer for someone enduring such suffering, knowing that the pain will be an entry way to eternal joy. Celebrate paradox, union and separation, joy and sadness, the stillness of the soul and the clamor of the senses.

The new birth you anticipate is one in which you all will assist. You are truly present at the creation. Be still and watch the light creeping over the dark horizon of doubt.

All for you this day.

Scripture: *"Whenever you are arrested and brought to trial, do not worry beforehand about what to say, just say whatever is given you at the time, for it is not you speaking, but the Holy Spirit."* Mark 13:11

Prayer: I have been "arrested" at times in that I have been put on the spot to respond to your message, or more often to respond gently to someone who is searching for the truth. Give me guidance.

Response: It is good that you see you can be arrested and it means be put into the spotlight where all ears are turned to you even if it appears those in attendance are not listening or that they dismiss your message in advance. It is at those times, and you have learned this from experience, you must draw in a breath and relax because if you are listening, you have just turned over your vocal chords, gestures, eye contact to me, and I will use what you offer to me to reach the person seeking truth.

How many times have you written or said something that seems so far beyond what you would have thought to assemble in response. It is on those occasions that I speak most freely. Your only responsibility is to keep your ego out of your voice, as well as all anxiety, judgment, and convey a peaceful visage. And do keep warm eyes on your audience, no looking away as if you are consulting a script.

Oh, I have so many examples in your life – in Berlin where you reluctantly addressed a group on prayer for the over-achiever and to this day your message, actually mine, still ripples among the audience and those informed later about the talk; in Afghanistan when you shared who you are with the Afghans, in Berlin when you touched the German executive who was contemplating suicide.

I am prompting your message, and in your writings I especially prod your sentiments and even your courage as you reveal what could just as easily remain hidden. You see I am with you and I mean all of you to turn you inside out for all to see. The soul that I help you reveal is a gentle soul, definitely not judgmental, compassionate, curious, patient, and conveying above all else love and respect. Yes, respect for differences.

You and everyone else seek to bring order so that everyone is in lock step of fealty. That is not my way or desire. I seek your love and the love conveyed to others in such ways that this love reveals the growing dimension of what love is. Let me tell you there is not a narrow definition available. And something else – love is not to be bounded but becomes more and more expressive and expansive like a smoldering campfire into a blazing conflagration in the souls of all of you. In time, this powerful love for which you are destined to experience will encompass all of you with colors not imagined by the most clever of you.

So treat occasions when you are "arrested," and there are many more than you realize, as occasions to relax and allow me to speak from your heart. All for today.

#133

Scripture: *"When you see the abomination that causes desolation standing where it does not belong – let the reader understand – then let those who are in Judea flee to the mountains." Mark 13:14*

Prayer: On this gray morning, the wind blowing from the sea, and rain in the forecast, please tell me the meaning of this verse.

Response: There are times when you don't want to consider the existence and activity of Satan in the world. This is one of those times. Satan has been successful in lulling you all with platitudes of easy words and concepts. You hardly realize what is happening like the frog being put in a pot of water that is then heated gradually before the frog realizes that he is being boiled.

You see it happening all around you with your daughter no longer seeking spiritual counsel, trusting that their method of parenthood will lead them all to the truth. And so it is with so many that have exhibited goodness and have allowed their acceptable behavior to believe that that is the sole reason they are on earth.

Surely Satan is not going to disturb this recruiting field that ultimately allows the subtle and not so subtle violence in your society to spread throughout the world.

For this verse consider deeply the existence of the abomination and its intent and purpose. The abomination is a threshing machine moving across the field. You are not blighted or dry wheat so please stay out of its path. And how do you avoid this crush – by being nimble, inquisitive, faithful, loyal, courageous, determined, and relentless. That is why I say, flee to the mountains. Because you see on the mountains you will see beyond tomorrow.

To recognize the abomination, pray for discernment. I do not want you on a street corner proclaiming the end is near. No, I want you in the midst alerting others of the danger, the subtle danger that seeks to lure you into complacency.

This verse is not a light verse, but one that reveals another side of Jesus, who alerted you to the danger and even provided you with a strategy of escape, and even in the process foretold that the time of travail would not be as long as you might and should expect.

In life this also applies. What you fear will turn out not to be anything as fearful as you imagined because on the mountain top you will find solace and refuge in my love. Let me end with the words: Be vigilant!

Scripture: *Therefore keep watch because you do not know when the owner of the house will come back – whether in the evening, or at midnight, or when the rooster crows, or at dawn. If he comes suddenly, do not let him find you sleeping. What I say to you, I say to everyone: 'Watch!'" Mark 13:35-36*

Prayer: Give me guidance on how I can be vigilant, and also some words related to my son's birthday.

Response: You are like the foreman of the servants or guards and you are training your son in vigilance. Do you know that it wasn't that many years ago – over forty – you were assigned to do exactly that in the Air Force? Remember driving along the flight line and encouraging the young troops, though you weren't so old yourself?

Well, that is what you are doing with your son and doing a fine job with a lot more energy than most of your biological age. It is time for you to bring him to the confidence to articulate his own prayers that are not memorized. This is a special year for him as he blossoms into maturity and he is blessed to have someone of your sensitivity and experience and wisdom to be at his side.

Now, regarding the scripture, it is the same. You are either training those under your care to be vigilant or you are accepting instructions from those more experienced. A word of your relationship – you are with someone in spirit who is serving as a guide to vigilance as you are supporting her need as well.

This scripture is not meant to constrain your activity or even concentration but to expand the perimeter that you can contain. As you expand you will discover that more and more people and souls will turn to your guidance. Your writing is especially important in reaching those who are not within earshot.

Consider vigilance as leading to great reward. It is not about being caught napping but observed as being alert and engaged in my work. And don't worry, I fortify my workers with sufficient food and energy and interest and curiosity and dedication and commitment. You might have difficulty believing this but the task of vigilance becomes easier the longer you are at it. So don't look back and ask when do I get relief, but rather forward and see how easy it is becoming as you free yourself from the distractions of the mundane.

.

#135

Scripture: *"Leave her alone," said Jesus. "Why are you bothering her? She has done a beautiful thing to me. The poor you will always have with you, and you can help them any time you want. But you will not always have me. She did what she could. She poured perfume on my body beforehand to prepare for my burial. I tell you the truth, wherever the gospel is preached throughout the world, what she had done will also be told, in memory of her. Mark 14:6-9*

Prayer: Please reach me this morning with your words, Lord.

Response: This morning I want to talk to you of death, my death – your death. As you read, Jesus calmly approached the event that would be the catalyst to spread his message throughout the world. See his foresight, experience his peacefulness, notice that he was not taken up emotionally in the "scene" that his disciples were creating.

His rebuke to them over the perfume incident is a gentle throttle to remind them to stay focused; stay focused on what is to happen and what they are to do following the event. *Throughout the world* are words that will resonate with them long after his crucifixion. Though relaxed, Jesus is alert to the events unfolding. He does not miss anything, especially the significance of the events leading up to his death.

Now, to you – stay focused. Attend to matters that linger and impede you concentration because I have much for you to accomplish in these next years. Let me list some of the leading assignments: you are to write and bring to publication sources of guidance for those on the path who are confused with the dark force's melody; you are to bring your son to maturation for the contribution he will make to this world; you are to pray diligently for the birth event that is preparing to take place amidst the violence of this world.

You are to be at peace. Allow events to unfold with grace. You will be surprised how smooth a ride if you do not seek to control. Read this line again because within are the elements so key to your life and others. Do not seek to control. Allow.

All for today.

Scripture: *Then Judas Iscariot, one of the Twelve, went to the chief priests to betray Jesus to them. They were delighted to hear this and promised to give him money. So he watched for an opportunity to hand him over. Mark 14:10-11*

Prayer: Lord, I have read these verses so many times. Allow me this time to understand more fully this scene in my life.

Response: You inadvertently provided yourself a great insight into the meaning of these words for you and others. Take the words as in the present time and that you are the main player.

Yes, all of you share some aspects of Judas. What are they? You like Judas feel sometimes that you are not appreciated and act with deception to rebalance this perception; you all experience greed that sometimes is not satiated and leads to envy; you all shy from obedience thinking that you know the way or the solution; there are times when you are impatient at the unfolding even if what is promised is beyond your expectations.

So here you have Judas intent on solving the problem, the anxiety of the people, the turmoil in the local environment, bringing peace with the Jewish teachers and chief priests of his tradition, finally making right with his family and those friends who questioned his sanity following Jesus. Yes, Judas found and followed a short cut that turned out to be an endless agony of betrayal.

So the lesson here is not to judge Judas too severely else you find yourself condemning yourself; allow the unfolding in your lives without anxiety, be at peace.

Though brief, you have much to consider this morning.

Scripture: *On the first day of the Feast of Unleavened Bread, when it was customary to sacrifice the Passover lamb, Jesus' disciples asked him: "Where do you want us to go and make preparations for you to eat the Passover?" Mark 14:12*

Prayer: Do you know, Lord, I have received so much from you in these days with Mark, I don't want to rush through the verses. Give me insights here as well.

Response: You are achieving a rhythm in your reading and prayer. As an aside, almost, I remind you of the importance to pray deeply for the situation in the Middle East where a cause for war could develop without your prayers and others that the British sailors[9] are returned without harm and this crisis is averted.

Next, I want to tell you to observe the scene as if you are viewing it on screen. Listen to the disciples ask Jesus of his plans and what they can do. They are becoming like lambs that listen to the shepherd without questioning. He tells them what he wants them to do and they follow his direction. Now, isn't that a change?

Remember how on the lake that they woke him for fear they would drown when the storm came up, or when Peter followed Jesus on top of the water only to lose heart and beseeched help at the last moment, or when they questioned him about the inadequacy of the loaves of bread. They all had a lot to say then, but now, they ask for his will for them and they obey though the directions are rather indecipherable. They don't even question – who is this owner that on the surface has such an intimate relationship so as to provide his room fully stocked at a time of the holy days of Passover.

Now, this is where I am looking to direct you . . . to a place where you spend less time trying to figure out my purpose and instead trust and accept what appear to be conflicting or at least obscure directions.

In your life as well as those around you, you have come to see the complexity of life, much as the tapestry image that you have used. Your mind's desire, even perceived need, to know and understand where you are going can be frustrating. So why not just relax in your spirit and heart. You should be thankful that you don't have to make all the preparations for the feast and celebration just as the disciples did not have to make the preparations for the Passover.

---

[9] British sailors were captured by Iranian Revolutionary Guards and after several tense weeks were released unharmed by their Iranian captors.

Just follow my directions and you will find a place reserved for you and all the preparations have been made. All you have to do is show up. Repeat that phrase – all you have to do is show up. And that is all I require of you – to show up. What that means is that you accept my word and guidance and you align your will to your soul where I reside. It's actually so simple. For today, just think a bit on what I mean by "it."

#138

Scripture: *"I will not forget you! See, I have engraved you on the palms of my hands."* *Isaiah 49:15-16*

Prayer: Bring me to understand more deeply these words.

Response: Begin by realizing and accepting that I do not forget you. You do not have to wait for some future consideration. At times when your prayer is a groan, a sob, or a tear that dries silently in the wind, I am present in your agony of the soul. You see I need no reminder of your distress. I don't have to look you up in an album to determine from where this urgent message is originating.

Your image is engraved on the palms of my hands. You are, all of you, my exclusive interest, and the object of my love. As you unburden your soul in wordless prayer, without pause or even consideration or deliberation, I receive you and recognize you as the one engraved on the palms of my hands, just as I unfold these very palms. And these same hands bless and anoint you; provide comfort and solace.

You will find at such times you sense a wave, energy, flowing even surging through your body. My blessing is palpable and present. All I ask is that you reserve a stillness of the heart to receive this special blessing.

Scripture: *"That will make your load lighter, because they will share it with you. If you do this and God so commands, you will be able to stand the strain."* Exodus 18:22-23

Prayer: Give me insight into your wisdom.

Response: There is something in your ethic that counsels you to go it alone. This day you are being counseled to see community as a great resource. For community encourages you to admit that you are not self-sufficient and that admission alone leads you to heart-felt, sincere prayer, gratitude, and to service—service to those who like you need assistance on the path.

For some your service might be literally carrying the load, providing encouragement, suggesting an alternative route less arduous than the one traversed, or perhaps leading the one struggling and yourself to stillness in prayer. A community of prayer! Think of it as an experience not dominated by the brick and mortar of an edifice, but soul vibrant as two or three or more clasp hands or simply remain in silence listening to or for my Word.

These lines offer you guidance in how you can lessen your load and your neighbor's, and avoid or at least endure the strain of daily life. Be open to sharing the burden of your heart and extending yourself to listen without judgment to another's plight, no matter how counter-intuitive it might seem for your culture; in doing so prepare to resume, I repeat resume, your journey in the company of like-minded, listening souls.

Scripture: *So he sent two of his disciples, telling them, "Go into the city, and a man carrying a jar of water will meet you. Follow him. Say to the owner of the house he enters, 'The Teacher asks: Where is my guest room, where I may eat the Passover with my disciples?' He will show you a large upper room, furnished and ready. Make preparations for us there." Mark 14:13-15*

Prayer: Lord, I want to thank you for this quiet, still time, to reflect upon your word.

Response: More will be given to you as you progress in meeting me within your heart and soul. Note the specifics of Jesus' direction. He leaves nothing to misinterpretation. The scene has played out in his mind, or is playing out in his mind, as he speaks to his disciples. This is meant to give the disciples an indication later that he clearly understood his upcoming seizure, scourging, and crucifixion. The verses are also meant to give you a hint of eternity where there is not past and future only an eternal present.

Think how the disciples must have been puzzling about his direction, yet they have reached a point of spiritual maturation that they are accepting, don't ask questions that would begin with *what if.* This is the point that I seek for you. No more *what if's* – all is ready in the eternal present. You have nothing to fear, nothing to be anxious about.

Your only obligation is to continue your journey, be at peace, love with a clear heart, pray for those less conscious of the miracle in their presence. Your prayers are needed to ease the crisis with Iran.

There are many symbols of importance in this reading. You have heard and read much about the upper room. Why upper? Upper room is to signify thoughts that ascend, are ascending, not tied to the earth. The upper room becomes a symbol of detachment. In a sense, once ascending those steps you become vulnerable in that easy exit and escape are less accessible. So walking those steps to the upper room requires a commitment that might be lost if you just wandered into a room and took a seat.

The water the man is carrying signifies the water of baptism and the water of new life and nourishment. The home itself signifies the retreat from the world where you can gather your thoughts, not unlike the "upper room" in which you now sit contemplating my word and the fountain sounding in the next room – again a symbol of the living waters in which you bathe.

Notice there is no talking or distracting noises greeting the disciples in search of the retreat. So it is for you to value speech and at same time value above all else times when you are quiet and free from the noise of life and responsibility. This quiet time is every bit as nourishing, even more so, than the meals you ingest.

Finally, notice again that the disciples are in a receptive mode. No questioning of Jesus, they simply follow his directions. All for now.

#141

Scripture: *The disciples left, went into the city and found things just as Jesus had told them. So they prepared the Passover. Mark 14:16*

Prayer: Lord, I am so reluctant to rush through these verses and yet Easter is only a week away and I will not get through the verses in time for the Resurrection. Also, my heart is with my spouse in honor of her 67th birth date.

Response: There is no rush, just attention, and I have your attention. Let us talk about your spouse for a moment. What a successful journey on earth, the love she spread, the understanding, the graciousness, the tenderness and gentleness. There is no cause to ponder her fate or to be emotionally down this day, but rather to celebrate a full life during which she overcame many obstacles to see the light.

As to a rush in completing the verses to fit an artificial schedule of events, dismiss such notions. Indeed that is a lesson for you in everything you do to become. I would not want anything to disturb the careful dwelling on my anointed word. Treat any views to the contrary that seep into your thinking as inspired by you know whom. Consider this advice as applicable to your life generally. You are fasting in a relationship that is special to you. Do you think that I have not noticed, and do you not realize that you have already been rewarded for your diligence?

Now to the scripture – see how the disciples follow directions. There is not even a word of their surprise. They enter the city and find everything as Jesus had foretold. The anointed word is there to tell you will not be surprised if you follow my word. Why? Because at the moment that I give my word what I have promised and foretold are present, though just behind a curtain that is already opening. If you listen intently you can hear the curtain being drawn back. So spend your time listening for the curtain opening and not wondering if you are in the right theater.

There is also a certain discipline displayed by the disciples. They leave, they enter, they prepare. Emphasize each of those qualities in your life – depart your old ways, enter my new life that I offer you, and prepare for life eternal.

.

Scripture: *When evening came, Jesus arrived with the Twelve. While they were reclining at the table eating, he said, "I tell you the truth, one of you will betray me — one who is eating with me." They were saddened, and one by one they said to him, "Surely not I?" Mark 14:17-19*

Prayer: Lord, give me the insights that I seek this morning in the quiet before dawn.

Response: Jesus is talking to you right this moment. He is speaking to all of you. He knows of betrayal and continues to sit at the table with you. His sadness is bolstered by his deep compassion. His compassion is only exceeded by his patience. So be encouraged.

You are like a young apprentice who is assigned to a master wood crafter. You are handed the implements; you listen, are distracted, are awkward, at times lazy, and yet this patient teacher — and that is what Jesus was called — is there to instruct you, and not for the purpose of making him happy, but for your eternal happiness as exhibited in the glory that you fashion under his guidance.

And surely you appreciate that there is risk that you will injure yourself. After all the implements are sharp and the work requires great concentration and focus. There are so many distractions in the woodshop and outside, but you are called to pay attention and to work diligently. The small cut in the wood is followed by another, but you soon discover that you must be with the first cut and not think of those cuts that follow. You also know that those egregious cuts contribute to spectacular artistic expression as you incorporate them into your design, since there is no way to erase the errors or to start over. Consider your environs an art shop of the highest and most demanding dimension.

Returning to the verses, imagine that instead of an upper room reclining, you are in this art shop and are just beginning to create under His guidance the art that will attract others to become master craftsmen, to attract others to reflect upon the beauty of the art piece you are fashioning to bring them to a deeper place.

This is the meaning these verses hold especially for you this morning. All that you are finds its way into the piece of art and yes it hurts sometimes, as you nick your finger or discover the sorrow and pain that surfaces in your art. How else to relate to those who wander the craft shop, looking for understanding and hope? Think of how many, an endless stream of observers, shoppers, you call them seekers, who have and do pause at the crucifixion. Indeed, it is pause that I seek from you and those who pass me in their journey.

All for now.

#143

Scripture: *They were saddened, and one by one said to him, "Surely not I?" "It is one of the Twelve," he replied, "one who dips bred into the bowl with me. The Son of Man will go just as it is written about him. But woe to that man who betrays the Son of Man! It would be better for him if he had not been born." Mark 14:19-21*

Prayer: Help me Lord with your grace not to betray you.

Response: Be as you are this moment and there is no fear of that. Judas had similar moments, then the dark force directed his full attention on this valued apostle. I tell you this not to unnecessarily disturb you but to plead, yes plead for your vigilance. You and others so inclined are reaching a stage in your life, spiritual life, life devoted to knowing me, that the dark force marshals all his forces to subvert you. He needs examples of his success and waylaying a poor, disconsolate wayfarer brings him little publicity and attendant fear and respect.

Do not walk about in trepidation, however, that would be just as useful for him even if you did not fall to his wiles. Instead move along with head held high not in pride but in the knowledge that I am with you and literarily legions of angels are at your left and right, above and below you. You are in the vanguard of the force that serves to vanquish the dark force, however powerful and wily he proves.

You see also he does not want to be defeated either, nor does he want his defeats, and they are also legion, to become known. Move ahead as if on a field of battle with confidence and determination, realizing that trust in me, faith, will create a momentum that could well force him from the field, vanquished, though ever watchful as to when he can next mount a counter attack. As you and others gather strength you will discover that his efforts are quite limited to attempting to disturb you with relatively minor feints that you can sweep from the field.

He has launched many attacks against you in recent years and though he checked your momentum, his forces suffered incalculable losses as you resumed the offensive. Among your most powerful weapons is the grace to which you have responded in reaching me in your most heartfelt moments of loss, at times when you question your ability to move on, your brief moments of despair. I will never, repeat, never fail you. I will extend your forces across a wide field of battle and your success will draw you ever increasing reinforcements and like dedicated companions as you prove the same for them.

So Judas to his credit faced overwhelming opposition from the dark force and his flaw was that he did not realize that the interest shown him by the dark force was indeed a compliment to him for his efforts on the field up until that moment of treachery. And with that first counter attack, he did not appreciate that I was there and am there to reinforce him and you to win the day.

Sorry to be so militant today but you must realize that this encounter with the dark force will only increase as you approach the gate of my dwelling. Realize, though, you are reaching the gate in triumph and not as a beleaguered column that is bringing needed reinforcements to me. What an enviable position you are in and that is what the dark force seeks to thwart. So be vigilant and courageous. Triumph is near.

#144

Scripture: *While they were eating, Jesus took bread, gave thanks and broke it, and gave it to his disciples, saying: "Take it, this is my body." Then he took the cup, gave thanks, and offered it to them, and they all drank from it. "This is my blood of the covenant, which is poured out for many," he said to them. "I tell the truth, I will not drink again of the fruit of the vine until that day when I drink it anew in the kingdom of God." Mark 14:22-25*

Prayer: These words are so familiar to me. Help me to reach a still deeper awareness of their meaning.

Response: Instead of focusing on the ritual that has been repeated for two thousand years; instead see those words, hear those words in your heart this morning. Allow them to resound; allow them to be my promise to you, my gift to you this morning and every morning. Consider this as an ever present ritual of love.

As I break the bread and pass it to you, you do the same in your actions for this day and don't worry about exhausting the supply. Remember what I do in such circumstances; multiplication is quiet easy for me – the same for the wine.

So each morning accept this sacrifice, actually the fruits of this sacrifice measured in the labor of love that produced both and share it with everyone you encounter, everything you write, all you think about, for all you pray. This is the communion for which I come.

Feel the stirring that is in your heart. This moment I am showering you with my love. All is possible. Though brief this morning, there is much for you to consider.

Scripture: *"You will all fall away,"* Jesus told them, *"for it is written: 'I will strike the shepherd, and the sheep will be scattered.' But after I have risen, I will go ahead of you into Galilee."* Mark 14:27-28

Prayer: Lord, help me to take in the significance of your words.

Response: Fall away. See the image, feel the image of free falling down, totally at the mercy of gravity, nothing to hold on, resigned yet still panicking over your situation. That is how it feels to refuse the hand that I hold out to you. But even here, with the shepherd no longer present to lead you, I do not desert you, and almost like awakening from a frightful dream, you awake to see me before you leading you to the home prepared for you. It is important to catch the full import of the falling in free space, totally helpless on the one hand, yet in my love that I exhibit in rising and leading you to safety – and much more.

Enough of falling from my grasp – continue to deepen your capacity to love that I cannot do for you. You are responsible for bringing to the surface the love that I implanted within you.

There is another image I wish you to consider. That falling away, helpless, is the ultimate act of faith, knowing that you will land safely and I will be there to lead you.

Finally, I want to consider how those words strike you today. I am telling you that there is a time when I do not seem present. That is how many spiritual men and women consoled their followers to be prepared for the time when I seem distant, yet they must persevere. You only become aware of that call to faith when you have progressed far enough along, otherwise the lesson would be lost on you. It is a process of refining, burnishing of your love. So indeed, there are times when I seem ahead or behind you, perhaps in the fog. Your knowledge of me will be like a lantern placed on a table in the dark of night awaiting my return. The lantern is a sign for me of your faith.

So greet these words in calm, unruffled acceptance.

All for today.

#146

Scripture: *When the Sabbath was over, Mary Magdalene, Mary the mother of James, and Salome brought spices so that they might go to anoint Jesus' body. Very early on the first day of the week, just after sunrise, they were on their way to the tomb and they asked each other, "Who will roll the stone away from the entrance of the tomb?" Mark 16:1-3*

Prayer: Come to me and help me to let go of all the casualness I attach to this event because it is a story that I have heard so often. Help me to be overcome as if I was one of the three.

Response: You are one of the three. Each time you ask to have the veils dropped from your eyes, I will do so. It takes courage to ask for this revelation. Why? Because it is a life changing revelation. How could anyone experience the resurrection deeply and still muddle through life?

So here it goes, as you would say. Approaching the tomb you are fearful. Fearful that all in which you have been engaged it seems has ended. And you can honestly say that were it so – there would be a relief, since my claims were/are so difficult to comprehend without my grace. It is as if I have given you a puzzle and told you that the solution resides with me that I give you daily.

So you do approach the tomb each day, like today, just after dawn. And you wonder who will roll back the rock. The rock is your doubt, your weariness though you have slept a full night. The exhaustion you feel is an emotional and spiritual exhaustion. At this moment you are thinking of solutions. The rock is an obstacle. In your mind you are wondering if you can pull the rock up and across the uneven surface. You are wondering if your hands, actually your fingers, will be able to grab hold of the rock as you expect it will be moist in the morning dew. Your companions, whoever they are, will not be able to grab a hold at the same time.

And on and on goes your deliberation, your analysis, your fear of failure. And all for what purpose? To show reverence to Him that offered and offers so much that transcends worldly satiety. You see this is not about where your next earthly meal is coming from, but from where will you receive the heavenly manna that Jesus so freely distributes among you?

With all these deliberations, concerns, nostalgia, feelings of loss, you come to the tomb that represents the hidden – what is not revealed, and you find that the rock has been rolled back. Rolled back! Do you understand? All your fear was ground away in the rumble of the rock being moved away from the opening of the mystery. There is no longer a mystery. Now it is for you to enter the tomb and discover in that dark place what you have sought and seek over a lifetime.

Think of the symbols: a rock tomb, an isolated place, early in the morning, an impossible – it seems – task, and most important a willing traveler who walks outside of the town to an isolated place to find me. Think over during the day as you work on our tasks this journey outside of town and see the resurrection unfolding in your life. You are ready to absorb the mystery in its full dimension of wonder.

#147

Scripture: *Now that same day two of them were going to a village called Emmaus, about seven miles from Jerusalem. They were talking with each other about everything that had happened. As they talked and discussed these things with each other, Jesus himself came up and walked along with them, but they were kept from recognizing him. He asked them, "what are you discussing together as you walk along?" Luke 24:13-17*

Prayer: Dear Lord, for many years that walk to Emmaus has captivated my attention. Please enlighten me further.

Response: It's rather astounding isn't it that I can be so close and you do not recognize me. They are my questions that pull you out of your concerns and distractions as I did and do with others walking to Emmaus.

Without a destination you might not take the time to reflect on events. You have done it all the time as you boarded a plane to San Francisco, to Kabul, to Boston, to Shanghai. Yes, traveling alone especially gives you the quiet time to ask and then even to answer the questions that I imprint on your soul.

The journey to Emmaus, any journey, gives you pause and though your journey is set, the pause allows you to prepare better. Prepare for what? Prepare so that you fully realize what you are about to encounter.

Think of my kingdom as Emmaus and you are journeying toward me. Don't get nervous, you still have time; you are not as close as you might imagine. There is still so much preparation for you.

And consider preparation not so much getting your belongings of the soul in order, but consider deeply what you must let go of. No, I am not suggesting that you sell your house and give the money to the poor. I am talking about the treasure within you that I want you to distribute. All of you have such treasure and it is the responsibility of each of you to distribute it to those around you. I want you to have dispensed everything of that treasure of love prior to your feet reaching the outer limits of Emmaus.

And please don't say that you don't know your treasure, or that you want to be reminded of it. You are not able to hide behind a false modesty of a child in these matters. Say your treasure aloud even if there is no one in the room with you. It is that treasure that I want you to distribute freely, and like the loaves of bread, I assure you that you will not run short.

So, be conscious of your "walks" that occur right now. Don't think that tickets are in the mail. No, they are in your hand and the departure date is not open. It is today.

.

#148

Scripture: *They asked each other, "Were not our hearts burning within us while he talked with us on the road and opened Scriptures to us?" Luke 24:32*

Prayer: So quiet this morning as the rains begin to hit the windows, the birds seemingly unaware that a storm is descending upon this area. Help me Lord to listen to you as I journey to Emmaus.

Response: Listen to that bird outside in the brush calling. It is calling as I for your attention. Just be still and listen and all will be clear to you. In clarity, efficient action follows.

You are to have no anxiety as to what you should do. I want the *should of's*, the conditionals that only serve to create turbulence in your life, to be dismissed. My guidance you will find is without any doubt. If you stumble off the road to Emmaus, I am there to recount the significance of your efforts and the significance of this journey. Each of you is on a journey of discovery. Emmaus is your destination. As I have said so often, the destination is not nearly as significant as the actual journey.

It is good to review your progress. This does not mean to lash yourself with past wanderings. I too am aware and see no need to question now a past when there is so much for the present. Listen to my inspirations that I give you in the moment. As your hearing improves so will your listening. That is what happened and happens to those on their way to Emmaus.

Hear the lashing of the rain that is increasing in intensity against your windows and listen to what you are being told this moment. Extraordinary how you are surrounded with these messages from the Father! In the rhythm of the rain you are literally slowing, controlling your body to fit within the rapture of nature that restores you and releases you from all anxiety.

Yes, that is what the two discovered and you discover as you trudge forward. Your pace is not increased as rather it becomes more solid and determined and confident. So confident that whether or not Emmaus is seven or seventy miles is of no significance. Reach into that present, and as you listen you discover other thoughts that I inspire that prepare you for entry into the Kingdom of my Father.

Nothing more this morning. Simply listen to the wind and rain, and know that they represent my love that washes and sweeps over you daily.

#149

Scripture: *While they were still talking about this (the experience of the two walking to Emmaus), Jesus himself stood among them and said to them, "Peace be with you." Luke 24:36*

Prayer: Help me to perceive ever deeper the peace that you offer.

Response: In any moment of time, if you will be still and call to me, you will experience that same peace. That peace is not a future gift. It is now, right now. All you have to do is ask for it. Sometimes, in fact most times, you are not so definitive, and you receive it just as fully. Peace comes to you watching a sunrise, in quiet prayer, providing a service to someone, through love.

This peace surrounds you. It is as if I am asking you to simply extend your hands and there it is – and during what you would characterize as the most traumatic of events. Call me at such times and you will experience a peace that knows no boundaries.

I offer you today that peace, and each day. That peace dissipates all confusion, anxiety, aimlessness. That peace provides or enhances your focus, restores your calm even if you are in a storm. It is with this peace that your ego, that part of you that wishes to dominate, is most attentive to your soul-felt desires and intentions.

Peace is what calms combatants and clearly you must pray for that peace in your world, and you see the results of your prayers daily. The depth of the violence requires simply more healing time to promote real change.

So do not take lightly the offering to others of my peace. It is a powerful invocation that those who receive it discover that they are changed and more receptive to my message of love that forms the basis of peace.

This peace is evident in healthy relationships whether the relationship be husband and wife, parent child and vice versa, friend and friend, and even friend and purported enemy. Allow peace to reign in my love.

#150

Scripture: *Then he opened their minds so they could understand the Scriptures. Luke 24:45*

Prayer: I am distracted this morning in the aftermath of yesterday's mass killing of students at Virginia Tech[10]. Help me to remain still in your presence.

Response: It is in that stillness, as I have explained to you previously, you must return to regularly whatever the tragedy you encounter – be it as you say man-made or natural. There is no divine plan to cause such calamity, but there is a divine plan for you to know my love and comfort in all circumstances. I repeat in all circumstances.

What you are experiencing at Blacksburg is the same chaos that is present when a parent or loved one learns of the death, whether the loss is experienced in American, Britain, Iraq, or Afghanistan. Death as you have come to realize does not discriminate on the basis of national identity. Coming to me in your helplessness, in your inability to understand the *why's* associated with the events or how it fits into my plan, in your inability to forgive, in your sorrow is evidence of my grace and most importantly your response to that grace.

At times like this, it is so important not to allow hatred to come into your consciousness. Nothing more quickly dissipates my grace and love as hatred. And further, it might come as a shock or an injustice, but hatred allows you to quickly descend into the chaos of the event itself and create a second more powerful wave of chaos that serves the dark force.

At times like this you are called to and reminded of my love that transcends any tragedy be it as I have said above man-made or natural. Your response serves to bring in my light as the sun rises above the storm clouds of doubt.

You will be inundated for days with media expression that will fuel your tendency to seek revenge or to sow suspicion, or to assign blame – as if chaos in life is avoidable. This time is a wonderful occasion to give lie to that tendency and instead as each photograph, word, or witness testimony are printed, praise God for the unfathomable mystery that He has shared with you and allow yourself to release anger. As you have written and I have prompted you –Be still.

---

[10] A student gunned down 34 students and professors this day at Virginia Tech University, located in Blacksburg, Virginia.

CHAPTER SIX -- STILLNESS

At seventeen thousand feet, approaching the base camp in the western Himalayas, we stopped to quench our thirst in a glacial stream. Standing hip-high in the rushing water, I cupped my hands and brought the water to my mouth and allowed the excess to flow over and cool me. I remember looking over my hands filled with a flowing presence and seeing the glistening golden rays of light through my perspiration in that power of nourishment.

Similar to the memory of a trek in western Nepal, each time I open Scripture, I sense a golden orb of God's light glancing off each anointed word to my nourishment as the pure glacier water did after an exhausting climb almost forty years ago.

#151

Scripture: *On one occasion, while he was eating with them, he gave them his command: "Do not leave Jerusalem, but wait for the gift my Father promised, which you have heard me speak about. For John baptized with water, but in a few days you will be baptized with the Holy Spirit." Acts 1:4-5*

Prayer: Help me to understand more deeply the power of the Holy Spirit.

Response: Yes, the Spirit is the force that blows over you and fills you with my love. This love is found in inspiration, the breathing in of this Spirit. The power of the Holy Spirit is such that were you to hear the spirit resounding you would have to cover your ears and you would feel as if the earth would open to swallow you up. Yet it is the same spirit that is as gentle as a lamb, tender as a feather drifting on the wind.

You are called to wait patiently and be filled with the Spirit. Any yes there is nothing territorial about the Spirit's reach – it flows across national boundaries and the boundaries you construct to hide yourself. This Spirit washing over you as a tropic rain in the forest, and this cleansing occurs as well within.

Feeling the presence of the Spirit is like that electric touch you feel when someone reaches to touch you after sliding across a carpet. This touch of the Spirit is like the hum you feel in your muscles after a workout, a long walk across a thick field in summer, a quiet conversation with a companion with both of you glancing up to the stars.

I wish your language was more expressive to convey the power and love of the Spirit – found in eye contact with a loved one, the power to leap across the sand further than you ever imagined, hearing a choir singing a familiar melody as if the orchestra were in the same room with you.

The power of the Sprit is not to be trifled with. Once you accept this infusion of love through the Spirit you are more inclined to discover a steady influx of that flow. Should you deflect it, you will discover that you become a deflective shield that is unable to absorb the density of love offered continuously to you.

So Jesus commanded his disciples to wait so that they would be empowered beyond their comprehension, and then dispersed them throughout the world so that you could hear in time.

The power of the Holy Spirit is not a benign god but the all powerful presence of the source in your life. All for now.

Scripture: *When the day of Pentecost came, they were all together in one place. Suddenly a sound like the blowing of a violent wind came from heaven and filled the whole house where they were sitting. They saw what seemed to be tongues of fire that separated and came to rest on each of them. All of them were filled with the Holy Spirit and began to speak in other tongues as the Spirit enabled them. Acts 2:1-4*

Prayer: There are times when I leave the distractions that surround me and am transfixed by your majesty. Help me to be in this scene in my life.

Response: This very moment you are in this scene that is repeated for you and others on a daily basis. You are seated in a theater, it seems, and you often spend your time focusing on one stage of many that surround and revolved around you, and fail to hear and feel the Spirit rising on a wave that penetrated your soul with every bit the majesty that the wind howled into the consciousness of those first witnesses.

The Holy Spirit is similar to a pulse that beats in and out in your life. Pause to feel its presence. You might not find yourself speaking in tongues; however, the impact upon you is just as miraculous.

How can you confirm this when you don't see a flame fluttering over your head? No one said the disciples saw the flame poised over their heads but those in attendance. So with you – the flames burns bright and warm above you and you now possess capabilities that are far more dramatic than speaking in tongues.

The Spirit's power is made manifest in all aspects of your life, and can be likened to cupped hands that support you in the battle of daily life. This is the power that Jesus promised. You can no longer be alone, nor do you desire this. You are now like a giant lumberjack who having finished some training is ready to fell the largest trees of doubt.

At times when you feel the Spirit's presence, pause and allow the rush of energy to flush through you.

Indeed, you live on earth at an excellent time in that you are contributing to the formation of a world spiritual community, hinted at in the speaking in tongues of the first witnesses. You are only to follow the lead, do not worry about added complications. Life just became simply this moment for you and those seeking union with me.

All for today.

#153

Scripture: *In the last days, God says, I will pour out my Spirit on all people. Your sons and daughters will prophesy, your men will see visions, your old men will dream dreams.* Acts 2:17

Prayer: Help me to see deeper meaning in a verse that I have read over several times. I miss the mystery of the words.

Response: Let me first address the difference between visions and dreams. There is none! I mean vision as what young people do with what they consider unlimited time before them. Visions are what contribute to their focus in matters of God. Now, dreams are more relaxed. Whether or not you remember the dream the next day of not, the dream calibrates where you are at the moment of the dream. The dream is a reminder that you are constantly being nourished by me even when you are sleeping. Both terms take you out of your worldly concerns to a dimension that is free from the anxieties the world contributes to. So don't spend an inordinate amount of time on these terms.

Next, in the last days – please do not pack your bags. The last days are now. Each day you live is your last day until the sun rises again the next day. There last days are so rich. They enable you to make a difference, to seed your environment with my love.

Most significant in this verse is that I am pouring out the Spirit over you. Feel in your life as it flows over your body, mind, heart, and soul. Feel its rush like the rapids moving across rocks and boulders on a mountain stream. Feel the power of the Spirit. It is making a tremendous difference in the world and in each and every life the Spirit touches.

Remember that I am pouring out this power on all people – on all people. Do you hear my words – on all people? So spend less time self-satisfied that you have the message, and grace your neighbor near and far with your witness to the Spirit.

The power of the Holy Spirit – truly words you should invite to take hold of your consciousness – the power of the Holy Spirit is like riding a white stallion – actually galloping on a white stallion is more accurate. Ponder these words and determine and or at least speculate what difference this power means in your life. I am not interested in an historical approach.

Much love from the power of the Holy Spirit.

Scripture: *David said about him: "I saw the Lord always before me. Because he is at my right hand, I will not be shaken. Therefore my heart is glad and my tongue rejoices; my body also will live in hope . . . "Acts 2:25-26 (from Psalm 16:8)*

Prayer: Though not David, I ask you, Lord, to allow me to know more deeply your presence and love.

Response: And much more, my friend. Yes, I am alongside you. There are times you look figuratively to the right and to the left to see if you are alone. And ask whether you have ventured too far out from your comfort zone only to be abandoned. It is good that you ask that question of yourself. Your faith strengthens becomes more resilient at times like that. Make no mistake about this though I am with you at all times even if you are unaware. As you mature in your faith you become ever more conscious of my presence like this moment listening to me.

Allow your heart to be glad and show that gladness in how you approach others, whether they are family, friends, or complete strangers. Rejoicing, the ability to see my presence, to feel my presence, to assume my presence – so special and that demeanor manifests my grace that I shower upon you.

Think of moments of rejoicing that you experience each day, even note them down. I did not come for my followers to make a list of their grief. And be aware, especially at this time of mourning, that rejoicing in the spirit in the knowledge that I am at your side, is the deepest, most inexplicable rejoicing of all.

Why did I say inexplicable? Because only those with the deepest faith can seize tragedy and turn it to my purpose. Rejoice in the prayers offered for the calamity in Blacksburg, for the reaching out across all ethnic lines in sympathy and hope and healing.

Now you see more deeply what it means to have me at your side. There is nothing you will endure without me. And let me tell you a secret – that got your attention – you will not decay. You are with me always beginning each and every moment. Your joy is to share this simple and profound truth with others.

#155

Scripture: *After they prayed, the place where they were meeting was shaken. And they were all filled with the Holy Spirit and spoke the word of God boldly. 4:31*

Prayer: Lord I am listening.

Response: For this morning I want you to recall the time at dinner in Tokyo when the light above the table began to sway and fear showed in the eyes of your friends who were hosting the family dinner. Something similar occurred as described in this verse. The difference is that though there was fear those present determined that this was not a natural phenomenon and was closely associated with their fellowship and the breaking of the bread. And so, in that instant they were changed, emboldened, assured.

It is difficult sometimes for you to appreciate that just as powerful events have occurred in your life that witness to the very real presence of the Holy Spirit at a special time. I do not reserve such instances to a formal Christian ritual planned and organized by church leaders, though I do not say that this outpouring of the Holy Spirit upon you does not occur at such times.

You may identify several occasions when the Spirit descended upon you. Think of the event as more a bird alighting upon your shoulder to give you rest. Yes, I said the bird alighting to give you rest. As you think back the alighting may have occurred at a time of great stress and anxiety, at a time when you felt celebratory over some thought or experience, at a time when you were so discouraged and wondered when everything would be made clear, before you were about to launch some enterprise, and even when you asked for a sign that you were on the right track.

You see the appearance of the Holy Spirit with all of its accompanying power and graces and blessings is not a one-time event. See the Spirit as a constant visitor that flaps its wings so that you notice it amidst your cares and concerns.

And yes, as it was for the disciples, the Sprit emboldens you to take chances, to risk mediocrity for excellence, to proclaim my word to those who squirm at my words but can no longer in the hearing claim that they never heard. And those words don't have to be exclusively in words. You spread my message, the wing flutter of the Spirit, in your service, smile, ability to listen, compassion, generosity, and most of all in your faith, that is, your conviction that you are doing my will. And when you find yourself in balance and harmony with me you will discover that your room shakes, the lights sway in my presence.

Spend some time reflecting how I alight upon your shoulder regularly, feel the flutter in recollection, and don't search your childhood – go back simply the last thirty days. .

Scripture: *Then Peter said, "Ananias how is it that Satan has so filled your heart that you have lied to the Holy Spirit and have kept for yourself some of the money you received for the land? Didn't it belong to you before it was sold? And after it was sold, wasn't the money at your disposal? What made you think of doing such a thing? You have not lied to men but to God." When Ananias heard this, he fell down and died. And great fear seized all who heard what had happened. Then the young men came forward, wrapped up his body, and carried him out and buried him. Acts 5:3-6*

Prayer: Perhaps, it is too early in the morning for me, but what purpose is served in recording this event?

Response: The easy explanation is the theater that the event represents. Better still would be to treat the event only in its historical context. But I am not with you to give you history lessons or to debate the efficacy of a commentary. I am here to bring you into the present moment and not allow you to escape into the past.

You are to share your innermost thoughts, desires, fears, and trepidations with me, if you choose to do. If you do, make doubly sure that you are speaking from the heart. Please do not disguise the truth. Don't be like Ananias who not only sold the land and appeared to give all to the community, but he wanted to appear to be something else with me. He was something else to me.

And in his deceit, at the moment preceding his death, he realized it and was saved. The turmoil caused by this realization and his great sorrow was too much for him and he died. So with you, it is so important, however you appear to others around you, in the most intimate moments in prayer be certain that you speak from the heart and all will be fine.

I am not suggesting that you will never be overcome when you realize that you have been fooling yourself, just don't attempt to lie to me. It is so critical that for your emotional and spiritual balance that you pray earnestly and truthfully. Our dialogue is essential to your salvation; don't compromise it by thinking that I am the shopkeeper down the street. All for now.

#157

Scripture: *"Go, stand in the temple courts," [the angel] said, "and tell the people the full message of this new life." Acts 5:20*

Prayer: Here is a verse that I do not recall from past readings. Do you have something to tell me?

Response: There is much contained in these lines. Temple courts mean that you are to go out into the world, your daily life, and witness the truth. Now, I don't suggest you wear a billboard and walk the streets, No, I want you to identify with whom you naturally associate, but spread the circle larger, and be who you are in my truth. Do not, I repeat do not, expect confirmation. Allow the seed to be planted. I will do the watering.

The angel represents the spiritual presence that surrounds you at all times and makes its presence known to you. How? In the coincidences, the experiences, the choices that become evident to even you when your eyes seem dulled. The angel is the whiff of surprise you sense in the air, the energy you suddenly feel though you woke sluggish. The angel represents not a mind altering drug, rather a heart vitalization that captures your attention when you find a moment to be still. The angel represents messages that come to you; break through the dimensions that for some are insurmountable barriers. Angels drift through closed curtains if you catch my drift.

The full message is not what you read or had interpreted without digesting. The full message is what this new life means to you. Please understand that I am saying clearly and directly "what it means to you." Not what it means to an institution, to a theologian who has spent his life trying to discover the interpretation. Of course, I am not suggesting that you dismiss the words and thoughts of those wise men and theologians. No, I am saying those after you rest in prayer, and think on the words of your preachers and scholars, then take the essential step, so essential, and decide what the words mean to you.

That is what I want you to proclaim openly and with gentleness, humbly, without judgment of another. Allow me to work in their lives as well; don't think you are called to that mission. Be always available, always, to share more deeply if asked for more explanation and more sharing of the wisdom that I impart to you in the stillness of pray.

And this new life is what you experience each moment that allows you to be accepting in love, charged in the light to share that love, and filled with the trust and hope that I endow you with in grace to cross the precipice without fear.

.

#158

Scripture: *All who were sitting in the Sanhedrin looked intently at Stephen and they saw that the face was like the face of an angel. Acts 6:15*

Prayer: Tell me more about the aspects of an angel that is being described in this verse.

Response: Aspect is the correct word. You are being reminded that at those times that your face is relaxed and a smile eases across your lips you reflect an angelic quality. Within that gaze is contained a knowing, an ease or patience, an extension of my love, an acceptance, a decision to be as I desire you. Anxiety is free of such an aspect. There is no anger or frustration. Each day unfolding is sufficient and is welcomed.

This sense allows deep breathing, calm reassurance, and is prone to listening to my stirrings that guide you along the path. The future does not frighten or threaten one so composed.

So today, I ask that you reflect to others the face of an angel and see what you experience.

In my love.

Scripture: *The eunuch asked Philip, "Tell me, please, who is the prophet talking about, himself or someone else?" Then Philip began with that very passage of Scripture and told him the good news about Jesus. Acts 8:10*

Pray: Sometimes, I think that I have neglected the Old Testament that I do not yet appreciate how these scriptures were a precursor to Jesus' appearance, death, and resurrection. Guide me.

Response: It is important to see the Old and New Testaments, so called, as my word, my anointed word. They form a treasure house of wisdom and guidance that is available to you today with the special meaning of today for you. Don't labor over trying to solve this mystery. There is no need, however, to try to piece all this together into an historical treatise. Rather see the scripture as marked for you. Do not consider the verse that you selected as applying only to the Ethiopian eunuch. Rather see it as written for you to open your eyes and clear your ears for my message of the good news.

Philip's willingness to rush down the road and almost intercept the eunuch's chariot is for you to drop everything when someone is "just up the road" troubling over a question related to his relationship with me. Drop everything to attend to his or her needs even if your ministering is found in the words of an e-mail, a poem, spoken at a meeting, and whispered on a telephone. You will have ample opportunity to administer and do not neglect the ministry of prayer. And as Philip was pulled from the eunuch's sight after he baptized him, so you must learn to allow the seed of faith to nurture in the person without badgering him. Trust the Spirit to cultivate the seeds that you plant.

It is also necessary for you to reread portions of the Old Testament with my guidance.

All for now. Be glad and celebrate the good news.

#160

Scripture: *As [Paul] neared Damascus on his journey, suddenly a white light from heaven flashed around him. He fell to the ground and heard a voice say to him, "Saul, Saul, why do you persecute me?" Acts 9:3-4*

Pray: Lord, I have used the expression being knocked off my horse on the way to Damascus to mark a humbling experience. Help me gather more from this scene.

Response: Maybe not as dramatic, but you have and will experience your humbling experiences. Some you create yourself and others are thrust upon you without you contributing more than being present. Life, as you have discovered, is filled with the unexpected experiences, death being the most surprising and dramatic, be it your death or that of a loved one.

It is not the event that is significant. Rather, what do you do or who are you after the event. You were knocked down at the passing of your spouse and see how your life and responsibilities changed, how you matured in your faith, in the deepening in your capacity to love.

In order to hold the significance from which you can profit, the event must affect who are and to become. Life lessons as deep are not meant to alter the doing as much as the being.

In the darkness Paul experienced he had much time to reflect on who he had become; those three days allowed him time to will to be something other than he was recognized before. Consider how such life changing events in our life also fill you, as they did Paul, with remorse and sorrow for past actions. Yet, as with Paul, you are energized with this remorse to become who you were all along.

Yes, life is a path of self discovery. It is shedding all the disguises you adopt or are thrust upon you. And that new emergent self is exactly who you have always been but did not recognize. Pray that those so well disguised in the world can have those disguises taken from them and that they can see once more with the eyes of a child.

Today, guide your life disguise-free.

Scripture: *After many days had gone by, the Jews conspired to kill him, but Saul learned of their plan. Day and night they kept close watch on the city gates in order to kill him. But his followers took him by night and lowered him in a basket through an opening in the wall. Acts 9:23-25*

Prayer: Help me to appreciate when I am lowered in a basket to safety.

Response: This verse is often overlooked. And yet it says so much about your life in faith. As you appreciate, the darkness is not as foreboding as you would imagine. Consider Saul/Paul being lowered carefully to safety though he still bumped against the wall, the rough brick of the wall.

Take these lines and see how I lower you to safety, gently, as your faith grows. How helpless you are in that time before you reach the ground. It is similar to your own experience when you jumped from an aircraft and waiting for the chute to open. That is what Paul experienced and that is what you experience – even right now.

Your long list of anxieties – does it ever get shorter? –is the reason I have placed you in the basket. Your journey down to a deeper level allows you to reflect upon your life detached from your immediate concerns. Just think – you are concerned about health issues, finances, confirmation that your chosen path of writing is correct, and of course relationship. Where would you or anyone else be if relationship, that is to share an insight, sunset, meal, conversation – didn't excite you?

Right this moment in your life, I am lowering you in a basket Yes, it is dark. Yes, the burlap basket is confining. Yes, you don't know how much further you will be lowered. Yes, you're not sure what you will meet when you reach the ground. Rest assured that I am lowering you to the place you are to be, where I want you to be. And this lowering is not only spatial, but most importantly deep within you so that you will experience treasures of the spirit that you never imagined. These treasures are what I want you to share with those with whom you come into contact.

So today, I ask you to suspend your anxieties and simply be in this basket being lowered and accept that you cannot at his point return to the point from which you were lowered, and cannot hasten the time required to reach the ground.

So breathe deeply and relax.

#162

Scripture: *"All the prophets testify about him that everyone who believes in him receives forgiveness of sins through his name." While Peter was still speaking these words, the Holy Spirit came upon all who heard the message. The circumcised believers who had come with Peter were astonished that the gift of the Holy Spirit had been poured out even on the Gentiles. For they heard them speaking in tongues and praising God. Acts 10:43-46*

Prayer: Help me to be astonished in your Word.

Response: Yes, that is a fine prayer and I will honor your request. In reflecting upon your life to this date there are so many instances where you have been recognized and I will see that more and more will fill the senses of your heart.

Especially, this will be so as you begin to influence those around you and those so very much distant, both in temperament and distance. Notice you do not read about whatever happened to those folks who listened to Peter and received the gift. Let me say that they carried the legacy of Christ to which you are heir this day.

You can thank those of centuries ago who stood on the shore of the Mediterranean as you stand on the sand of the Atlantic for their receptiveness, their courage and their commitment. Romans, Jews clutching the Holy Grail of Christ and passing the cup that would never be empty as they passed it forward to the present.

You have the cup in your hands as many around you. Please do not even consider that this cup is to remain in the safe quarters of the look-a- likes. No, you must pass this to the Gentiles of today and don't necessarily think that the Gentiles are in Afghanistan or Iraq. They are in Sandbridge, Virginia, and the US. Worse they don't realize they are Gentiles and are often puffed up in pride and judgment.

It is your contribution to break down this wall of ignorance even if it is discovered in your family. Please don't withhold your message from those you love. Does it really matter if some might think that you are losing your grasp on reality? Pity those who grasp the illusion of the material and forfeit the knowledge of my love as found in your heart and those around you.

Let me close by telling you, instructing you, that you are to reach the Gentiles in whatever form they take, in whatever robe they wear, in whatever color they bear, in whatever religious tradition they follow.

And you ask for a sign. Take this specific instruction as another sign for today. In my love I leave you.

#163

Scripture: *[Barnabas] was a good man, full of the Holy Spirit and faith, and a great number of people were brought to the Lord. Acts 11:24*

Prayer: Help me Lord to be a good man and fill me with the Holy Spirit.

Response: Being a good man or woman is within everyone's grasp. Your free will allows you to convince yourself that you didn't understand the direction, your mission, or your responsibilities. In a sense, when you act in this feigned ignorance, you are taking cover in the darkness. What you do not realize that you bring into the darkness in your flight, is my Light. You are quite visible even to yourselves when you pause and do not allow frenetic activity to distract you seemingly, I say seemingly because even then you recognize your decision.

Indeed within you is the Observer who witnesses truthfully. This Observer is like the little boy in the fairytale who observes, "The Emperor has no clothes." It is the childlike observation with no guile that is my grace to you which is available at all times.

Treat this light and this innocence as your grace and do not, I repeat do not use this insight to judge others. They too have their witness and it is not for you to condemn them without you knowing the inner workings of their heart. Yes, you could present me a scenario that is tilted to condemning the actions of another. To the extent possible stay clear of condemnation and risk the vulnerability of being honest and allow your light to shine in whatever circle you move.

What is a good man – one that is and appears to hold dear love and compassion? With these aspects of the soul visible no harm can come to such men and women though the world might think otherwise.

Incidentally, you might have already concluded this. Filled with the Holy Spirit is manifesting those traits, and manifesting them means that you are overflowing in abundance of my love.

.

#164

Scripture: *[Paul and Barnabas] preached the good news in that city and won a large number of disciples. Then they returned to Lystra, Iconium and Antioch, strengthening the disciples and encouraging them to remain true to the faith. "We must go through many hardships to enter the kingdom of God," they said. Acts 14:21-22*

Prayer: I shy away from hardships, it seems, and still consider them a burden. Help me to see how hardships speed my conversion of heart.

Response: Well stated. You are undergoing a conversion of heart. This conversion applies only to you; the rate of the conversion or its thoroughness is not something to compare with those around you. It is a singular thing as a potter fashions a piece of clay to fit the texture of the clay and the intuitive desire to create.

You see my creation of you did not end when the first human species came to life, nor when you were conceived and later born. No the creative process continues as I use the potter's wheel to continue my creation.

Hardship is also a unique quality belonging to each of you. There is no value in comparing the intensity of the hardship. It all varies and meets the needs of my creation. The beauty of my creative involvement becomes self-evident in time, made manifest first to the subject and later to those around him or her. There is resilience in my creations as if the sinews that bind together body, mind, and spirit.

Each hardship experienced is selected and assigned to bring you to fullness. Today address your hardships with confidence that you are drawing ever nearer the kingdom of God.

Scripture: *From the ends of the earth I call to you, I call as my heart grows faint, lead me to the rock that is higher than I. Psalm 61:2*

Prayer: Yes, Lord, lead me to the higher rock because there are times that I feel faint and wonder if I am alone on this quest.

Response: Silence does that you know. Without the clamor, your aloneness is magnified. Yet, notice I didn't say but it is in the aloneness that you find me alongside. In fact, I never leave your side.

In deepening with the image of climbing, I am alongside you nudging you, motioning to you, leading you along this path to a higher realm. Think of that. And how do you know that this is so? Before I tell you, this higher realm is every bit as magnificent as the shadow of this beauty you experienced climbing in the Himalayas. You know because indeed your breath gets shorter at times, puzzling over the direction; you do get weary and must stop to regain your strength, and you do find my support all around you. All that is required, and I do not minimize the effort, is for you to stay focused. Notice I did not say obedient. Stay focused and all is well.

Do you know that your path might seem arduous at times? For each of you the path fits your conditioning. Sometimes it appears that someone is undertaking a simply grueling journey to the higher rock late in life. That journey is needed to condition his or her soul for the higher climes.

There is no standard to apply to determine where you are on the climb or how conditioned you are. You will sense both with the insights you receive to move you higher, the purpose you experience in continuing the climb, the opportunities you have to share your journey, the abandon and trust you exhibit to yourself as you reach an altitude you did not think possible previously. And the beauty of this climb, you don't have to negotiate the descent. Think of that. I've made it easier for you.

So today, continue your climb. Be exhilarated in each and every step along the path. Allow nothing to discourage you though there are obviously rocks strewn along the path. I assure you firm footing; focus on the path and regale in the panorama that I am spreading before you.

In my love.

#166

Scripture: *Because you are my help, I sing in the shadow of your wings. Psalm 63:7*

Prayer: Lord, this morning I seek to sing, knowing that I am in the shadow of your wings, that I am doing your will.

Response: You seek assurance. I understand. You all you, are crafting your way and for the most part know, you are following the path I seek for you. As you stretch way out from the mundane, and I mean the worldly, you question your sanity, yes sanity. It seems as you venture so far from the fold of humanity, you have second thoughts about the wisdom of leaving the conventional, the hearth that seems to have an unlimited supply of wood, if you conform, follow the prescriptions that require you to devote your entire being to the distractions, yes, distractions that keep you from me.

Rest assured, and I mean this literally. Rest and be assured. Yes, the landscape may at times seem stark, even barren. When you have been in such climes, how many times did you take in beauty that would have been overlooked had you used the glitter glance of the world? When you reached into the sand or stone to see a bud or flower that would have escaped your attention – one beyond description – had you not paused, focused on your environment, become still.

Remember how you spouse would stop in her tracks along the pathway in Vienna to which you had become so accustomed and spot a bud in a field of weeds. That is what I am asking and encouraging you to do in all aspects of your life. Allow nothing you experience to become routine. It is in this practice that you move far beyond and above the routine of humanity, and that is where I am asking, directing you and others to lead my people. I did not create you to see you holding hands around a warm hearth of the routine. I am looking to have you boldly break those boundaries of comfort whether it be of material or mental comfort.

I ask, yes direct you to embrace the paradoxes, the conflicts, and even the hypocrisy in your midst. In so doing what I ask, you will find yourself in what appears to be a lonely, stark, dry place. Pause and you will discover the waters flow freely, the sustenance is sufficient, my presence will fill every crevice in your heart, and just to be sure, you will feel the flutter of my wings shielding you from oppression of any kind.

Be focused this day as I have described and be satiated in the abundance that I stretch out for you.

#167

Scripture: *On my bed I remember you; I think of you through the watches of the night. Psalm 63:6*

Prayer: Free of distractions reach me at the deepest level.

Response: After you turn out the light, consider our closeness. Lying here helpless and vulnerable, you are most inclined to listen to my melody. In this verse, I am reminding you the times when your business can not interfere, intrude on your calm.

Think of the quiet of the night, what you once experienced when you were the night manager in the motel during college. Each segment of time flowed into another and before long your night was completed.

This evening, in your weariness, remain still. Listen to me. I have much to tell you. Physical tiredness serves you because this lack of energy slows your doing and you listen with more relief. Sometimes – like now – your hearing lacks the immediate words to describe or narrate, so there is an advantage of meditating on my word in the morning when you are fresh. However, now I have your attention and most importantly your willingness to discipline your body to listen.

Your concerns all, I say all, serve to correct your course, modulate your prayer, calibrate your engine of concern.

Let us take each concern that you have. Before I address each one notice how the list or at least the priority order changes.

Highest on your list is one of doing, yes, I said doing. Never in your life have you devoted more energy to being and you have less to show in the doing area. For example you produced a whole bevy of decoys now you are designing them, so much time performing tasks and now you consider alternatives, more concern with what you read in the headlines and now you pray for relief, for a dissipation of the violence. You are dusting off yourself for a long journey and allowing your pack to be small, manageable, and are allowing the baggage you accumulated in the past to be left at the side of the road.

If you need a reminder that I want you writing and teaching those who yearn for the word I transmit through you and the wisdom that you have accumulated in your adversity.

This evening you will dream deeply. See if you can extract, capture the dialogue occurring.

213

#168

Scripture: *Lord, you have assigned me my portion and my cup; you have made my lost secure. The boundary lines have fallen for me in pleasant places; surely I have a delightful inheritance. Psalm 16:5-6*

Prayer: This day help me to realize how you lead and sustain me.

Response: There are times when you all look around at someone else's portion in life, not even knowing the secrets of that person's journey. Yes, I have assigned you your portion and cup. It is as if you line up daily and I dispense with the nourishment that will carry you forward during another day on the road. I am with you during that and every day and this can be measured and noticed as you sense a second and third feeding during the course of the day. My advice to you is to take the sustenance in slowly as you would if seated at the finest dining room. Be still and leisurely reflect upon my presence as manifested in what you receive.

See for this moment, not looking to the future, and experience the delight of this morning, be gracious with others as you share this bounty that is overflowing. Be in expectation of days upon days and an eternity in which you will and do experience my love and bounty.

Your acknowledgement is found in your generosity with others directly and through prayer, and these others include those who suffer and have suffered mightily. You are called to ease that suffering by distributing my bounty as I distribute the bounty to you. And one last comment, there is no end to what you receive daily. No end. My storehouse stretches on and on and I have no purpose but to nourish you.

Be in smile and love this day.

Scripture: *Therefore I tell you, do not worry about your life, what you will eat or drink; or about your body, what you will wear. Is not life more important than food, and the body more important than clothes? Matthew 7:25*

Prayer: I pray that these words really penetrate my consciousness.

Response: Worry is a hesitation on the path that you know is correct though fraught with challenges. Worry is studying a subject and concern that you will not pass the test. Worry is the fear to risk success. Yes, I said success.

All that I teach you has direct application in your life for one purpose to promote love. How easy is that? You know what the test is. It is all about you and there is only one answer. In all that you do, every action of the day the test is repeated.

How do you love me? You love me in every gesture you make toward another, in the patience when you really listen to another and feel his or her concern. The time you make free to pray for others and for the situation in your world, and yes for yourself. You see, it is all about love. My mission is understandable to all even those bound by fear and violence. And that is love.

Worry is the muscle spasm, the cramp that hinders your movement. Stretch out in love and the disability even temporary evaporates. When worry seeps into your field of vision wipe your eyes or glasses and look directly into the eyes of the person or people with whom you are and listen to them, alone become the sunset or the sunrise, or the wind blowing through the field of experience.

Do not lose heart, do not become discouraged. Easy for me to say, yet I support these words with a promise. Whenever you are worried, or worry, become still and listen to me. Do not be surprised if a smile stretches across your face, or one of my many graces in the form of a coincidence happens in your life, like someone offering cooling waters along a desert road.

There is a purpose to worry and that is it places my message of love in stark contrast to a message of hopelessness. I offer you love, I encourage all your efforts especially those that promote the stirring of love in those bereft, and it seems to them, of favor.

So today all of you mark those instances of love you experience and the coincidences that just "happen" it seems.

In my love.

Scripture: *Having received the commander's permission, Paul stood on the steps and motioned to the crowd. When they were all silent, he said to them in Aramaic: "Brothers and fathers, listen now to my defense." Acts 21:40*

Prayer: Help me to be silent and listen to you.

Response: When you hear me, like this morning, it is as if I am talking Aramaic, a secret language of the heart. My language is one that is always clear, you are only required to be still and listen. As the crowd on the steps of the temple who suddenly stopped what they were doing and listened?

What does it take to listen? First, you experience a need to fill a gap. This is the initial motivation, and it is when you experience recognition. For those before Paul, it was a language that they understood and one that they heard in the synagogue. Next, his message of Christ confirmed the rumors that they had heard, and finally Paul spoke words that hit a deep recognition in their hearts.

You don't have to travel to Greece to have a similar experience. You are silenced by my presence this morning. You have stepped from the crowded activity of your mind, and paused, directing your attention toward me. I speak in a language of authority, one that you understand from your youth, a holy language for you. Nothing for this moment is more important than to be still.

In the course of the day, I pull you aside with this strange language of the heart to reassure you, to prod you further to understand and embrace my love, and to generously share this love.

There is such an urgent need to pray for those experiencing despair. You can understand that despair among those who have up until now not heard and even if they did could not comprehend the words of Aramaic I speak to all.
You are to pray in your words, in your thoughts and gestures throughout each day. Not as some robot but as a gracious individual who allows my love to shine forth. In the process you will come to understand that your Aramaic is improving.

This day is an especially opening day where you will find that the isolated compartments of your life begin to integrate in a startling fashion, where you no longer consider writing, worldly chores, reading, and relationships as separate areas of your life. All is coming together as a tapestry of my love.

In your peace today.

#171

Scripture: *It is hard for you to kick against the goads. Acts 26:14*

Prayer: Lord, I do not remember ever reading these words previously. Please give me some insight.

Response: You discover daily how just a few words, collected in a verse, even half a verse contains much for you to consider. There is a paradox contained in this thought. A rich paradox at that and it does not escape Paul.

First, realize that Paul is explaining his conversion to an exalted king who appreciates the vigor with which he pursued perceived enemies of the Jewish faith. Consider the weight that now the shame he carries on his soul in the persecution of those from the same heritage who chose to follow Jesus, The Way. So he establishes with the King his loyalty to the established religion and even reveals the increasing intensity of his efforts.

If you step aside you can see a flood emerging in his basement and floundering about trying to seal the leak, or better, a ship beginning to sink though the water is calm and unable to stem the flow of the water. From persecuting Jews of The Way locally, he travels far a field and that is where he experiences the blinding white light in broad daylight, brighter that the noon day sun. If that was not enough a voice booms, *It is hard for you to kick against the goads.*

Consider what I have contained in those words and have anointed with my presence. First, The Way is one of self discovery and in your dawning consciousness of my love a path is laid out for you to return to me. Please do not consider that this path in any way thwarts the direction you choose. In fact this path is also self discovery for me in that you reveal your love for me. Once on the path, and you are all on it, you recognize the path and journey to a greater or lesser extent. The goal is that over time, if that is allowed you, you understand more fully each day the path, the experience of the journey in the moment, and my love for you.

This awareness, I prefer consciousness, creates the goads that offer a reminder, a check, that keep your attention to the path before you. You have ridden horses in the past so think of the slight flicker of the crop, the knees that offer correction as well, and of course the reins, all encouraging you to continue on the path however winding it is through mountain terrain. Think of this journey as a trail ride, the scenery is spectacular with all its ups and downs and hardship and joys.

The goads are an indication, a real indication, that you recognize the path, you know my love, and that you are eager to know my will. And so it was with Paul though his experience was dramatic. He needed a strong correction and he received one – but how changed he was after that. Though do not think that he did not continue to receive those corrections in the future. Because as you can appreciate, I do want you to move along the path and not linger away munching grass at noon when there is still much distance to cover before night fall. I should say with you it is afternoon, I did not say late afternoon, and you have still a long distance to travel.

In my will and love today.

Scripture: *Now get up and stand on your feet. I have appeared to you to appoint you as a servant and as a witness of what you have seen of me and what I will show you. Acts 26:16*

Prayer: Lord, help me to understand these words as spoken to me.

Response: Well, I tell you that they are, with every bit directness and intensity as I spoke to Paul. Consider these words as being spoken for the first time this morning and written for you so that you can reread them and not depend upon memory alone.

Notice the order of my words. First servant and that means service – service in a family, service in work, service in sharing wisdom and knowledge, service in prayer for those enduring trials. About trials, isn't it interesting that what you observe you suffer and what you suffer you can offer for those less aware and conscious of my grace and love?

Now, a word of witness – some are called to be Paul on the fringes of what might be considered safe. Most are called to witness first to themselves and this is done in prayer, in the reflections of my love that might fill a day, in accepting what is unfolding though it does not yet seem clear. That is where many find themselves, yet to encourage you, see how any discovery whether it be across an ocean or climbing a peak for the first time has you traveling in uncertainty. Your trust and faith allows the surprise and wonder to be even greater when you witness what I have in store for you.

Witnessing is not I must tell you performing on a stage of life. Witnessing to others is a quiet connection though you might be on the stage of life. Another paradox you say. Witnessing from the heart and not the ego seeking recognition is what I seek from you. And witnessing does not have to be even seen. Such witnessing can be heard, read, and thought about in reflection. You didn't see Paul in person and though you read his words, the real impact of his witnessing is now where you become present with him and listen to him across time.

True witnessing has no time or space dimension. You see, real, genuine witnessing is eternal and of course assumes a community of at least one more than the witness. Remember I said that space and time are not ingredients or even factors of witnessing.

So first witness to yourself and then reach out onto whatever path presents itself and share what you experience.

All for now.

Scripture: *May God be gracious to us and bless us and make his face shine upon us, that your ways may be known on earth, your salvation among all nations. Psalms 67:1-2*

Prayer: Lord, help me to praise you as your face does shine upon me and guide me to fulfill your will in my life.

Response: This morning as you experience the first rain in so many days and weeks, see my face shining upon you even in the rain. It is at times like this that you trust the sun rising though you cannot see it. So I work in your heart and soul, nurturing you though you are unable to tell what is occurring in the light – so dismal is this day of bounty hidden in the rains.

Approach days like this with thanksgiving that you are being tested on another level. My guidance is measured on your commitment to trust my love. You will reach dazzling heights as you continue to trust. As I have told you previously, this is no competition. Each of you is suited to the metaphorical rain to a great or lesser degree. I am at each of your sides to guide you, just you and you and you. And as you become more conscious, you find that my guidance leads you to others so that in some instances you are offering a model to them and in others you are influenced and are being led by their example of trust, confidence, and love.

The important thing for you today is to be in the rain. Hear the steady fall and the accompanying wind. Be in the rain as if you are in a protective bubble of my love and sense what that means. Hear and feel the rhythm of its beat, catch its beat as the beat of your heart. Be one with creation that is far removed from anxieties magnified by the ego. Sense the cleansing that is occurring at the deepest level – this cleansing allowing you to become more present to my love which is eternal.
So today allow yourself to be in a listening mode. Hear my voice that will be especially distinct today.

In my love.

#174

Scripture: *Indeed, when Gentiles, who do not have the law, do by nature things required by the law, they are a law for themselves, even though they do not have the law, since they show that the requirements of the law are written on their hearts, their consciences also bearing witness and their thoughts now accusing, now even defending them. Romans 2:14-15*

Prayer: Guide me as I reach across to those who are the Gentiles of today.

Response: In reaching across to those who are in ignorance and delusion, be respectful, do not judge, see the divine spark within each. Do not be surprised if their understanding of the law and my truth is deeper than yours though they have arrived at this truth by another path. It is so important for you to discover your connection in my love with another who on the surface is not in faith than to win a debate. Gentleness must be a mark of your actions and your prayers.

It is understandable how you could become frustrated in discussing with others your experience of a spiritual nature acquired outside your Christian circle – like a modern day Paul, and all of you who are comfortable ranging in foreign circles, are modern day Paul's. However, realize that you are also modern day Paul who stay right in your local environment and share quietly and gently your faith with those who have drifted from the truth of their fathers to continue their search.

While I am not talking of idols and golden calves necessarily, I am talking about the longing for union that spurs those to travel so far a field when I am found within. Yes, within the quiet of your soul. You ask for signs and I tell you to be still without distraction and you will hear me. My message is carried on the wings of the Spirit and right this moment encompasses you in my truth and love.

So with all you encounter be they Muslims, ethnic (as you call them) Christians, agnostics, supposed atheists, and those of other traditions, extend your hand, listen to them, pray for them – not as being superior but as one who needs as Paul did the reassurance and companionship and community – however diverse it is – of you all on the path to me.

That is all for today. Travel gently but with footsteps that are clearly left in the sand. In my love.

#175

Scripture: *Shout for joy to the Lord, all the earth. Worship the lord with gladness; come before him with joyful songs.* Psalm 100:1-2

Prayer: After the storm last night and experiencing the rising sun on the flowers and the birds delighting in the abundance, help me to be joyful without a *because*. Let me simply be joyful in your presence.

Response: It is good for you to de-link your responses from an event. You do mention the beautiful morning that is before you. See if you can go deeper and experience joy without being prompted by the externals. You might be surprised to discover that you are joyful more often than you imagine without it being *caused*. You see that is true joy that arises within because it is within that we are one.

It is this joy that you bring into the world as the birds of the morning do likewise. To be a peacemaker which you desire is to find first the peace within and then to bring it into your environment. I came to bring you that awareness of the power that you possess within and that power is based on – is formed – in my love.

You cannot be joyful without joy within. Sounds simple doesn't it? When you are not joyful you have lost connection with me as your source. It is like forgetting to drink from my fountain regularly, moment by moment. Whenever you feel disengaged with this source, stop, breathe deeply, listen and drink deeply of the joy that resides within.

This might seem sensible in a meditative state but it is even more important as you engage in the world. My joy is with you in all corners of your life, even confronted with a life and death situation. You see that inner joy is access to me and my love. At this stage of your consciousness, I am guiding you in principles that seem almost too simple. So here it is, joy, inner joy, is available to all at every moment of their life. You discover this joy at all stages in your life and is manifested in your demeanor with others.

All for now.

Scripture: "... *but we also rejoice in our suffering, because we know that suffering produces perseverance; perseverance, character; and character, hope. And hope does not disappoint us, because God has poured out his love into our hearts by the Holy Spirit, whom he has given us. Romans 5:3-5*

Prayer: May I say to you this morning, I am suffering – with doubt, anxiety, second-guessing decisions that I have made. There are times – like this – when I feel overwhelmed. Please give me pause to persevere in your love.

Response: Sometimes the stillness before dawn allows the shadows of doubt to infiltrate, with certain logic the conduct of your life. It is times like this, however rare they might be, for you to lift your voice in praise, to see beyond the cloud of doubt, the horizon where the dawn is about to erupt in the brilliance of my love. At times like this expect, hope, be determined, be intent, focused. Vigilant is the word. At times like this, you are on the brink of discovery.

Discovery of what? My love especially manifested in your life and in those around you. No need for you to seek explanations of what motivates, spurs, stirs that love. The timing and expanse are mine to decide. You are being brought to the edge so that you realize once again your dependence on me and my love, and equally important, you realize like the young bird standing atop the precipice that it is time to leap – as Kierkegaard once said – *into the absurd.*

Please do not look back – though your past is filled with riches – rather look forward to where I am heading you. Your staff is sharpened or defined with your responsibilities that you readily assume, by consciousness that declares your prayers and intentions, by your love unfettered that is becoming more and more filled with forgiveness and compassion.

So today celebrate as if you have been invited to attend the exclusive banquet of the king; for that is what I have invited you. Celebrate and praise exactly when you feel discouragement, in your shouts of praise you roust the enemy from its positions and they flee in fear as those who were arraigned against Gideon[11] and his lanterns. Sweep through their abandoned encampments with your shouts of joy. Hallelujah!

In my love.

---

[11] Judges 7:15-24

#177

Scripture: *Let the morning bring me word of your unfailing love for I have put my trust in you. Show me the way I should go, for to you I lift up my soul. Psalm 143:8*

Prayer: Indeed, I feel I have discovered an immeasurable resource to tap into your love. Help me this morning to feel that love.

Response: These words of scripture are there for you to help you to go deeper in understanding and acceptance. It is not so much their existence and the anointing that accompanies them as you sit quietly and read and reflect upon them; rather these words are like keys that open various doors within you that you might have allowed to remain locked. It is like living in a mansion and never getting to the lower floors where the treasure awaits you. My scripture provides the keys to such exploration, but first you must have a desire to leave the upper, actually surface floors.

This morning your prayer is answered and will be throughout the day. For in opening the doors on the "treasure corridor" so much will be made clear to you. You have asked the question in your heart that so many will not address. The question of how my unfailing love is manifest in your life is a question all should ask and in all circumstances of their lives, from where they are, what they are experiencing, in their strength and in their frailty. These words are for the twelve year old, the successful businessman or government worker, the woman in labor or alone, or the person in failing health approaching the release in death.

The prayer contained in that verse is always, I repeat always answered. It doesn't need any formula requiring you to send it to seven individuals, or performing some ritual thought up by someone seeking mechanical solutions. No, simply reading this verse deeply, quietly whether in a group or alone as you are this morning at dawn, and I hear you as if I was and actually am sitting opposite you. You can whisper the words, cry the words, shout the words, or simply repeat the words in your heart without them being audible.

My love for you celebrates your every prayer as these words contain. But please don't think that these are the words above all others. This verse is another example of how the scripture is anointed and is your shortcut to my love.

What a treasure you have uncovered in the lower rooms. Take your time to go through each room, each treasure chest. They are all aligned in rows for you to examine at your pace.

Much love this morning.

#178

Scripture: *But if Christ is in you, your body is dead because of sin, yet your spirit is alive because of righteousness. And if the Spirit of him who raised Jesus from the dead is living in you, he who raised Christ from the dead will also give life to your mortal bodies through his Spirit, who lives in you. Romans 8:10-11*

Prayer: Explain more deeply Christ's presence in me.

Response: Christ is in you like the blood flowing in your veins, like the air your lungs take in, like the thoughts that inspire you to write, the words that you seek to pray, the work that your hands engage, the eyes that land softly upon those who suffer, the compassion you extend to others, the forgiveness you exercise for those who have hurt you as well as for yourself when you have not measured to the standard of your new life.

Christ is present in the boldness with which you embark on a new adventure and leave behind the pursuit of youth. It is like hunting in the King's domain. Indeed, you could continue to hunt the ground-hugging game and in doing so continue to be fed. Christ in you is providing you the inspiration to seek the more elusive game that requires courage of the spirit, unflagging desire, commitment, determination, and perseverance.

Christ in you changes all, like taking on a new identity and the clothes that accompany. Intent you are vigilant, look forward, exhaust your resources to discover that they are replenished beyond what you depleted. Christ in you is to embrace the world about you for the purpose of leading those around you to a higher plane in which to view and refashion it in Christ presence.

Indeed, with Christ in you, the old ways of neglect and ignorance and unconsciousness are past. The music you hear now is the rapture of creation audible in your heart as the sensors of Christ within you are enhanced.

You are blessed and in my love this day.

Scripture: *In the same way, the Spirit helps us in our weakness. We do not know what we ought to pray for, but the Spirit himself intercedes for us with groans that words cannot express. Romans 8:26*

Prayer: Help me to understand the groans and the Spirit's interaction.

Response: There are times that what you pray for is what your mind leads you though deep within you know at that intimate level the longing of your heart. This is when the Spirit gives voice to those prayers of the heart with groans that are unintelligible except to the heart.

These groans are recognized by you and often are accompanied simultaneously with tears, the gift of the Spirit. There is nothing for you to do to prompt these groans. Rather, your steady resort to prayer, both for your own condition and for those around you, and for an easing of global violence in all its manifestations bring such prayer to fruition.

The groans are an easing of the pent up frustration of not being able to articulate the prayer that resides deepest within you. Once uttered those groans though they appear, or at least you think they are external, are really in harmony with music that is not heard outside of your heart longing.

The groans this morning, though you did not hear them, were ringing as the pealing of bells on a mountain top as you viewed the rising of the sun as it penetrated the low cloud cover. Groaning is the primordial utterance of the soul and takes you back to the creation story that you are manifesting in the present.

How reassuring for you to realize that it is not a pattern of prayers that I require but an inclination to prayer. The groans the Holy Spirit lent to you makes up in a manner the prayer of praise that requires no formula or for that matter no ritual, incense included; no panoply, simply sitting, standing, walking in awe of my love for you.

All for today.

Scripture: *For I am convinced that neither death nor life, neither angels nor demons, neither the present nor the future, nor any powers, neither height nor depth, nor anything else in all creation, will be able to separate us from the love of God that is in Christ Jesus our Lord. Romans 9:38-39*

Prayer: What a statement! Lord, help me to take this in as fully as I am able this day.

Response: In this statement you are led to understanding the significance of Christ's Love and that of the Father that encompasses all eternity. These words strive to break the boundaries defined by life and death, angels and demons, height and depth, and encourage you to pull all those contrasts that you can identify and there are innumerable, and to conclude that there is not one example you can discover that puts in doubt my love nor your separation from that love. What is not said are the words, *if you so will.*

Before I address these latter words, let us focus on the non-dual nature of my love, a term that you have tried to grasp in the past. By non-dual I am trying to explain with the limitation of mind vocabulary that which are truly heart-reckonings. By non-dual, I mean that in the regions of the heart and soul all is one and further, seeks union with the source of love. This source is not outside the heart but is one with the heart.

Therefore, my love for you is your love for me and is one. You cannot be separated from that love by circumstances outside the heart – the heights or depths where you travel, or the past and future that are elements of perceived time, or the forces of good and evil that seem to coexist in your environment.

Your journey inward promotes union with me, love and compassion and this is what you see as the source of love that is ever replenished, is ceaseless as you generate that love and compassion in the world that you inhabit. This is a difficult concept or truth for you to fully grasp, especially so early in the morning, but accept that you have an inner source of divine energy within you like a nuclear power plant. The only difference is – among many – is that there is no issue of spent fuel. In my love you have an absolutely endless supply of warmth, love to generate with no fear of running dry or empty.

Let's get back to *if you so will.* Nothing can prevent the smooth generation of power of love unless you *will* to cease generating that power. And believe me when I tell you it would be no small effort to cease the operations of this very elaborate power plant of love, but of course I have left you that option. On a lighter side, it would be more difficult for you to turn off the generators of love than you might imagine. It is like my safety check that is designed to continue the flow of love than to stop operations in a cautionary state. You see, in matters of the heart to disperse love no caution is to be observed.

So for today linger on the union, the non-dual nature of your love, and realize that I am here to encourage the smooth and ceaseless flow of love within you and in your external environment, if you so will. Lastly, don't make this too complicated. This operation is so smooth that you can even dispense love unconsciously, just like breathing you might say.

All for today.

CHAPTER SEVEN -- LISTENTING

I was introduced to "centering prayer" in the writings of Thomas Merton, a Trappist Monk. He has influenced my pray life from the time I was a high school student to the present as I continue to read and reflect upon his work.

Simply stated "centering prayer" is placing oneself in the presence of God and then listening. There are no verbal formulations though in the early days I employed the phrase – Come Lord Jesus in Aramaic (Marianatha) to busy my mind so my heart remained in a listening mode. Selecting a time and place for this practice was of enormous assistance in establishing a routine that knew few lapses. For example, I once crated a quiet place within a cluster of Blue Spruces behind my home. There I placed within an all-weather chair. For twenty-two years, rain or snow, I would trudge the forty paces before dawn wrapped in a camel's hair cloak to my sanctuary for this period of listening.

For many years, I have reserved a weekend each year to visit a Trappist Monastery located beside the Shenandoah River in Virginia. There the listening blends with the rhythm of the routine of the monks who begin the day in chapel long before dawn.

Listening without any agenda or expectation leads me to a consciousness that enters a space-less, even time-less dimension, and appears as a portal to eternity in God's presence. The concerns of the upcoming day and even what could have happened in the past are let go for a time. It is a time of nourishment in the Father's presence. What I do as a person pauses, and who I am surfaces and is nourished in this respite as I listen attentively to God's words. Here was the birth of my praying fingertips.

#181

Scripture: *So Sarah laughed to herself as she thought, "After I am worn out and my master is old, will I now have this pleasure?" Then the Lord said to Abraham, "Why did Sarah laugh and say, "Will I really have a child, now that I am old?" Is anything too hard for the Lord? I will return to you at the appointed time next year and Sarah will have a son." Genesis 18:12-14*

Prayer: Lord, I guess you are telling me something about age and your power that lingers about me.

Response: Lingers about you. That is an interesting way to describe my love for you. Yes, this verse is also about age and how important for you to consider age irrelevant to the present moment. *Irrelevant for the present moment,* I repeat so that you realize that age is only a factor when you fold into your consideration the past and the future. Dispense with those notions; no longer be held by the fantasies of youth past, or old age future. You are ageless in my love. Quiet a concept isn't?

I am asking you to be conscious now, this moment, and listen. Listen, listen. I have so much to tell you and to guide you. There is nothing impossible for me to accomplish. You wonder sometimes why your prayers are not answered. Let me tell you why. They are not bold enough, not confident enough, do not serve the love that resides within you, do not serve to kindle the love that resides sometimes flickers/wavers within those you meet.

I accomplish through you, repeat through you, miracles of faith that are far more magnificent than bearing a child in a seemingly impossible biological age. Only if you trust, tap into the inner presence, and allow your prayers to come forth gently, boldly, loudly, in tears, in joy do you catch my attention. What a simple proscription. You are my fingertips, my vocal chords, my embraces, my tears, my laughter. And listen carefully, and I am your fingertips, your vocal chords, your embraces, your tears, your laughter, and much beside.

So greet each day as a staging for another, actually countless miracles. And as Sarah does, laugh at the absurdity of your prayer, your concern, and hold on for another miracle. Because you see, in addition to being described as the God of judgment and compassion, I am whimsical as well.

In my love.

Scripture: *But who are you, O man, to talk back to God? Shall what is formed say to him who formed it, 'Why did you make me this?' Does not the potter have the right to make out of the same lump of clay some pottery for noble purposes and some for common use? Romans 9:20-21*

Prayer: Lord, help me to accept this lump of clay and praise you forming me as you did.

Response: I want to give you an expanded notion of what it means to be in the hands of the potter. That lump of clay also represents the circumstances of your birth, your race, sex, health, religion, and the chemistry that in inheriting your ancestor genetic pool provides you a physical and emotional visage.

Take note of everything I have mentioned and since I didn't mention specifically eye color you can estimate the ingredients that have made you up; I did not define or confine your will to turn away from me. So with all these elements, there is one at first glance missing, your will to reject or accept me.

Is the ingredient missing, or another perspective, is it a void like a turbulent whirlpool, like the black hole in the galaxy? Think about it. See the free will and all its aspects as a creation point in which I have allowed the "it" to be in true union with me as a co-creator. That is why I say or said yesterday that you are my vocal chords, my fingertips. You see in the *missing ingredient,* your free will, I have granted each to you, Christian, Muslim, black or white, short or tall, male or female, its own creation point found in a void of sorts that you call free will.

Now if you accept what I am saying, consider each creation point residing in such diversity on this globe and consider what would happen if there was union of these void points, let's say, in harmony and peace, and then consider what would be the result, and in love. The void in harmony promotes love to a depth not imagined, to a cellular level, if that makes it any clearer to you. Don't dwell on it, but consider alternatively what happens when these void, creation points unite in disharmony and violence.

So, yes, I am the potter, and you are the clay. I have the intention to create and in each one of you I have created a void of creation that stirs as the open sea on the darkest moonlit night. You are essentially that stirring and through my love and grace I seek to see you to stir love.

All of this morning.

#183

Scripture: *What then shall we say? That the Gentiles, who did not pursue righteousness, have obtained it, a righteousness that is by faith; but Israel, who pursued a law of righteousness, has not attained it. Why not? Because they pursued it not by faith but as if it were by works. They stumbled over the "stumbling stone." Romans 9:30-32*

Prayer: Please help me to understand the "it," the righteousness by faith.

Response: What is righteousness, you ask. Righteousness is finding that the creative point about which I have been talking these last days is in harmony with my will, that your will is in harmony with my will. Following a law, without plunging deeper so that your very essence that which defines and distinguishes you, is surface allegiance that disguises true intent.

What I am calling you to do is to bring your essential being into union with me and in that harmony you discover that it is not the law but your faith, your realization that I am with you. I am with you in faith and you discover through faith that I am within you, talking to you, consoling you, counseling you. Such intimacy cannot be achieved through a law.

I call you to an intimacy that is deeper than any intimacy that you have experienced with a loved one. And I do not legislate intimacy through a law, though I could. I call you, invite you to this intimacy by appealing, yes appealing, to your trust, faith, willingness to suspend your ego's call to rationality.

You don't have to go anywhere to prove your righteousness. It resides in faith within you. And therefore there is no stumbling against the rocks strewn in your path. No matter where you are, I call to you and in listening you hear me by your faith.
That call is like the chapel bells sounding in your heart. Listen to them and be present in faith. You will see great wonders worked in your life in that hearing.

So faith is the essential message I have for you this morning. Not faith in a formal religion, rather faith in hearing my words that you then share with those in your faith community.

How simple I have made it for you. There is much more I could say on faith, but let me give you pause and allow you to digest these words. If you have any questions, simply listen and I will scatter the doubt.

In my love.

Scripture: *We have different gifts, according to the grace given us. If a man's gift I is prophesying, let him use it in proportion to his faith. If it is serving, let him serve; if it is teaching, let him teach; if it is encouraging, let him encourage; if it is contributing to the needs of others, let him give generously; if it is leadership, let him govern diligently; if it is showing mercy, let him do it cheerfully. Romans 12:6-8*

Prayer: Help me to identify my gifts and to use them generously.

Response: Becoming aware of your gifts is a significant step for someone. So much has come before that awareness. First, exposed to a board of wood does a person realize that he or she has the gift to become a craftsman? No, first you receive faith in your life and then you become aware of where you have talent, a special gift.

Think of writing. When first you wrote a sentence, or in drama, the first time you memorized a line, in drawing, the first time you picked up a pencil, and I could go on - - in a dawning awareness of your talent, your special gift is made aware to you.

Then, a very critical step, with courage you seize the gift and use it. You are especially blessed when you use the gift deliberately for my word, to extend my message for which it has fallen if at all on deaf ears. There is so much to do to reach those who in their self- righteousness have closed their heart to my word, from my love; self confident, they are on a path that leads to destruction. At a minimum, I can say that they are on a meandering trail that they aimlessly follow, but the destination is not clear, their goals are not set.

The gifts that I speak of are all extensions of my reach. As we discussed days ago, as you become my vocal chords, my fingertips, my eyes, so too do your talents and gifts. Prophesying is a special gift that blossoms from those who reflect upon my word not as a learned document, but in the heart, allowing my anointed message to them burst forth to those huddled alongside the road seeking nourishment before they continue.

Recognize your gifts but do not harbor pride in their possession lest you lose the gift. Keep the ego far from the manifestation of the gift in whatever you do. The gifts are essential to the expansion of awareness of my love. And the gifts vary in the individual as well as in the course of your journey. Be accepting of these shifts lest you become wedded in pride with one.

#185

Scripture: *Therefore, as God's chosen people, holy and dearly loved, clothe yourselves with compassion kindness, humility, gentleness and patience. Bear with each other and forgive whatever grievances you may have against one another. Forgive as the Lord forgave you. And over all these virtues put on love, which binds them all together in perfect unity. Colossians 3:12-14*

Prayer: Bring me closer to what you mean of perfect unity.

Response: Notice that I did not say that in perfect unity you all became alike. Compassion, kindness, humility, gentleness and patience all are manifested in the diversity of each person and are prompted by the circumstances that you encounter and the capacity that you have to extend. All of the manifestations create a union of love without disturbing the distinctiveness of each of you.

From showing these indications of love, you indeed become one body with me, no less diverse than a finger from an eye, a toe from an ear. So each of you play your instrument or sing clearly and loudly with your voice in my divine choral orchestra. Allow me to direct the performance. And if you sound a bit off key at times, your individual performance will meld into that of those around you into heavenly acclaim.

Another word about union. It begins in a family, and then reaches out to friends and strangers. It cuts across relationships at all levels – work, church, play. It works union among you all for my purpose of love.

See in your day how you contribute by your attitude and actions to union. Yes, you contribute to union in your prayers, in your work, in your writing, in how you greet people who are meeting you for the first time, or those whom you have known slightly or deeply, yet the relationship must be nourished, re-invigorated.
Union is what I seek for you without in any way disturbing the grand diversity that I have created in you.

.

Scripture: *When my spirit grows faint within me, it is you who know my way. Psalm 142:3*

Prayer: Lord, this morning I feel weariness and seek your nourishment.

Response: You are rewarded for your perseverance. Though discouraged you continue to trust and hope and those qualities of the Spirit are more and more manifest with you. At times like this, it is so important to fix yourself in the present. As you move about the garden in silence watering, and return your attention to me, clear your mind of anxiety because that is where it resides. Your heart is clear and steady in my love.

Consider each step you take today as a step to take and to be completed. Imagine, if you will, that you are setting out on a journey and at nightfall you will have reached where I intended you to be, though I must say that each step you take is exactly where I intended you to be.

Today is a day to clear out the web of tasks that seem to accumulate especially when you are entertaining family. Do not consider the backlog but rather the graces extended to others through your attentiveness.

Be prayerful today especially of those about you and those who linger and suffer so far from home. Be especially peaceful today, gentle in your speech and every action.

You will find me lurking along the road in the smiles you encounter and in circumstances that will fold in your path to ease the journey.

Be of gentle cheer this day.

Scripture: *And do this, understanding the present time. The hour has come for you to wake up from your slumber, because our salvation is nearer now than when we first believed. The night is nearly over; the day is almost here. So let us put aside the deeds of darkness and put on the armor of light.* Romans 13:11-12

Prayer: Help me to understand the present time.

Response: Over these last years, you have become more attuned to the significance of the present. Today I would like to focus more on the night as almost passed and the dawning light is upon you. This alone should stir you in anticipation; give you the energy to sort through what you spend your days on; select only those to keep your attention on that prepare you for the dawn.

Be prepared to shed your masks and the cloaks you wear to disguise that startling glow within you; do what you must to lift the burdens you carried in the night so that you can leap across a meadow and not worry as you did that you would fall into a crevasse. Be prepared to look up and around you and embrace the sights and those around you that up until now you missed in the dark.

Yes, it is time to wake, pull yourself from slumber and unthinking and that unconsciousness with which you justify your sloth. Being present means choosing your every step and not making excuses that you could not see one step in front of you. This is a time when you must be able to shout to someone distant, but can see in the light.

Remember we are not talking about an end of the world scenario, but rather a dawning of light that affects you right now, this minute. And as I conclude, take on the armor of light that empowers you to reach out with courage and love to those who still slumber, whether they be in your family or stand afar in a distant land.

Scripture: *Accept him whose faith is weak, without passing judgment on disputable matters. One man's faith allows him to eat everything, but another man, whose faith is weak, eats only vegetables. The man who eats everything must not look down on him who does not, and the man who does not eat everything must not condemn the man who does, for God has accepted him. Who are you to judge someone else's servant? To his own master he stands or falls. And he will stand, for the Lord is able to make him stand. Romans 14:1-4*

Prayer: Lord, this is the first time I notice these message. Please me a deeper message.

Response: You are a meat-eater, so you know where you fit. Isn't it interesting how you say quite often that in all your years you have not found a food that you didn't like? Well, let me say this morning that your eating inclination is also symbolic of your faith. You are indeed curious and that inquisitiveness allows you to sample a wide spiritual expanse without affecting the integrity of your love of my message.

You and others so inclined must be attentive to those who are vegetarians. Do not assume that it is simply a matter of clarification and all would be like you. That is not the case. Great patience on your part is called for. You must hone further your listening skills.

In this verse I am also explaining the need to be inquisitive and questioning to the extent that you are able and are comfortable. There are countless reasons why someone is restraining his or her vision, so you must avoid the perceived need to judge or make judgment on the efficacy of their actions. It's as if some wear a self-repellant garment of faith and others are comfortable in the self-absorption mode.

Realize that is so very important to remain grounded in my word. Your capacity to eat everything is not encouragement to be everything. I am seeking witnesses who can move freely among the lost and to extend the hand of truth and love. Such witnesses would not do well if their diet was too constricted.

Scripture: *Many have undertaken to draw up an account of the things that have been fulfilled among us, just as they were handed down to us by those who from the first were eyewitnesses and servants of the word. Therefore, since I myself have carefully investigated everything from the beginning, it seemed good also to me to write an orderly account for you, most excellent Theophilus, so that you may know the certainty of the things you have been taught. Luke 1:1-4*

Prayer: Help me to catch the excitement in this opening of Luke's gospel.

Response: The excitement, the anticipation that you feel is for the anointed word that gathers no dust with age. This morning, the sun already high, the birds joyous in the garden, it is no less an opportunity for discovery. You are Theophilus opening this missive across the reach of time.

It seems to be a theme that I constantly refer to in our dialogues so forgive me if you need no further reminder. You have in your hands Luke's account and believe if you will that you have just received the package because that is in fact the truth. Luke's account was written especially for you. So in these readings ensure that you have reserved a quiet time free of distractions to hear my word as transmitted through Luke as your writing transmits my thoughts and instructions to you.

Luke's account brings order to the accounts of Jesus that circulated the known world as you would describe He is methodical and there is a certain tempering of his enthusiasm to give as accurate accounting without allowing his own fervor to color his description. He understands the weightiness of his task and clearly understands in an inspired sense that he is laying a building block upon which later commentaries and interpretations will be built. There is a certain mater-of-fact quality to Luke's writing.

Speaking of fervor, Luke is so taken with his assignment that he chooses each word as if he were reporting on a cure that he was recommending to a patient. Luke is providing you with that cure and he treats his assignment seriously to write clearly of what he has discovered.

How many times have you read over this introduction to get to the meat, so you think? But this time, don't overlook the import of his words. He has investigated; he has drawn up what he has learned from eyewitnesses and old believers in an orderly fashion – actually a linear approach rather than a thematic approach, his style of writing is for those without the background in the Old Law.

Yes, he is writing for someone that fits your profile. All you are required to do is to read each word carefully. There is no rush to complete the book because as with your journey to Emmaus there is no completion. In the reading and reflecting you are on this spectacular journey home. .

Scripture: *The angel answered, "I am Gabriel. I stand in the presence of God, and I have been sent to speak to you and to tell you this good news. And now you will be silent and not able to speak until the day this happens, because you did not believe my words, which will come true at their proper time." Luke 1:19-20*

Prayer: Give me the patience to wait for the proper time.

Response: Waiting for the proper time is a sign of patience, trust, and hope that all is well. Waiting for the proper time is confidence in an unfolding that involves you as a key ingredient as you all are. The proper time demonstrates how all is connected. Every action that you do in love prompts a further revelation of my love.

So it was for Zechariah, the faithful priest, and his wife Elizabeth. Quiet acceptance with a wry smile, perhaps an inward smile, is the ultimate demonstration of confidence in my word.

Zechariah was silenced when he allowed his analytical, rational mind to interrupt the revelation that Gabriel was announcing. So too in your life, don't interrupt the revelation that comes to you through events and friends and by your own efforts. Be accepting of the miracles in your life as you are of the sunrise appearing suddenly through a cloudbank or over the top of a hill.

Life is filled with wonders, miracles that must capture your attention with devotion. In the silence see what Zechariah experienced. Not able to express himself clearly – what he had seen and heard – he was confined to listening and see in silence what was unfolding. Do the same. In silence see what is unfolding in your life. Be quiet and allow my grace to wash over you as a morning rain.

#191

Scripture: *Deep calls to deep in the roar of your waterfalls; all your waves and breakers have swept over me. Psalm 42:7*

Prayer: Lord, counsel me with this verse.

Response: As you walked the beach this morning at dawn, you sensed a seamless connection with my creation. The ocean filling the sand pockets as the tide rose, the birds skittering along the wet sand, the sun gaining energy as it reached above the low lining clouds, the dredger anchored off the beach – a resilient calm extended over your path. That scene is the roar of the deep that I ask you to enter. See if you can plunge below surface calm to experience the calamity and chaos of creation. That is where I reside most clear; where I am most present.

You will find in entering that domain which incidentally doesn't mean that you leave where you are. You see all is one and in union. Entering ensures that you are turned inside out and it is in being turned inside out that your praise of me is most genuine and authentic.

Why praise, you might ask? Good question. Your praise tells me and you that you seek union with me in my love – and as I have told you, you are not forced to seek this union. Turned inside out you become the waves churning off shore and meet your true self on the sand as you skim across it. Your unlearning must include realizing that you are one with my creation.

Today, catch snatches of your union with the nature that surrounds you: that nature that is within you. See if you can turn yourself inside out and allow the breakers of my love wash over the barriers of your heart and mind.

Scripture: *The neighbors were all filled with awe, and throughout the hill country of Judea people were talking about all these things. Everyone who heard this wondered about it, asking, "What then is this child going to be?" For the Lord's hand was with him. Luke 1:65-66*

Prayer: Lord, help me to see your graciousness as John's name means.

Response: You are more inclined to take in the meaning after walking on the beach for an hour. Graciousness is that easy calm that comes over you at such times when you find there is no need to speak, make sound. Graciousness is my communication with you and my demonstrated easy love of you as you are present in the silence.

Graciousness is a confident acceptance of who you are and in that realization and acceptance that you are present to me. Graciousness is a beautiful rhythm with the life that you experience whatever the circumstances. There is a confidence, hope and faith that all is well. It is like greeting far more guests than you have prepared for and realizing everything will work out.

Graciousness in life is not trying to control things and people. Though the term is used too often and for little purpose; graciousness is going with the flow. The flow is the path and not a scattered, spastic direction.

Graciousness follows and manifests heart direction.

So John, later to be the Baptist, comes into the world and is named for graciousness. A mighty characteristic of the God you have come to know. And what was this child to be? Ask the question of yourself but starting from this moment on. Who are you to be? That is the question to ponder, and let me say many are seeking that answer to that question. More importantly, they ask it of themselves wherever they are on this journey.
My love to you today.

Scripture: "*And you, my child, will be called a prophet of the most High for you will go on before the Lord to prepare the way for him, to give his people the knowledge of salvation through the forgiveness of sins, because of the tender mercy of our God, by which the rising sun will come to us from heaven to shine on those living in darkness and in the shadow of death, to guide our feet into the path of peace.*" *Luke 1:76-79*

Prayer: I was struck by the imagery of the rising sun coming to us from heaven. Please deepen my knowledge of these verses.

Response: As I have pointed out to you what you see on earth offers a hint of the heavenly realm. So the sun rising reflects the light from heaven. So when you watch the rising sun as you do so often, appreciate that the sun represents my light emanating from heaven, and that light is love that vanquishes the darkness of hate and violence and ignorance, if you will.

As I say, if you will, because my light warms, you are responsible for reflecting that light on those you encounter and on the environment in which you live. Let me talk a bit of the darkness that envelops so much of your world. The darkness swirls in pockets like ground fog on a valley caught between high cliffs. Though quite thick in regions of your global heart, my wind and the warming morning sun can do much to dissipate the blackness.

And this is my call to you. How do you do this? How do you reflect that light? Through your heart-felt prayers. I mean heartfelt, informed prayers that are filled with generosity, compassion, understanding, free of fear and ignorance. Yes, I expect you to pray for those you love and to whom you are close and for those whom special petitions are raised by friends and those in authority. However, I am directing, yes directing your prayers to those you do not know, those you fear, those who have hurt you or threaten to hurt you, for those you have hurt. I ask you to direct these prayers without any sense of hopelessness. I want your confidence and faith, your humility; toss out any tendency to judge and any claim that you are gifted or endowed.

Why do I want this? Because you are the ones that translate my light, my warmth, my love, my forgiveness, my compassion, my hope, my presence into action among those who have never heard me speak as you are hearing me this moment.

Consider this day, yes, Independence Day, as a day of forgiveness. Humbly ask me in prayer to gift you with my blessings to flow across your troubled globe. Yet, in this globe, many like you take the time to see the sun rise reflecting from heaven to work miracles.

In my love.

#194

Scripture: *O Lord, what is man that you care for him, the son of man that you think of him? Man is like a breath; his days are like a fleeting shadow. Psalm 144:3-4*

Prayer: Yes, Lord, that is a mystery to me. Help me to understand with more clarity.

Response: We are in agreement. It is a mystery for you as is the mystery and power of love. You are a single breath and a fleeting shadow as measured in time and space. In the eternal rhythm over which I shower you, your capacity for love is without boundary.

It is good for you to see in a breath and fleeting shadow my love for you. In your youth you used to describe life as a whisper. You were not far off the truth even then.

In the time remaining I want your shadow to be a noticeable shadow that drags others to the depths that you have and are reaching. And breath? Be deep in breath that alters your surroundings and the sense of gloom and violence that lingers as a morning fog. Be the burning sun that lifts the fog.

A fleeting shadow is also a call to make a difference. And that is what I call you to do. And this call is to all of you. Make a difference in your communion with others.

You ask for clarity in your life? Here is the formula. Embark on any path or let me be more specific, the path that leads you to heal. Alone or in company, your path is to heal.

.

#195

Scripture: *So too, at the present time there is a remnant chosen by grace. And if by grace, then it is no longer by works; if it were, grace would no longer be grace. Romans 11:5-6*

Prayer: Help me to comprehend grace.

Response: Now, indeed, that is a question for this early morning. First, you must accept that grace is a mystery. Not only trying to describe grace, but just as mysterious how grace is conveyed, and most important of all why grace is conveyed, and to whom.

Let me begin with the last, to whom is grace conferred? Rather than look around and attempt to conduct a poll of those around you who are graced, accept that you are graced and graced mightily. So you have the answer to the last question – you are graced. Before leaping to the next question, allow a moment to take this in – you are graced sitting, standing, sleeping, working, loving, consoling, being consoled, struggling, laughing, crying, healthy, ill – and every other aspect that might describe you for a time. You are graced.

Now, why is grace conferred on you? Notice I did not say was conferred on you. Grace is not a one-time transmission. Grace is as essential to you as the air you breathe, the water you imbibe, the sustenance you ingest. Grace is the love that pours out over you and within you – and you can't seem to identify the source or the depth of the stream that you seem to have entered. Does a boulder in the middle of a mountain stream churning down the mountainside ask why me as the water cools in the blazing sun? Maybe a better question is why are you positioned in the middle of the churning water? So perhaps a hint to the answer lies in where you are, not what you are doing.

How is grace conferred? Imagine an oversized canvas and along side is a palette with the most vibrant colors – no grays or dark browns or blacks. And a collection of brushes – some wide, some narrow to depict subtlety. And who do you think the artist is approaching this huge canvas? Right! With broad strokes I enliven – don't miss this word – the scene in which you participate. I lend you a season of color to enlighten your adventure and it is that light that you use to navigate your journey and to lighten the path for those that follow. That is how grace is conveyed.

The last question – actually the first – what is grace. Pure and simple, with no attempt to disguise its import, grace is divine love. Is, repeat that word, is divine love. So you see, the mystery is lessened, though it will take more than this early dialogue for you to comprehend the depth of my words. Accept it on faith that grace is divine love, conveyed in the brush strokes of your life because of you – not because how you look or what you do. If you continue to puzzle over why, I suggest that you simply say thank you.

Scripture: *I cry out to God Most High, to God, who fulfills his purpose for me. Psalm 57:2*

Prayer: It isn't me fulfilling my purpose but you fulfilling your purpose in me. Help me to understand these words with new meaning.

Response: In the quiet of this morning before your day begins filled with tasks to be performed, responsibilities to be addressed, consider yourself as an empty vessel into which I pour sustenance for you to meet my purpose.

This purpose is not for you exclusively. Far from it. I need your energy to reach those distant and close to me and of course distant and close to you. Imagine if you will that you are resuming a journey, which you are this morning, this day. I have prepared your transportation, providing your provisions, and now you are about to head off. This is my purpose for you. In no way am I controlling your decisions as to the direction you will take, nor do I limit the amount of time that you will spend with each of my people, but journey you will. And in journeying you are fulfilling my purpose for you.

It is like hiking in the mountains of Montana. As you journeyed through the snow and reached higher altitudes and your breathing became regularized; your span of vision is expanding; your reach in a sense has widened; and all of this is happening without focusing on an end or return point.

So it is with you now. You are to be robust in spirit and allow me to spread before you this panoply of opportunities to touch those in need of my healing. You are in such cases my minister, and in accepting this vocation you truly fulfill my purpose for you.

Today, note all the opportunities for my purpose for you to be fulfilled.

In my love this morning.

Scripture: "*I assure you that there were many widows in Israel in; Elijah's time, when the sky was shut for three and a half years and there was a severe famine throughout the land. Yet Elijah was not sent to any of them, but to a widow in Zarephath in the region of Sidon. And there were many in Israel with leprosy in the time of Elisha the prophet, yet not one of them was cleansed – only Naaman the Syrian.*" Luke 4:25-27

Prayer: Lord, help me, if it is your will, to understand your will.

Response: Knowing my will for you is quite clear. I do not keep it hidden from you. To understand this will, you must be still. You must listen. See the signs that I lay before you in those you just happen to meet when you once thought that coincidences existed. See my signs in what you read, what thoughts inspire you, and what enters your heart when your mind is busy. Yes, my will for you is clear. Your responsibility is to have and nurture the courage to follow my will.

Seeing the will for others in their actions is more difficult because you are reaching beyond your singular responsibility. However, do not dismiss the effort you make to perceive my will there too and in the process see those external signs of my will as a feather you would find across your path, in a blazing sunrise, or in the wind.

As you reach beyond yourself with purpose you will see that my will is what brings you together into community, a community of love.

This scripture verse is meant to push a closed minded community – believing that only the "hometown," be it of Jews or Christians – to appreciate my working out beyond the reefs, touching those who are not kin. The scripture is meant to fire you with energy to go outside the comfort of your family, friends, and social communities to see evidence of my presence and it more than seeing that presence. More important, it is meant to pull you into a wider circle of souls who support and sustain my love in their presence.

The question for you to ask is, can you see miracles in your midst where are they occurring. Let me assure you that there is no leveling off of my miraculous works in your world. In fact, the miracles abound. Soften your eyes to see me in your midst.

.

Scripture: *"Put out into the deep water, and let down the nets for a catch." Luke 5:4*

Prayer: Lord, give me the courage to leave my comfort zone and follow your will for me.

Response: Yes, I am asking you all to leave the safety of your homes and touch those who long to hear my message of love. Leaving the comfort zone might be just raising your eyes and observing what surrounds you in grief and loss of those around you, patiently listening to them and to me, extending our touch in sympathy and compassion, smiling gently on the oppressed so that they see your understanding.

Letting go of your nets into the deep is my expression to encourage you to descend into your consciousness as you are doing now to hear me clearly outside the babble of your mind and the distractions that your life engenders. Descend deep and reach wide. Quite a paradox!

In reaching wide and descending deep you are releasing your hold; you are letting go of control and grasping of what is illusion.

And notice how the exercise of letting go of the nets reaped a catch beyond the expectations of Simon. So it is for you. Allow me to surprise you this morning.

Scripture: *And the power of the Lord was present for him to heal the sick. Luke 5:17*

Prayer: What is that power, Lord?

Response: That power you see daily in your life – in the manifestation of what you experience daily as you prepare to see another sunrise, stand in awe to watch the full moon rise above the ocean, in the voice you hear when you are still, I am the thread you clutch as your guideline through the chaos, the blessing you receive in relationship with children, friends, and those you happen upon.

The power of the Lord is seen when the ordinary and expected gives way to my will, when compassion and joy overcome revenge and sorrow. The power of the Lord lifts you to another plane of existence and potential. The power of the Lord speaks directly to your heart where all distraction subsides.

This same power Jesus holds, and by referring to the power as if it existed outside of him is to remind you that this power is available to you. This same power is showered upon you daily in the form of grace that arises within. How? In the thoughts that turn your glance to my love.

The power of the Lord is a call to your trust and love. For today take each moment as wrapped in my power and see what unfolds. You see, recognition of that power brings you into a conscious and direct connection with it and you become inseparable to this power. When this occurs and you are conscious, just imagine what is possible. Perhaps, you won't be telling a cripple to stand up, but you just might find that the emotionally impaired and hurting individual arises in the awareness of my love.

Go in peace today.

Scripture: *While Jesus was in one of the towns, a man came along who was covered with leprosy. When he saw Jesus, he fell with his face to the ground and begged him, "Lord, if you are willing, you can make me clean." Jesus reached out his hand and touched the man. "I am willing," he said. "Be clean." And immediately the leprosy left him. Luke 5:12-13*

Prayer: Lord, help me to comprehend the full scene – the man with his face pressed to the ground, his plea, and Jesus' willingness.

Response: You all have been the man with his face to the ground at some time. Recall such instances and recall the immediacy of my response because you see I am not only willing, I am eager.

I have for you in these verses a formula for prayer. Recognize your situation that you want corrected. This requires some introspection and honesty in the quiet of your heart, not prodded by those around you or even custom.

Next you must humble yourself in prayer. Be still and alone or with someone who knows your heart and vocalize, if you are with someone, or even quietly allow the sentiments and plea to resound wordlessly.

Notice the confidence with which the man approached Jesus. If you are willing were his opening words. He recognized the power of God within him. And he also accepted, though he wanted to change his situation, that perhaps Jesus would not be willing. And in his humility, he accepted that outcome as well.

Now, listen to Jesus' words, "I am willing." There you have a connection between the divine and humanity. I am willing. Hear it always when you approach me in prayer. Think on, reflect on, this connection. I am willing.

Then see the results. He is cleansed and departs after receiving instructions to go to the temple and fulfill the obligation, as if his cleansing was routine in a sense. And the healing was routine in a sense – the result of sincere heart-felt prayer.

So what would you pray for this morning?

#201

Scripture: *In the morning, O Lord, you hear my voice; in the morning I lay my requests before you and wait in expectation.* Psalm 5:3

Prayer: Lord, I have not yet spoken a word aloud this morning, but you know my heart, especially this morning that marks what would have been my 43rd wedding anniversary. Help me always to be before you in expectation.

Response: Be gentle with yourself today. Take in as the air the full breadth and scope of your life to this morning. Breathe deeply and feel me rushing into your lungs with healing grace.

Yes, as the words of the Psalm proclaim I know your solicitations before they are spoken. I know your hesitancies, I know your loneliness, I know your love, I know everything about you.

The silence rings with the clamor of excitement as you reach out to fulfill my word. As a sign of my listening – and it is more than listening, it is knowing – I ask that you take note of each signal that you perceive of my attention to you and your pleas this day.

You might think that so many years have passed since you stood in front of the chapel at Fairchild AFB waiting for Donna to join you, but it is an instant in time. The fruit of that moment is that it lives within you and has affected you the same as the genes of your ancestors are responsible for your energetic outlook, your once dark hair, and your height. See events that shape you as present in your DNA, so to speak. You will never be what you were.

This day praise that moment in time for how it fashioned you to a commitment to another soul, to children and grandchildren, to friends, to strangers. Think how that moment in time affected how you read literature thereafter, wrote poetry, sketched, endured privation. You were no longer and are no longer the fellow who stopped along the way during a race in New York to observe an accident though really sought to avoid the risk of losing the race. See where you have come, how you have been affected, and how you willingly pass on this wisdom to all within your circle.

Today is a day of celebration and acknowledgement.

Be at peace today.

Scripture: *"Blessed are you who hunger now, for you will be satisfied. Blessed are you who weep now, for you will laugh." Luke 6:21*

Prayer: Please, Lord, apply this verse to my situation where on a material sense I have plenty to eat, and on an emotional surface level I laugh.

Response: There you have it – on a surface level. I am talking about matters of the heart that transcend the surface level that is fading even for you with the energy you generate.

Your hunger, that of all of you, is one of the deepest, heart hungers that I have blessed you with. *Blessed you with,* I repeat these words. It is that hunger that brings you out onto your deck at dawn to see the sunrise in silence; it is that hunger that ponders relationships fulfilled and unfilled, ended, and begun. It is that hunger that nudges you to a path as your poet once observed to a path not traveled. Hunger both of the physical and spiritual keens your interest, makes you alert, has you reflect on how best to satisfy this hunger.

As far as weeping, I am talking about heart weeping and from those interior tears is produced the paradox of joy, laughter, love. If you were to live for a thousand years, as you say ascribing the words to a Sufi wise man, you will still have much to ponder and so much laughter and joy to extend – that is, if you continue to devote quiet time to the sorrow, grief, and loss you have experienced. This paradox is worthy of your time in stillness.

Do not be troubled where solutions are not yet clear, where the path still seems to meander through the thick forest. Realize as you have that there is no rush, in the darkness you are not lost – in fact you are found. Be still and allow the other senses of the heart to be your guides.

Lin my love.

Scripture: *"Give, and it will be given to you. A good measure, pressed down, shaken together and running over, will be poured into your lap. For with the measure you use, it will be measured to you."* *Luke 6:38*

Prayer: Help me to be generous and understand "shaken together" in this verse.

Response: The words of this verse have a melody and rhythm and that is what your generosity should reflect. No ponderous pre-thinking, but spontaneous giving from the heart. Shaken together connotes abandoning the careful measuring you would undertake if you were looking to conserve profits. I am asking you to throw aside such notions and give, love, with no thought of what you might receive in return.

And then I tell you, oh, if you follow my prescription, you will discover that my generosity exceeds what you might have ever imagined. And this applies from the material to the emotional. Give of yourself in your loneliness and discover companionship from the heart.

And anyone so giving will appear a bit odd. That is what I want in my followers. I want you to be odd, to stand out, for people to ask who is that generous giver; who is that generous lover? Why does he laugh and smile when he gives all away? That is what I want you to model yourself after, and in doing so you will receive so much in return to give out once again.

.

#204

Scripture: *"For out of the overflow of his heart his mouth speaks." Luke 6:45*

Prayer: Help me to speak out of the overflow of love and compassion in my heart.

Response: What a simple formula to test the vitality and health of your heart. Focus on your own words and do not use this verse to judge others. You best know yourself. So each day, if you remember, recall what you have spoken and what you have written to gain an insight as to where your heart is. And I mean by this you can tell if you are drifting into illness of the heart just by the words you use with others.

If you find that voice is irritable, angry, harsh, elevated, you know that like an illness you are coming down with something. At times like this and it happens to all of you, take precautions. It might be a quiet walk, a simple meditation, reading something that nurtures you, an admission to yourself and perhaps to the person who heard your words of your imbalance.

Don't get discouraged because how best to understand your health unless there were times you experienced fever.

I am brief but to the point this morning. One final point, a heart that reflects humor and wisdom is one that is overflowing with my love.

Scripture: *"Lord, don't trouble yourself, for I do not deserve to have you come under my roof. That is why I did not even consider myself worthy to come to you. But say the word, and my servant will be healed."* Luke 7:7

Prayer: Few scriptures have I reflected upon as much and have had more meaning as I repeated them – Lord, I am not worthy to receive you, but say the word and I will be healed – before communion. Tell me again, again, how your word heals me.

Response: It seems you want a discourse of many pages, but I will keep my comments brief. Invite me into your heart and I will heal you. I will and do make the difference that encourages you when you falter; I do nourish you in your driest moments; I do show you a path when at first glance none seems visible. I am with you at your darkest hour, and just so you don't think that I reserve my appearances to the bleak times, I sit alongside you in your joy, in your laughter, at times when you reach out in love.

You see what the centurion learned is that I am not confined to space and time. He unconsciously understood this and it became clear to him when his servant was healed.

I do not have to come to you to lay hands on you. I am already with you with my ear cocked to your deepest longing and prayer.

Note though you say I am not worthy to receive me, you make bold to ask that I say the word. And I do much more. I embrace you in my love.

It's all so simple, you see. Invite me into your heart and I am there. Eliminate consideration of time, distance, feasibility, worthiness. Simple invite me and your prayer, your plea is answered. What will it take for you to believe, to have the faith that a miracle awaits your every utterance?
In my love.

Scripture: *Then he went up and touched the coffin, and those carrying it stood still. He said: "Young man, I say to you, get up!" Luke 7:14*

Prayer: Help me to rise, Lord, when I am discouraged.

Response: How could you do anything differently when you observe the rapture of another sunrise only this one more magnificent that yesterday's and I promise the same for tomorrow? The verse is significant because the young man could have remained in the coffin despite my urging and power to the contrary. Remember, he was not a robot nor are you. That is what is so special about our relationship that grows deeper daily, minute by minute.

This short verse wraps so much of my teaching in it. I am present alongside you when you are especially in need. It is important for you to state that need even in your heart without words or through the prayers of others for you. And it is so important for you to hear my call; some would say command. And then, notice your response. He sat up. What are you going to do?

Take the short cut in reaching me by stating in prayer your needs. Not that I do not hear until you vocalize them; the uttering of the prayer raises your consciousness of your essential, heart-felt needs and your realization that I am close when you realize them fulfilled.

Today, pray deeply for what you need to fulfill my expanding will for you.

Go in peace today.

Scripture: "*Blessed is the man who does not fall away on account of me.*" Luke 7:23

Prayer: Lord, help me to understand a verse that I have read before and never paused on what you mean.

Response: As you have come to learn, each verse has the power to reach you and anyone else at just the right moment in their lives. I am saying to you this morning that blessed is the person who upon hearing of me, my works, and my love embraces my message and does not give up the path because he or she considers it too arduous.

Blessed is the person who accepts that I will be there by his or her side in the most difficult times and does not lose hold.

Blessed is the person who perseveres, exhibits patient endurance and does not decide or allow him or her to be convinced that it is an impossible way.

Blessed is the person who hears my voice and accepts that all is possible under my guidance. Blessed is the person who accepts that I am a companion for eternity who will usher that person into the kingdom of God.

You see, I realize that all of you have the will to say this path is far more arduous than you thought and decide to turn back in clatter confusion to the world's demands. I am blessing you this morning for upon hearing my call do not turn back.

Peace to you this morning.

Scripture: *"Though your sins are like scarlet, they will be as white as snow."* Isaiah 1:18

Prayer: Bring me to a fuller understanding of your forgiveness.

Response: You will find understanding, a deeper understanding, by reflecting upon the forgiveness that you have extended and the forgiveness that has been extended to you over time. By not dwelling on the many times that you have received forgiveness, you tend to remember more clearly when you have forgiven. It is necessary for you to put a balance into your concept of forgiveness.

I forgive you for your failings, the deliberate ones, and am most forgiving when you are aware and contrite. But please do not see me as a ledger God, one who keeps a balance sheet. In your life experience I am watching, if that is the word, your progress in developing compassion, extending forgiveness especially when you have been wronged without provocation.

I am asking you to forgive in your heart those who have injured you and are unaware of the harm they caused, or are no longer in a position to extend their sorrow and request to be forgiven.

Concentrate in this verse on the words white as snow because metaphorically that is what your soul becomes as it moves into my light. It is not so much a transformation of you but rather your will to move into the light, where nothing would be possible other than to be as white as snow.

And where do you think Isaiah saw the snow about which to write? In the mountains where the air is crisp and cold and you can see for miles. Be in my grace and you will see for miles – you will almost feel like you can fly.

Scripture: *After this, Jesus traveled about from one town and village to another, proclaiming the good news of the kingdom of God. Luke 8:1*

Prayer: This seems to be such an ordinary verse. How many times have I heard "proclaiming the good news of the kingdom of God?" Bring me to a deeper meaning.

Response: In this verse see the power of the Holy Spirit in your life, proclaiming the good news in words that sometimes don't seem to be your own, but apply directly to the situation you are in.

Proclaiming the good news is sharing the truth that you have come to accept on faith and through the grace of discernment that I shower on you and those who are attentive to my word and promise.

For the less conscious, the kingdom is a place, for others the kingdom is the totality of their being, like the blood flowing in your veins, the air you breathe, the awareness you have in this moment of my presence within you.

See the kingdom of God as my domain without boundaries of time and space. Kingdom of God is my presence and your decision to be in that presence. The kingdom of God is all loving, all compassionate, all forgiving. The kingdom of God is without fear.

You enter the kingdom of God in prayer and do not leave unless it is your will to do so. The kingdom of God reigns over all from above and within.

In your deepest moment of stillness you are present in the kingdom of God and it is within your power, yes I said power, to remain in the kingdom of God though you operate through the tasks of refinement and fashioning that you experience in life. When it is time for you to leave the earthly body, taking with you the lessons and soul consciousness that you acquire, the transition, if I were to call it that, is seamless. You go from a state of wearing reading glasses to full vision without assists.

See the kingdom of God in your midst, especially within. .

Scripture: *"Still other seed fell on good soil. It came up and yielded a crop, a hundred times more than was sown." When he said this, he called out, "He who has ears to hear, let him hear." Luke 8:8*

Prayer: Please explain more of what goes into this good soil.

Response: Good soil is soil that receives the seed and nourishes the seed. The seed constitutes my word to you in expression – be it in scripture, something you read, hear, observe, a relationship that encourages you or one that teaches you – you see they don't have to be the same. The seed represents the blessings that I shower upon you when you least expect it during times of joy, great sadness, low energy, high energy, in all patterns of weather.

Now let me talk of the soil. Deep rich, black earth is best for planting, moist with tears, with decaying dreams that enrich your acceptance of the present where I reach you in eternity. Planting soil is soil that receives, that is prepared to receive. It is soil that has experienced the turbulent weather, survived drought, has not been swamped away in floods, has pressed down in the blazing heat, has coalesced in the frost, has generously offered refuge to the plants and animals of the forest.

Now why is some soil of the receiving variety – soil that can receive my seed and nourish it to a bountiful harvest? Read again the last words of this verse. It is soil – you are that soil – that listens and hears my word. And again, that word is not limited to a text but can be found imprinted on your heart.

One last word – remember that the seed once impregnated in the earth, grows to maturity and is harvested. So with you and so with the bounty that matures in your field. So in addition to hearing my word, you must give of it freely in the harvest that I have ordained.

CHAPTER EIGHT -- SURPRISE

When I was in college Bob Brown conducted a seminar on Hemingway. On the first day of class, he distributed copies of what Hemingway wrote as he was returning late one night from a newspaper assignment. Hemingway had spotted a conflagration in the rear- view mirror of his car. He turned around the car and sped off, thinking that it was a fire in the stockyards at the outskirts of the city. As he reached the crest of a hill, he realized that it was the sunrise.

I too have been surprised by sunrises – on a pristine beach on Pangkor Island in Malaysia, during a predawn walk along the Atlantic, and in the mountains of West Virginia. I am in awe and feel chill-bumps when the brilliance irresistibly breaks through a dark cloud bank on the horizon and diffuses the dense formations in a sad heart.

I see in nature unexpected reminders of God's love as I do in life's accidental events – accepting there are no accidents – when I find a discarded Beatles' CD in the sand and hear a prompt answer to a prayer, meet a stranger and discover a life-long companion, perform a routine task and witness its transformation into something extraordinary.

Each morning I am amazed by the words of Scripture I encounter and upon which I reflect. A familiar or not so familiar text takes on a freshness and intimacy that convinces me that the message is meant, it seems, for me alone that morning. And, as with a sunrise, I am surprised.

Scripture: *"Who is this? He commands even the winds and the water, and they obey him."* Luke 8:25

Prayer: This is my prayer too as my mind wrestles with understanding. Please help my heart to understand.

Response: You are required to lose your balance, allow your mind to become engaged in solving this puzzle, while you allow yourself in heart to be transported to another realm. In this realm all is in harmony.

If it helps, see yourself floating as if in a gravity free state. In this realm hear in the deepest reaches of your soul my voice. It is a rumbling voice that you recognize in the crashing surf, or in the wind that thunders across a mountain height, or in the blistering heat of a desert, or the monsoon rains you experienced in India. These extremities allow you to catch a glimpse of my power and with no intention of promoting fear see how dependent you are on me.

Instead of creating fear that freezes your moment, see me as the one of love. In commanding the winds to cease, I am also the One who bounds the seas, who bounds the chaos, and even the violence, but releases love. Releases loose love.

So in your darkest hour, understand that the darkness is bounded and the light is without end in an eternity of love. If you will there is darkness but it is like a fly-blemish on an endless canvass of which you cannot take in at first its full dimension of light.

Be at rest today and see my presence in your life, controlling the outside elements that would or could cause to limit your mission of love.

#212

Scripture: *"Where is your faith?" he asked his disciples. In fear and amazement they asked one another, "Who is this? He commands even the wind and the water, and they obey him." Luke 8:25*

Prayer: I return to this verse – the full verse. Help me to have faith.

Response: You are early today in the darkness before dawn. In that silence consider the wind when it is quiet and the sea when it is flat, and feel lingering my power – both to stir and to return both to tranquility.

The only way your mind can deal with this is to take in what happens without seeing the cause except as explained as scientific phenomena. The scientific explanation suffices if you limit the explanation to the atmosphere, but when you attempt to go further into the galaxies that surround you on your spinning orbit of dust, your explanation becomes less precise; and then if you can even range in your imagination beyond the galaxies, end even to other dimensions of creation, your mundane, worldly explanation seems so childlike.

Instead accept in faith my power beyond what you can yet conceive with all your education and reflection. Accept that I direct the forces of nature as if I had a control panel before me. Now, not stirring fear in you, allow yourself to accept deeply my majesty. And my majesty is not something to sit back and observe as you would a circus performance. No, my majesty is there for you to ponder like now in the absolute silence of your early morning.

And then, it is so critical, that you bring this majesty into your life and accept that you are like the fingertips of a wave crashing upon a beach and the whistle howl of the wind in my embrace. And that all you do is so connected to me. I am your intimate partner. We are in a dance together and you have the power, yes power, to show the world steps and movements unthought-of, actually uncreated earlier, as you do my will as revealed to you.

So, bringing this guidance to you now, do not fret and concern yourself about whether anyone would attend your series of seminars on grief, rather be that fingertip. You do not realize it yet but you have already influenced those who received and will receive your message.

Be bold and hold the confidence of a wind that does not falter and a sea that knows no hold, no restraint.

In my peace.

265

#213

Scripture: *"Where is your faith?" Luke 8:25*

Prayer: I don't know what's wrong, but this morning I am so anxious with everything I must do and concern about money. Please help me today.

Response: I am pleased that you return once again to this scripture. It contains the question for all of you. Where is your faith? Did I not promise that you are to rest and rely upon me? There is nothing troubling you that is not the scattered thoughts and anxieties encouraged by the dark force to encourage you to change course.

You are sailing into a brisk wind, the sea is a bit choppy but you will find that by altering your sail a bit you will literally fly across the water and will hardly notice the bumps. Hear the wind howl as you gather speed, feel the wind in your faith, the water splash, lean back and create that stability to make the most of the vessel in which you ride.

All your concerns are hooks that are trying to snare you from the past, or anxieties that you have about the course that you have chosen and affect what you perceive in a very narrow sense the future. Today will be a great unveiling of my purpose for you. So please be attentive.

In my love.

Scripture: *"Return home and tell how much God has done for you." So the man went away and told all over town how much Jesus had done for him.* Luke 8:39

Prayer: Help me Lord to appreciate all you have done in my life and give me the courage to tell that story.

Response: Do you not find it amazing how your eyes and heart rest on a single line of scripture with deep meaning overlooked. Rest for a few moments on the significance of those words written two thousand years ago and anointed for you this morning. What a colossal statement. God is Jesus. Can you imagine how this was taken when first read or addressed to the crowds? Think of that scribe working quietly to copy this text in a monastery in the dim light of a candle and he comes upon this text. Think of how many scribes paused, put their quills down and pondered the meaning of these words, before resuming with renewed vigor their assigned tasks.

So with you. You are a scribe of sorts and you have paused over the meaning of these words. In fact you have pondered them deeply. Rather than stay in a sleep state, you approach this new day energized just as the scribe. In fact the comparison is not far off because you copy on paper words inscribed in your heart. And further, the text is endless so you will not exhaust the text – your earthly life – that you are copying for others to ponder.

I ask you to approach each day as another text to translate or copy for others to read and contemplate.

All for this day.

Scripture: *My soul yearns for you in the night, in the morning my spirit longs for you. Isaiah 26:9*

Prayer: Lord, give me understanding as to my purpose in life, especially in view of the long and healthy life that you have granted me.

Response: You are where you are in this point of time to bring peace to those around you and afar. You are to ease the suffering that infiltrates your world. You are to show, to demonstrate a deeper stillness to a world rattled with noise and distraction, to introduce a joy that so many cannot yet even contemplate.

And you are to understand that joy and inner peace yourself. No longer are you to question why you are not working in the traditional sense. You are to continue to reach out through your website, through e-mails, and personal contacts. All this will require discipline, dedication, and action.

You are to expand your experience and knowledge base as a twenty year old. And most of all you are to love without grasping and in fear that you will lose something.

So much is happening in your life, it is good that you record your experiences so that you can see what is happening, evidenced by the graces that I am showering on you.

As to your longevity, you will as you live now vibrantly without end in eternity. How is that for an answer to your question?

.

Scripture: *"Show me, O Lord, my life's end and the number of my days; let me know how fleeting is my life. You have made my days a mere handbreadth; the span of my years is as nothing before you."* Psalm 39:4-5

Prayer: Lord, show me the path you would have me on in the years remaining me.

Response: You have been granted long years and it almost surprises you. Think not in the long years that have passed, but rather the moment that unfolds before you now.

You are as if on a merry-go-round, turning, turning as you reach for the rings that are just out of reach. As you grow in wisdom your reach extends and more is within your grasp, not to hold, but to extend my love.

Your reach, imagine if you can, is like reaching out and touching those just witnessing the ride. Some stand in awe, some in dread, and some even in fear. It is your responsibility and chosen path to reach them all, gently, with a touch that invites them closer and not one that would have them shrink further from the turns that you make. You are like a whirling dervish in an ecstasy of my love.

So it is not a question as to how many turns you have remaining on this ride of life but rather how you can infuse each turn with the power of my love aimed at reaching those most reticent, most troubled, most grieving. Pull closer with your smile those who observe in trepidation or even in awe; see what you can do to have them leap in faith on the carousel and take a seat alongside, in front, or behind you so that they too can grow in wisdom and reach further still to those who hesitate.

So for years remaining, think more of turns remaining where you once again face someone stalled in doubt, wounded in grief, abandoned in their loss. If your ride were to end today – and think in those terms – reach out that much more in the hours and minutes preceding your call home.

.

Scripture: *"Who touched me?" Jesus asked. When they all denied it, Peter said, "Master," the people are crowding and pressing against you." But Jesus said, "Someone touched me, I know that power has gone out from me." Luke 8:45-46*

Prayer: Do you feel me when I touch you in prayer that is without words.

Response: Especially then. I know those times when the words do not form, when you feel without purpose; when all you want to pray for or about seems too complex to simply in words. That is when I hear your heart.

A step in faith is to realize my closeness. I am within. You are riding in a train compartment through the night and I am the silent companion sitting opposite. If you desire, I will engage you in conversation like now. At other times, I sit quietly seemingly lost in thought but I am really lost in you.

Never for a moment become frustrated because you forgot a name or person for whom you had wished to remember in prayer. At that instant that person is blessed through your love.

As you are learning to remain in the present, do so also in prayer. Don't indulge in recriminations of the past or anxieties for the future; simply be in the present and my love.

So you see Jesus feels the power leaving him to reach you, and the supply of power is endless. In a sense he cannot control his love for you. That is the point here. He loves so it would seem that for you to ask there is no possibility of him refusing.

Be in peace today and in the present.

Scripture: *But Herod said, "I beheaded John. Who, then, is this I hear such things about?" And he tried to see him. Luke 9:9*

Prayer: In my thirst, help me to see you.

Response: Reflect upon Herod's confusion. How could this happen – that this itinerant preacher, despised by the Jewish leaders, is said to heal people, even bringing them back to life. See confusion as the inspiration of the dark force. You embark upon a path, follow a direction and then something happens that creates doubt and causes you to question the first step that you took in this new direction.

For Herod, the pause could have led to his repentance, given the atrocities that he committed. In fact, the comment that he tried to see him shows that even this was possible though not probable. With all his power and the resources that he could command the fact that he did not see him at this time demonstrates that it was a half-hearted attempt.

More often you experience "confusion" and second thoughts when you are on a path to me and the path becomes arduous and you wonder if you have lost your mind. In fact you have and are guided at such time by your heart. The dark force attempts to influence your mind to take back control and move off the path or reverse your steps.

You are trying to see me, and keep trying. And you find me at dawn in the sun rise as you pray and hear my voice and your confidence that your prayers are heard increases. Take these words of scripture as the brief longing of a very powerful man to reconcile with me and despite all his authority his inability to leave the appearances of power to humbly beg forgiveness. Think of what such a conversion would have meant for the people of that time. Use Herod as a model for your life in that you have the opportunity to influence others in passing word of my love to them. You do not want to be remembered as the fellow you would of, could of, but rather did and does. Action exceeds any notion of understanding.

In my peace.

Scripture: *"But what about you?" he asked, "Who do you say I am?" Peter answered, "The Christ of God." Luke 9:20*

Prayer: I sense that you are asking me this question this morning.

Response: Yes, and every morning. Begin each day with my question and you will find that each day unfolds with my declaration to you that I am the Christ of God. You experience it in the love that surrounds you. You experience it when I help you through grace to become aware of the power of your prayer.

Who I am is the special ingredient that I fold into you, if you are willing to experiment. Yes, will to experiment with my goal for you that is to inherit my kingdom. I am offering you residence in my heart and I in yours. Think of stirring a recipe as you fold in all the ingredients. Well, in this case, metaphorically I am preparing a special celebration recipe and I am working with who you are and at the last moment I am adding that special ingredient that makes you so unique in my love.

Once added, realize that I must put you in the oven so that the ingredients are fully cooked and mixed, and it is the heat that you feel as apparent setbacks, but there are no setbacks. You are rising with the yeast that I added and you will not recognize what you become and you ask where did this originate, how is it possible, yet, there it is.

The ingredients manifest themselves in all you are being asked or invited to participate, the thoughts that come to you to pray for those in stress, and those for whom you are asked to be responsible.

So who am I? I am your loving God who stays quite close to you, nudging you in one direction or another, whenever I see that there is a need that you can provide assistance and love.

#220

Scripture: *"If anyone would come after me, he must deny himself and take up his cross daily and follow me. For whoever wants to save his life will lose it, but whoever loses his life for me will save it. What good is it for a man to gain the whole world, yet lose or forfeit his very self? If anyone is ashamed of me or my words, the Son of Man will be ashamed of him when he comes in his glory and in the glory of the Father and of the holy angels. I tell you the truth, some who are standing here will not taste death before they see the Kingdom of God." Luke 9:23-27*

Prayer: So early this morning I sit before you after sending out e-mails as I try to find a place for my daughter to heal. So much is contained and so special for me in the reading for today. I didn't know where to focus so I included the words of Christ spoken in their entirety. Please enlighten me, especially as they relate to my life and responsibilities for my son and daughter.

Response: Not contained in the words above, remember that I stand at the door knocking. All you have to do is to open the door and I am with you and more I embrace you.

You do take up your cross daily and what's more you do it with a smile and not with a heavy heart. It is beautiful for me to see how far you have come on your journey to Emmaus. Your insight on this mystery is deepening especially when you refrain from comparing the size and weight of the crosses; and do not try to estimate or compare distances traveled. Continue to walk the walk, beginning with the gray dawn through the day until retiring at night, and as I mentioned, do so with a light heart.

You have taken in well about the value of this life experience in the cultivation of your soul qualities, not focusing on material acquisitions, though you find that material necessities follow what you need to accomplish my mission for you. Praise those who supported and educated you who passed on this deep wisdom that some never attain. And isn't it interesting that you come upon the same line about the taste of death – its impermanence. This applies to you of course and those with whom you come in contact. You see, I am with you for eternity. There is no interruption so how could death be any more than a taste, bitter or sweet doesn't matter.

Living with that thought and insight in mind, greet everyone with whom you have contact, whether in person or through writing, with the knowledge that there is no interruption in my love. That is my message and you are one of those chosen to carry that message in your life. Be at peace today. All is unfolding as I desire and you are a worthy extension of my will.

Be at peace today.

Scripture: *Two men, Moses and Elijah, appeared in glorious splendor, talking with Jesus. They spoke about his departure, which he was about to bring to fulfillment at Jerusalem. Luke 9:30-31*

Prayer: Help me to comprehend the significance of these verses.

Response: Here is a wonderful example of the past, present, and future merging into one time dimension and as such this scene provides you a glimpse of eternity.

Catch the casualness and ease and relationship these words of scripture depict. There are no introductions, no surprises, all is known.

And so it is with you. All is known and your acceptance of this allows you to experience the same equanimity, peacefulness that the scene reveals to you.

"His departure," are words that convey in acceptance the crucifixion and resurrection. So casual that clearly we sense a return and he does return to each day.

Jesus introduces his disciples and you to the relationship to be experienced in eternity; it is more that a calling together of close friends to swap stories, but rather it is for the purpose of expanding your consciousness, for you to become enlightened, even fired by God's love for you. No wonder the apostles were sleepy – they were experiencing more than they could absorb.

In your life see the past merging with the present, and see the same for the illusion of future.

All for today. Know that all is on a path for you and you are on that path.

Scripture: *"No one who puts his hand to the plow and looks back is fit for service in the kingdom of God." Luke 9:62*

Prayer: Lord, I am one who from time to time looks back from the plow. Help me to be more confident and committed.

Response: It is a long field that you plow. Consider how steady you are over time. And for the most part, during those long furrows when the heat is oppressive or the wind bone-chilling, you have kept your hands wrapped tightly on the plow. You do have an advantage that you sometimes do not appreciate. You have twin horses in front of the plow and they represent my angels that keep the furrow straight and there is little in the way of hidden stumps or ferns that they cannot negotiate their way through.

Do realize also that you are not riding a tractor, but walking the long lonely stretches in all variations of weather; that what others consider warm and delightful in the sun can be oppressive for you in the heat; while in the cool of autumn you are quite comfortable, even in the light rain all is well.

Look at your hands that grip the plow handles as the grip of your heart and soul onto my message. Look at your hands as representing the forward thrust into the dark and unknown, and you do this on faith; see your hands as your protection from a fall.

Feel the newly ploughed earth as you walk ankle deep through it. See the stain it makes on your pants and feet. It is in this blend of earth that body and spirit are mixed in this divine alchemy that I call the consciousness of my love.

So keep your focus forward, anticipate the rises that lay before you or the deep ruts; hold firmly the plow but with an agility that does not sap your strength; keep your shoulders loose, free of tension, always appreciating that the two steeds before you are there to lead.

In my love.

Scripture: *"Go! I am sending you out like lambs among wolves. Do not take a purse or bag or sandals; and do not greet anyone on the road."* Luke 10:3-4

Prayer: Give me the courage to go out among the wolves. Also, inform me why I am not to greet anyone on the road.

Response: The meaning of the last verse is quite simple. Keep in mind why I have called you, why I have dispatched you. I implore you, urge you, and do not become distracted. You have a mission and that is what you are to fulfill.

There is a timeliness that I speak of here. Surely, one could argue that I took a detour or another route because of the good I expected to undertake. I am saying that often you use those side trips as a justification for the distraction that they are.

A word on courage – courage is shoring up your confidence and not allowing doubt to cause anxiety. Courage is not only demonstrated on a battlefield, but also when one states his or her truth despite the sense that such expression will not be greeted by the audience. Courage is being who you are without diminishing your stature because you are in the company of those with less stature.

.

Scripture: He answered, "'*Love the Lord your God with all your heart and with all your soul and with all your strength and with all your mind; and 'Love your neighbor as yourself.' *" Luke 10:27

Prayer: Help me to take in the full meaning of these words and not glance off them because they are familiar.

Response: Sometimes or even most times, you take these words to mean that I expect you to sit quietly and repeat over and over again "I love you, God." I am not dismissing the value of these times occasionally entered upon; however, let me tell you that love is how you rushed around to take the wash out of the dryer, put a new wash into the machine, woke your son, reminded him to wash his hair well, rushed upstairs to place out the still damp napkins and dining table cover to dry, and then returned to your prayer.

You see love is measured in action. Repeat that phrase again. Love is measured in action. I can't love you unless I display that love through action. The action becomes a witness of my love. That is why Christ became man. He did not come to be among you; but rather to act among you.

So how do you love me with all your heart, soul, strength, and mind? Through your daily actions is the answer. Be conscious of me and your love as you listen to another's problems, as you pray deeply for those in need, as you commit your body to undertake a mission, and you devote your mind and understanding to bring about peace.

That is . In my peace.

Scripture: *"What good is it for a man to gain the whole world, yet forfeit his soul?"* Mark 8:36

Prayer: Lord, this quote is familiar to me since my years in high school, over fifty years ago. Please help me to understand why this verse has stuck with me.

Response: Many years ago I wanted to brand you as my follower and this is one of those word imprints on your soul that you have retained. It is like the ridge of a scar long healed that recalls the incident without enduring again the pain.

Over your life time you have touched that ridgeline of your soul which has served to remind you whose follower you are. Further, the ridgeline has afforded you access to a hidden valley that you frequent. This verse has served as your pathway forward. Interesting isn't it that you have not tarried long in the land of distraction?

You must now take that verse and ask if seeking and forfeiting all to gain the world is not worth forfeiting your soul. Who should you be to be worthy of the soul you are?

Spending time with that question clarifies so much your purpose in this life. It reduces considerably choices over which you labor to those which advance your soul, contribute to a raised consciousness that is measured in compassion, love, prayer, service.

So for all these years you knew the message and repeated the words of this verse that served to nudge you along the correct path; at other times pulled you from your sloth to resume the journey; and other still pushed you suddenly from behind. These words also served to clear debris before you.

Once repeated these words acknowledge your commitment to seek my kingdom without reservation, regret, but filled with hope, grace, and gratitude.

So keep reminding yourself of these words as you journey closer to my kingdom. These words have proved to be your reliable compass as you have journeyed across the sometimes arid landscape.

In my love.

Scripture: *The Lord is my shepherd . . . Psalm 23*

Prayer: Lord, I have read this Psalm so many times. Bring me, please, to a deeper level of understanding.

Response: I want you to read it once again and then we will take it verse by verse.

Notice the Psalm is not written in or for the past. Its words of love and caring are for you right now.

The Lord is my shepherd . . . You are being guided by me and my focus and intention are fixed on you as if no other existed. I have no other cares but for you.

He makes me to lie down in green pastures . . . I am conveying to you a tranquility of spirit that you experience in my care when you rely upon me completely, totally.

He restores my soul . . . Yes, I restore your soul to the innocence and openness before the fall; and you know this, yes, really know this as I guide you on the path I intended. See how far you wandered and see where you are now for confirmation of these words.

Even though I walk through the valley of the shadow of death . . . Notice I say *walk* and not *have walked* or *will walk*. Yes, daily you walk through the valley of the shadow of death, take heart; a shadow has no substance and dissipates immediately in the Light. And I do comfort you, today, yesterday, and tomorrow. And when the shadow seems most impenetrable, understand that the cliffs on either side of your path are highest just before the rising sun surrounds you as it rises above at dawn. Also, I do not require you to climb those cliffs; simply catch the full majesty of your dawn. Dispel fear as the Light dispels darkness.

You prepare a table before me in the presence of my enemies . . . Sense the bounty that I lay before you without any regard for those who would thwart you. And I anoint you as my own; you are blessed, chosen, and loved. Indeed, your cup overflows into eternity.

Surely goodness and love will follow me all the days of my life . . . How could it be any differently?

Now do you have the deeper meaning of my love poem to you?

In my love to you this morning.

Scripture: *Surely you desire truth in the inner parts; you teach me wisdom in the inmost place.* *Psalm 51:6*

Prayer: What a source of wisdom I receive daily reading your word. Shine light upon these words this morning.

Response: In this short verse I remind you that you cannot claim ignorance when faced with the dilemmas of life. In your inmost parts you hear my word and guidance. It is there that your wisdom grows in silence.

Consider how you sit now in silence before dawn and I sit opposite it seems. What a precious moment for you and for me. It is this time that proves all is right for you in this time of uncertainty because all is certain in my arms.

Let me tell you more about wisdom. Wisdom reflects the fruit of one who spends, rather devotes, the time in silence and reflection, not disturbed by events that seem to challenge him. Wisdom is truly a gift of my spirit. Even you recognize that wisdom cannot be acquired by study. Wisdom seems to fall on you from within as if you experience an internal and external fall of snow. Think of a first snowfall and you are outside walking in it. Well, wisdom occurs similarly and spontaneously within you. Right this moment you are walking in such a snowfall.

Feel the silence, the feel on your cheeks and uncovered head; hear its softened cushion for your feet that sometimes thud along on the path; see the beauty of its fall caught in the light of a distant star and moon.

I will see that you are bundled up and free from anxiety to witness the fall within.

In my love this morning.

Scripture: *I can do everything through him who gives me strength. Philippians 4:13*

Prayer: This is the selected verse of one of the facilitators on Stephen Ministry. Give me its deeper meaning.

Response: I am not talking about walking, running, and eating, but rather of things of the spirit that generates the action. Your spirit is like that of a race horse awaiting the start of a race. It has always been like that. You are being acted upon to free that spirit as if it were a race horse and allow it to rush along the path that I have chosen for it.

I have guided you, strengthened you, and nourished you for this event that leads to eternity. You are touching eternity right now. I am asking you to loosen the reins, give your spirit its freedom to do my work. Put aside all those second thoughts, those anxieties created by the dark force, and reach forward in your saddle, go for the gold as they say.

You have all you need to rush along the track, keeping to the inside and in the straightway, which is where you are now, give full throttle; allow your spirit to thunder on the track, the path. Wake those observing so that they too will mount up. You have every resource you need right now and more will come to you to sustain this race of your life into eternity.

Use this quote in every endeavor you undertake – raising your son, healing your heart and body, discovering resources to sustain your life requirements, reaching out to others in your writing and messages, praying for the multitude you pray for. You have no want. All is provided and stretches before you. Your cup does overflow.

In my love.

Scripture: *When Jesus spoke again to the people, he said, "I am the light of the world. Whoever follows me will never walk in darkness, but will have the light of life." John 8:12*

Prayer: Help to see the light within.

Response: The light within magnifies and manifests a new consciousness. You experience this new consciousness regularly now. It is the pause in the walk along the sand and praising me as the sun creeps through the clouds announcing another opportunity of love. It is found in the pause where you notice a pod of dolphin two hundred yards out feeding, as the feeder fish dart for the safety of the shore where the gulls wait. It is a ripple free peacefulness of spirit. That is the light that you have sought. That is the peacefulness you experience.

The light within is brighter than the sunrise, reaches further than your eyesight, is not confined to the minutes of its rise but reaches back to the past and into the future – a dimensionless time-scape; the light within guides you safely, enriches you with inspiration to heal and to love; the light cauterizes those dark corners that have yet to see the light.

The light of life is confirmation of your path and opens opportunities as a torch held aloft in a dark forest. With the light of life there is no fear; serenity and acceptance, and detachment prevail.

The light of life warms you in chill grief, energizes you in loss, has you to smile when all within seems dark.

Finally, let me say that the verse means more than possessing the light, you become the light.

Scripture: *But he said to me, "My grace is sufficient for you, for my power is made perfect in weakness." Therefore I will boast all the more gladly about my weaknesses, so that Christ's power may rest on me. 2 Corinthians 12:9*

Prayer: There are times when I do feel weak. More specifically, I can't seem to see the path, or find that I need more signs – is it grace – to continue this journey in your will. Help me to understand deep your words as quoted in this verse.

Response: I do make my power and majesty perfect in you and especially at those times when you feel most powerless. You are only, and I repeat the word only, to keep to the path, don't be surprised at the turns you make in the forest. You are not lost; in fact, those observing are caught in the power and grace that you display.

And who are these observers? They are your friends, casual acquaintances, those who have only heard you mentioned in conversation, they are those who receive my particular blessing prompted by your prayers – and they don't even know your identity but experience a special blessing for which they have no understanding of its prompting; they are those who have passed on and are so pleased to see your commitment in love; they are your spirit helpers – the angels – that surround you and are ever ready to lend you support; and of course me in all my love.

So, shout to all who will hear of your weakness, and the resounding voice, my voice, strengthens you beyond all measure. Be at peace in this knowing. For you are loved in my grace.

.

Scripture: *To keep me from becoming conceited because of these surpassingly great revelations there was given to me a thorn in my flesh, a messenger of Satan to torment me. Three times I pleaded with the Lord to take it away from me. But he said to me, "My grace is sufficient for you, for my power is made perfect in weakness." Therefore, I will boast all the more gladly about my weakness, so that Christ's power may rest upon me. 2 Corinthians 12:7-9*

Prayer: Lord, this is one of those times that I give pause to reach deeply for your message. I copied this text from a footnote in the biography of Mother Teresa that I recently read and only now see it includes the same text that I meditated upon two days ago. Help me to understand more profoundly its meaning for me.

Response: The thorns in your flesh are the constant concerns with which Satan pricks you, and you flinch each time. One prick is your financial concerns, and a second is your worry that you are not doing all that is possible in the raising of your son. Each thorn is provided, yes, I said provided, so that in your weakness – after each flinch when the thorn is pushed or you feel it – you will turn to me and discover that your weakness is strength in my grace.

You don't need to do anything, but be aware of how I keep you from boasting. Satan performs a service to you because he keeps your attention focused on me without in any way limiting your participation in your path to me.

See the thorns in your daily life, anticipate them, and smile at them. I have given you the answers to the puzzle of life and you can confirm that is what is happening and unfolding. It is as if you are walking a winding and arduous path and you anticipate a way station around the bend and find it as you expected. Well, these thorns are way stations because they do two things, they confirm that you are on the path and have not wandered off into the brush, and they lead you to me, your true nourishment.

The thorns are not fixed. In time they will lose their sting, but be aware they will always be replaced. They become your companions on the road that insure your alertness. I do not want you tumbling off the path in a stupor. No, these thorns will not allow that. They keep you attentive. If you ever doubt their sting, measure the depth of your prayer and you will be able to decide for yourself.

In my peace.

Scripture: *Surely you desire truth in the inner parts; you teach me wisdom in the inmost place.* Psalm 51:6

Prayer: Thank you for helping me to identify the inmost place.

Response: When you are still you discover the range of that inmost place. And as you know still means keeping the chatter of the mind quiet without distraction, turning your heart ear to catch a voice from afar that at first seems to so faint. You are becoming able to hear over the conversation that you would experience in a crowded room. Remember the first time you heard your son address you as Dad. You were standing some feet away in a crowded check-in place of an inn and your mind seemed poised to catch his first "Dad." Well that is what you do in your inmost part.

And in that special place I have much to tell you. Not all what you want to hear, but much to confirm your path and your intention. You are not all Doctor Jekyll or Mr. Hyde. It in the inner classroom I expand your capacity for my knowledge and my knowing. It is there that I help you to see gradations of your life, examine your anxieties, and hold for you the promise that keeps you on the path.

And your inmost parts are the motivating impulses and desires that encourage you even inspire you to offer consciously gentle words to those who struggle, like your words to your son's birth father last evening, encouraging him in his job change and at the same time encouraging him to take care of his relationship with me by suggesting that he join a church. Your advice issued as a father will have him report back to you soon that he has done exactly that.

Realize this trial for you is to further hone you, fashion you to my purpose. Much is asked of you.

In my love.

Scripture: *"So I say to you: Ask and it will be given to you; seek and you will find; knock and the door will be opened to you. For everyone who asks receives; he who seeks finds; and to him who knocks, the door will be opened." Luke 11:9-10*

Prayer: Give me the confidence in prayer to realize and to accept that you respond to my boldness in prayer even if my prayer *comes in the middle of the night.*

Response: I hear your prayers before they are uttered in the silence. I hear them in the dark, like now before dawn, on a walk alone where you are only able to groan as you did when you lost your wife; I hear you at those inconvenient times. For me, I am as if your sole companion. So in that knowledge of which I must constantly remind you, pray to me often, unceasingly.

There are times when you hesitate to ask for the loaves of bread that are in my cupboard because you need the sustenance for yourself. Be free to put before me your special requests. Why, you ask? Because in your prayers you reveal to yourself your needs and aspirations that underline your desire to meet the fullness I have planned for you. Notice that it is in prayer when no one is listening, or someone with whom you share such honesty, you come closest to touching your soul's intention.

So today, yes pray for the many souls you remember daily, but pray deeply for your own intentions.

In my peace.

Scripture: *I can do everything through him who gives me strength. Philippians 4:13*

Prayer: How can I measure the "everything" that Paul mentions?

Response: That is a good question. *The everything* is what your soul desires most intensely to express. That is the short answer. A longer response is that *the everything* is what you were destined to accomplish or contribute during your time on earth. The everything is your mission, a mission that you first must discover in the quiet of your heart; listening to that quiet voice or soft voice, that speaks to you of my truth and love.

So it would seem sensible, or should seem sensible for you to spend time regularly in that quiet space and listen. Please understand that this is not a one-time message but one that accompanies you on your journey as I accompanied those on the walk to Emmaus. Your *everything* unfolds as you become more conscious. Clearly a child's consciousness has not yet matured to see *the everything* with the heart of someone of your age.

However, it is also important that you not regret the past, or better said those years when your vigilance at hearing my voice was not as attuned as it is now. Isn't it interesting that when your hearing was good, it wasn't so good, and now when it is not so good it is improving dramatically? Paradox is the rule of life and of my love.

See the paradox of my message, focusing on those one would have thought lost, and rejecting those who one would have thought saved.

Now let's get to the power or strength that I afford you at all times. Let me repeat, at all times I am there, alongside you to lend you strength. Another paradox: I am there to support you when you surrender. When you admit to yourself your weakness, I make you all powerful. Just as at this very moment. There are not reserve forces that I dispatch to you. They are forces that are with you at this and every moment.

So take to heart that you need nothing more than the strength that I lend you, and I mean surrender to you daily, in each moment. Power I surrender to you. Another paradox.

So delight in your weakness because it is in your weakness and surrender that I make you whole, wholly powerful, wholly in my love.

Scripture: *It was not through law that Abraham and his offspring received the promise that he would be heir of the world, but through the righteousness that comes by faith. Romans 4:13*

Prayer: Please help me to understand deeper what you mean by righteousness.

Response: Righteousness is accord, accord with your soul, with the voice you hear within, the movement that stirs within you to undertake an action. Yes, I said action. Do you think that a man is righteous if he hears the voice and does nothing? You are not spirits floating about as some would picture you, floating in and out on the breeze of time. No, you are my creation that I stir to action in love.

So righteousness is right hearing. And to hear, you must listen. You must listen to even what you don't want to hear. Yet, even here I say to you "hear me out" and you will find that my words reverberating in your heart are not punishment. My words lead you to a place of harmony and love. Trust me through my words and you will discover this truth every time. Yes, I said every time.

So righteousness brings you back to the stillness of soul you must cultivate in your life. If you were to ask, and you didn't, what is your primary purpose for enduring all of life's blessings and seeming setbacks? It is to teach you to listen, ever more deeply to me. And this is not to form you into robotic worshippers, but rather to create in you a reflection of the divine spark that I breathed into you in all of your works, thoughts, and endeavors. In so doing, you indeed become the source of great pride in me that I have, and truly enjoy a righteous family of those who grow in my love.

Not much more to say today on righteousness. There will be more on this topic later. Just review what I have taught you this morning.
In my love.

Scripture: *Through Jesus Christ the law of the Spirit set me free. Romans 8:2*

Prayer: This is a verse that means much to a colleague. Help me to understand *the law of the Spirit.*

Response: The law of the Spirit could as easily be stated as the ever or all presence of the Spirit. Like the wind is rushes through and sometimes is not even noticed so calm is it. Like the wind it is a source, the primary source of refreshment of your spirit. Sometimes you feel it strongly like the bluster on a mountain peak or along the beach in as storm tide. But at other times it works its way in a flutter that catches you, like finding a shiny penny on a solitary walk in the morning.

The law of the Spirit is above all. It is your intimate connection with me, a seamless connection that eliminates all time and space that serve to separate you from your environment.

In setting you free, the Spirit acts as that breeze that generates your sails with wind power; the Spirit is the inspiration that has you retrace your steps to do a good deed that you had previously overlooked; the Spirit is the motivation for compassion and forgiveness, especially when no one will notice your act, prayer, or intention; the Spirit reminds you in your freedom of the power of prayer and clears you to acknowledge that meeting your prayer was not a coincidence.

You are free through the law of the Spirit. See yourself as the sleek sailboat or skiff that has reached the outer limits of the protected harbor, and now with the sails up you are underway, no sound to interrupt your divine purpose. The law of the Spirit endows you with a power you would be hard-pressed to realize except in the stillness of your heart.

All for now.

Scripture: *"No one lights a lamp and puts it in a place where it will be hidden, or under a bowl. Instead he puts it on its stand, so that those who come in may see the light. Your eye is the lamp of your body. When your eyes are good, your whole body also is full of light. But when they are bad, your whole body also is full of darkness." Luke 11:33-34*

Prayer: Lord, help me always to put my lamp on the stand.

Response: Note that the light is lit when it is dark. You live in an era where there is much darkness. Upheaval, violence, greed seem to encompass wider and wider circles of humanity. Yes, I could say that darkness abounds and your newspapers and media seem to reinforce that assessment.

Yet, why else do you have lamps? You have them to ward off the darkness, to be a beacon for others to follow or to be attracted to; to provide warmth of the type that brings family and close friends around the table. Why else to light candles when adequate light still flows through the windows?

See the lesson in this verse, to be of singular importance is that you through your eyes, free of deception, open to love, are able to attract, willing attract to your table those who have not felt that light and warmth previously, or if they had experienced that light extinguished.

As you know a beacon does no good if it is covered. Therefore, I urge you to be open to others, not with some preconceived script of conversion, but in the light of my love, innocent to the process that occurs in the heart of the one so attracted.

This verse is meant for those of you who nurture an atmosphere of light and you have been rewarded. Now is the time to gently share that light, hold that light up high so that others can see and be similarly led to my table.

All for now.

Scripture: *But everyone who prophesies speaks to men for their strengthening, encouragement and comfort. 1 Corinthians 14:3*

Prayer: My dog woke me at 4:30 AM to go outside. I came back into the house and tried unsuccessfully to get back to sleep. So here I sit. Help me Lord to touch on the meaning of prophesy.

Response: Prophesy is bringing my word to a clear understanding to those who are listening in anticipation. Prophesy is being able to move deep into the mine shaft and to bring to the surface the minerals of exceeding value. And as you know, the value of the minerals is based on their rarity and their durability.

So it is with my word. My word is not strewn about the surface as rubble or discarded artifacts, but rather is a treasure that you are to seek, strive for, extract though all of these actions require perseverance, commitment, and an ability to withstand adversity. Yet, the reward is great.

And for what is the reward? Is it to enrich you with wealth? No, it is for you to give away as soon as you reach the surface to those who have not labored in the mine, to those who might not have persevered, to those discouraged, and even to those who are lazy.

What a paradox. And as you distribute my treasure freely, openly, generously, you discover that you are unable to exhaust the treasure. And there is something else you might discover – those who receive stir in their heart and become at whatever stage in their life, no matter how despondent and discouraged they have become, no matter how many years they have endured, no matter how frail, they become renewed in their passion to serve in bringing to the surface and distributing my treasure that I offer to all.

I guess the word today is to put aside all apprehension and anxiety and enter the mine of my love for you.

Scripture: *When he had received the drink, Jesus said, "It is finished." With that he bowed his head and gave up his spirit. John 19:30*

Prayer: This morning I, not the dog, woke up before four AM. Help me to see the meaning of this verse as it applies to me.

Response: Your drink is found in the experiences of your day and life. Some of them indeed seem bitter, and they sometimes are offered when you are weary. And there will come a day when you will bow your head as did your father and say or think the words, *it is finished*.

Jesus was a model for you all. His life like all of you had a beginning middle and end, filled with moments of time that you are called upon to be or at least become conscious. It is as if you were provided at birth with a secret ingredient that would take hold and transform you. And it has. It is called grace of the spirit that took up residence within you. That spirit flowed throughout your interior at all times, even those when you realized that you were feigning ignorance about my love.

This day be aware of each moment and discover how the spirit works, especially when you are conscious. Begin from the very moment you set out for your walk and complete the exercise when you lay your head on your pillow this evening with the words, this day is finished.

Every second of Jesus' life that is recounted offers you a model to follow in that he represents total, as you would explain it, total consciousnesses. Your goal is to reduce the moments of unconsciousness where you do not praise God for his love of you. I am not saying that you are to ignore responsibilities, but rather that you must enfold this consciousness into whatever you are attending to in your daily life. You have a special ingredient that has been added to your body and soul system. Your actions, thoughts, aspirations, and desires, and intentions must come to reflect that special ingredient which is my love.

All for today.

Scripture: *Jesus reached out his hand and touched the man. "I am willing," he said, "Be clean!" And immediately the leprosy left him. Luke 5:13*

Prayer: Help me to catch the immediacy of your help.

Response: I am ever at your side and you are ever the recipient of my love that is many times manifested by those "accidental" happenings that fill your life and your incredulity. You have often said, as if you discovered a great truth, "it isn't supposed to be complicated." And it is not. The more often that you naturally turn to me, the easier it will be to see my love manifested in your life to heal you. Please do not give me the solution. Allow the forces of love to work in your life; if you must, you can later see the depth of the healing in the events that surrounded what appeared to be a trauma or tragedy.

And remember my healing is meant for all of you. My healing takes into account the healing of the injured and the one causing the injury – and it is never that easy. My healing reaches in Divine mixture the catastrophe and all affected by that catastrophe. And I use that word to catch your attention. Let me bring you into a secret knowing. There are no catastrophes. All you experience directly or indirectly, externally or within, are experiences that serve to bring you closer to consciousness, consciousness of my love.

Yes you can point out a truly horrible event or individual, yet I say to you that all works to bring fulfillment to my plan for each of you. No need to fret or be filled with anxiety or to turn away from the reality that faces each of you. I ask though that you be relaxed in my love, be confident, be filled with warmth and love, be at ease, and trust that in time you too will understand the depth of the transformation I seek in each of you.

That is , and it all began with the words that *I am willing.* In my love.

CHAPTER NINE -- SERVICE

Within weeks of arriving in New Delhi, we joined our church's project to white wash the Home for the Destitute and Dying that Mother Teresa's Sisters of Charity maintained. The building was only large enough to house ten individuals who had been abandoned at the railway station by desperate relatives who hoped that they would somehow reach the holy Ganges River in death.

We carted out of the building long suffering Hindu men and women on charpoys — wooden frames with crisscross strands of rope for support — and returned to climb ladders and wield large paint brushes of white wash across blackened walls. We were told that the average stay for the visitors was three to five days before death. In that time the Sisters of Charity bathed, clothed, fed, and loved them, while at the same time fully respecting their Hindu heritage.

It sometimes seems attractive to withdraw to one's attic of the mind to contemplate God's mystery and leave service and action to the professionals, to those more qualified to build and repair homes for the poor, to teach the unschooled, to minister to the downtrodden and vanquished in our midst, to promote peace and reconciliation.

Indeed reading the Scripture does give one respite, does sustain and even nourish us when weary. But the Scripture is also a call to action. Scripture encourages, prods me to service in His love. How many times has the not-so-subtle message of the Gospel roused me from my slumber to reach out to those less privileged, to participate in projects that alleviate suffering and bring joy to the joyless?

We were blessed to bring a two year old girl from Mother Teresa's orphanage into our home. She returned to America with us where we adopted and raised her as our own along with our four other children.

Scripture: *When Jesus saw her, he called her forward and said to her, "Woman you are set free from your infirmity." Then he put his hands on her, and immediately she straightened up and praised God. Luke 13:12-13*

Prayer: Lord, I feel pressed down this morning with the tasks that are outstanding, from uncertainty. Help me to straighten up in your praise.

Response: Sometimes your mind goes in overdrive and you keep scanning the tasks that you have not completed, or tasks that you feel obliged to complete but have put off attending to them. At such times you are vulnerable to the questioning that you are experiencing now. "Am I worthy?" you ask.

At times like this you are to step back and consider how much you are in conveying my love to so many, your reach to friends, family, and strangers. It is especially important for you to remain precisely in the present, not anticipating a phone call, an E-mail announcing something that you had been expecting, a note of encouragement.

Today is your test to be alone in a crowd. Think about those words. Today is the day for you to attend to all your responsibilities and not depend upon outside influences of whatever nature to survive. Today is the day during which you prosper in my love.

You have so much to be thankful – another grandson is born, bringing new love into your family and into the world. Praise God.

Scripture: *You will seek me and find me when you seek me with all your heart. Jeremiah 29:13*

Prayer: It seems that more and more I seek you with all my heart. Please give me guidance.

Response: My promise is a solemn one, one to be taken seriously. Seek me with all your heart and you will see me. You will see me in your loneliness, in your doubt, in your weariness, in failing health, in your dismay. You will also see me in your rapture, confidence, and encouragement.

You see me means that my presence will be palpable. You will literally touch me and I you. Seek me in a quiet walk alone, in prayer, in gestures of compassion and generosity, in unselfish actions, in commitment, and I could go on. Seek me unceasingly because seeking unceasingly is praying unceasingly.

Seek also connotes the search for treasure. You do not remain immobile, transfixed by distractions but move out in the heart.

This promise is clear. You do not need to ask scholars for another translation or track the various usages of the words contained therein. Seek me and you will not be surprised to discover that your treasure is near.

In my love.

Scripture: *By the rivers of Babylon we sat and wept when we remembered Zion, there on the poplars we hung our harps. Psalm 137:1-2*

Prayer: Oh, Lord, how rich is scripture stretching back so many years to enrich me. Help me understand these verses more deeply.

Response: It is important for all to realize that each verse has a message for you today. I repeat this thought often so that you appreciate how important it is for you to catch my word for you today. No need, as I have said, to consult biblical scholars or geographers to pinpoint Babylon or to investigate its history, unless you will. It is more important for you to dwell on what your life would be if you were exiled, cut off from me.

The harp represents your heart strings, your soulful expressions of love, or better your ability to express that love, to extend that love, to pass on that love – briefly – to love.

In exile, cut off from me, you would miss most – and you would be conscious of the loss – the inability to love. You are surrounded by a society that is diminished by its incapacity to love. And in that, they are in exile. Their harps, heart-strings, are left hanging on the branches of a polar tree in winter.

My message to you today is to snatch the harp from the poplar; hear me speaking to you in the stillness; and allow me to instruct you in the composition of my love song that you will play. Yes, it might sound plaintive to some, perhaps a dirge to others, but keep playing it – in your smile, gentleness, compassion, voice, instruction, listening – and especially in all your efforts to communicate my love.

It is within your capacity to free yourself from exile at any time. Seize the harp and free yourself from the bounds of exile at any time you feel that the enemy has captured you. I will play a lilting melody to lead you from whatever distress you experience. Let me repeat, from any distress you experience.

Of all the traits that exhibit this freedom from exile is one of joy. Show that joy in all you are.

.

Scripture: *You have made known to me the path of life, you will fill me with joy in your presence, with eternal pleasures at your right hand. Psalm 16:11*

Prayer: Fill me with your joy today as my day seems already to be divided among meetings and responsibilities with hardly a moment to pause.

Response: I praise you that this day you will experience the joy that I talk of. Your only requirement is to slow your gaze and sense the joy in your life that supersedes any meetings that you are scheduled to attend. See yourself as guided into various circles to offer and receive the light.

Let me talk of the path of life. Here I mean a direction and most importantly a pace, a holy pace, that nourishes each moment at all hours of the day and night. See yourself carried along and nurtured at all time. I am present. It is like I am holding a light for you as you walk through the darkness on an unfamiliar way, or hold that same light while you are in repose. My light offers warmth, solace, understanding, and is a beacon to attract others to your campfire or to our path.

Feel pure joy today not diluted by anxiety. Breath in deeply my love. And be present to me, be in my presence through the whirlwind of activity.

All this morning.

Scripture: *Then Saul dressed David in his own tunic. He put a coat of armor on him and a bronze helmet on his head. David fastened on his sword over the tunic and tried walking around because he was not used to them. "I cannot go in these," he said to Saul, because I am not used to them." So he took them off. Then he took his staff in his hand, chose five smooth stones from the stream, put them in the pouch of his shepherd's bag and, with his sling in his hand, approached the Philistine." 1 Samuel 17:38-40*

Prayer: Give me the courage to choose my own *five smooth stones* to do your will.

Response: What I ask of you is to listen to me and trust that I provide you everything you need, material as well as the inspiration and thoughts that serve to guide you. Of course, it takes some resistance on your part to overcome the world's desires for you in the form of pressures to perform according to the script that all around you would have for you.

It is only in the silence that you can distinguish my desires for you, but more, the magic moments I have scattered across your path. You however would not recognize the graces I shower you with if you did not first recognize your responsibility to seize the moment in my love.

Five smooth stones represent an arsenal of my grace and love for you. David only needed to use one, but see he had backup support if required. So it is with you. In silence you allow me to reach you clearly. Realize and accept that there is no obstacle, challenge that you are not able to overcome in my love. Let me repeat – no obstacle or challenge that can keep you from my path and union with me.

Note the clear water. Cleansed they were, pure, and deadly against those who oppose the path that I have determined for you. Be comfortable in that assurance that I will never desert you even when you face a nine foot giant who is heavily armed. Think only of the crashing sound he makes falling to the ground in his arrogance.

.

Scripture: *"You must also be ready, because the Son of Man will come at an hour when you do not expect him."* Luke 12:40

Prayer: Lord, guide me in each action so that as much as your coming is a surprise, I am waiting faithfully.

Response: The secret of my command is that you take each moment as the only reality you address. And if you focus on this one moment as if it were your last, you will not experience the trauma of what could have been.

I say this to you not to make you nervous dealing with an unwieldy weight. In fact, my words are meant to calm you. Like this moment. See as if you were an observer, this man sitting by his desk, still chilled from the walk in the brisk, cold wind. Measure his breathing. Hear the deep breath he takes. Catch the rhythm of his fingers on the keys of his keyboard. Slow this moment down to its real time. It is not the time he will spend making breakfast, getting dressed, and all the tasks that await him. No, it is this holy moment of pause and is to be extended throughout the day, buried as it were, in each moment. That slower pace – and it is really not slower (compared to what?) – is what creates watchfulness, wakefulness in the servant. And that alertness is what is rewarded.

Be in the rhythm today so you are watchful to catch the words uttered to you in an e-mail or face to face, so you notice a gesture, respond to a need, and all this quietly in my love.

Scripture: *Again you will plant vineyards on the hills of Samaria; the farmers will plant them and enjoy their fruit. Jeremiah 31:5*

Prayer: This verse attracted my attention this morning. Is there a lesson for me here?

Response: Relax in my presence and listen. *Again* is a key word. I could have said *again,* and *again* and *again.* I am always at your side, before you, ready again and again to reach you in words, thoughts, inspirations, and even touches. I use, employ everyone and everything around you. Yes, of course, the spectacular sunrise, bursting through the clouds, but also the word *again* sitting before a verse. So realize that you can't *shake* me as if you were under surveillance. I am with you.

Next, I do not reserve my message for only the meat and potatoes and life. No, I am here for you to celebrate. In the planting of the vineyards I tell you first you must identify the right land with the proper moisture – not too much – with the right winds – not too much – and then acquire it. This of course takes some diligence and commitment. Next you must prepare the soil and make the plantings, keeping proper distance. There is you see a certain protocol to follow.

Next you must be patient in caring for the seedlings over time awaiting the first fruit. Next you must choose the fruit and allow it to ferment once picked. And this also takes patience as you wait for the proper time. Finally, I plan for you to celebrate. The celebration actually begins with the identification of the proper land – your dream. And all the next steps leading to the drinking of the wine harvested from your grapes describes the path that you are on.

Selecting the land is of course the first step. It is there that you decide to invest your resources, realizing that additional resources will be required before you realize the bounty. Selecting or identifying the land symbolizes that you have heard my call to you and you recognize the call, you accept the call. Please don't make it more formal than that; I am not telling you this to have you to reduce my instruction to a neat formula. Your diligence in the field and your study of the right elements that make up a fruitful harvest are all indications of your first calling and your growing acceptance. I say growing because when you decided to be a vineyard keeper you clearly did not realize fully what that meant in the hard work, the bitter cold and torrid heat in which you would toil to save my harvest. Yes, I said my harvest.

If you can, do not limit yourself to linear time. Realize that I ask you to celebrate throughout your journey, throughout your work in the vineyards. And celebrate you do, or at least are encouraged. As I said earlier, you celebrate in a quiet walk, in a intimate conversation with a loved one, in reaching someone far a field in need or a kind or understanding word, in viewing life's passages in humor.

So read this verse once again and celebrate.

Scripture: *And suddenly with the angel was a multitude of the heavenly host, praising God and saying, "Glory to God in the highest heaven and on earth peace to men on whom his favor rests." Luke 2:13-14*

Prayer: As I sit here recuperating in silence, speak to me.

Response: This is a special time for you. What silence. Those shepherds also felt the silence in the middle of the night and then it was interrupted and they turned inside out with fear. The words of scripture capture a stunning event reserved not for theologians but for uneducated shepherds with no guile or intentions other than to report what they see.

You also are in a field late at night. You too pause and look up into the heavens and wonder. You too have that wonder explained in the coincidences that crowd around you and remind you that the empty music chamber that you sit in is actually replete with like companions and angelic forces; the music hall is brightly, even brilliantly lit, with gold crosiers, and the resounding chorus of praise heard throughout reverberates in your heart. No fear do you experience but modesty, even humility to be in the presence of this spontaneous praise offered.

I also want to say that you are favored. Now don't going running around spouting the words, "I am favored." Simply realize that it has been made known to you and many around you that you are favored. What does that mean? It means that you have been entrusted with the mission of healing individuals and areas of the world that still do not realize or experience the healing light of my love. So, your task, if you are willing to accept it, is to continue to be diligent in prayer and in action.

Whenever you wonder what is going on in your life with all the confusion, pause and put yourself in that that dark field and catch the hosannas of the angelic host and realize that host is not distant but in your midst.

All for now.

Scripture: *The king said to Daniel, "Surely, your God is the God of gods and the Lord of kings and a revealer of mysteries, for you were able to reveal this mystery." Daniel 2:47*

Prayer: Lord, cultivate in me the awareness, the consciousness of your power.

Response: Your very request demonstrates to me and of course yourself your consciousness is deepening. It is no surprise, nor should it be, that your diligence in prayer and in the silence listening to me, are contributing to your enhanced consciousness.

The real question is for what purpose. Do you think that I want you to acknowledge this power as one would the feats of a showman? I think not. I desire your acknowledgement so that you can advance, transcend, if you prefer the word, to a state that you have truly left behind the attachment to the illusion of the corporeal. Once my power is truly evident to you, you will discover that all who you are reflects that greatness as the divine spark that I planted into you before even your mother and father were born.

For me, you and for that matter everyone are the focus of my love in a union that surpasses understanding. You have been invited to a celebration and so many of you remain in the dark and do not see the festive candles lit all around you.

Your acknowledgement of my power serves to expel the darkness from the room; see the blazing torches on the walls; hear the spectacular chorus singing my praises that rebound and resound in your inner sanctum of love.

My power is manifest and will become even more manifest in your life and others who listen in silence to my words. .

#250

Scripture: *He said: "Look I see four men walking around in the fire, unbound and unharmed, and the fourth looks like a son of the gods." Daniel 3:25*

Prayer: Help me to see that you are the source of my protection.

Response: I am the source of your protection and I look to guide you as well as I am doing now. All you are required to do is to be patient. Carry a preserving spirit. Trust in me.

Right now I am influencing you and communicating to you in the depth of your heart the theme I wish you to develop about this new writing project. You will serve my purpose and love to encourage those sleeping to awake and embrace the legacy of their lives, that is, the reason that that each of you has been granted the gift of life, which is the gift of love.

You can't yet imagine how far you have come in realizing this purpose and the reason for this is that your legacy like everyone else's is suited to you particularly and once you are silent it is as manifest as a sunrise on the horizon.

So see this new project to be another manifestation of your legacy. And what should be interesting to you, your legacy is the same you had standing before the church, only now with your experience you see detail in it that was lost to your developing heart so many years ago.

I am the fourth wandering about in the flames, reassuring you that all is well. So I say to you this evening, all is well. In my love.

Scripture: *Cast your cares on the Lord, and he will sustain you. Psalm 55:22*

Prayer: Lord, one of my daughter's sent me an e-mail message that contained this verse, and I was astounded to discover that I made a notation in my bible when I received the same verse in an e-mail message some years ago. What am I to take from this?

Response: First, do you see how I use all people and events to remind you of my special messages. And this verse contains a most special message. It is of no significance who sends you the message as a wind blows a valuable piece of paper into your garden, or for that matter out of your garden. It is the message that is important, not the bearer or driver of the message.

This forced relaxation for you as you recuperate is an occasion when I know I have your attention. Go to Daniel 4 now and find the verse that echoes this thought, this divine instruction.

His dominion is an eternal dominion, his kingdom endures from generation to generation. Daniel 4:35

Yes, that is the verse. Please understand that I am all powerful. All powerful. Do you understand? Now, before you begin to quake, understand and take deeply these words, I am all loving. So with the power of an all powerful God, I say to you and anyone who will listen that I am all loving. I did not say that I love all. I said that I am all loving.

Now combine these two verses together. Realize as truth that I am asking you to cast all your cares onto to this all powerful, supreme God who is all loving. That is quite an alliance we have formed. I asked for you to depend upon me and I am all powerful and all loving. I just have to add almost as an aside, you cannot lose.

#252

Scripture: *The blessing of the Lord be upon you; we bless you in the name of the Lord. Psalm 129:8*

Prayer: This verse from the Psalm appeared in a get-well card I received. Give me guidance here.

Response: You are blessed and this manifests to you in how I touch you and your consciousness. You are also blessed through me through the hands and sentiments of those who convey my blessing to you like the sentiments of the card that you received this morning.

It is so important for you to convey such blessings to those you meet in your home, on the street, and through e-mails that you exchange with those living many of thousand miles distant. You know best how to convey that blessing so that their hearts opens to the warmth of my love.

While it is so important to extend my love, sometimes it is more important, like now, for you to receive my love through the blessings and kind gestures of those around you. Be relaxed and not apprehensive or anxious about anything. Everything is being attended to by a bevy of angelic host. We have much for you to be active in these next years.

Continue with the legacy and you will see it mature as it unfolds, and your purpose will become clear.

.

Scripture: *"Because he loves me," says the Lord, "I will rescue him; I will protect him because he acknowledges my name. He will call upon me, and I will answer him; I will be with him in trouble, I will deliver him and honor him. With long life I will satisfy him and show him my salvation."* Psalm 91:14-16

Prayer: This morning, following the holiday, I feel a deep need to call upon you – to bring clarity to my path.

Response: Your mind is clattering with concerns, about what you see you must do, the *could of's* and *should of's* of life are almost overwhelming you. Your incapacity from your operation is contributing to your restlessness and even a feeling of helplessness. As you correctly surmised earlier, you are leaving this year helpless, immobile, and dependent on friends.

It is time for you to focus on the present moment, not on the past or even the future. Allow the future to be filled with hope; hope in my love for you and allowing good in all aspects of your life to materialize. Why? The answer is to further my message of love far out from the concentric circle of your existence.

So in these closing days of the year, realize that between Christ's birth and the presentation in the temple there was much travail, and so for you. You are blessed and will be freed from the entanglements that seem to restrain you and soon. Simply continue to call upon me in your loneliness, in your questioning of your path, in consideration of your financial situation.

A new dawn is dawning in your life, brighter and filled with more warmth than you could have envisioned.

.

Scripture: *For he has rescued us from the dominion of darkness and brought us into the kingdom of the Son he loves, in whom we have redemption, forgiveness of sins. Colossians 1:13-14*

Prayer: With the sun rising over the horizon, help me this day to realize the depth of this rescue.

Response: The rescue is more dramatic than you yet understand. You get hints of it each day you wake up and wonder "what am I doing." Darkness is that sense of hopelessness, even a hint of it seems to arise out of the emptiness. And that is my point; you are no longer in the emptiness.

Listen to her words that Satan seeks to bring you discouragement to pull you, ensnare you. However, Oh the difficulty Satan has with one so committed as you. And that is just why he pursues you. To bring you to your knees in hopelessness is the reward he seeks because it would influence and discourage so many who listen for your word spoken aloud or read in your writings.

I make you a promise today. You will see signs that no one can doubt of my personal attachment to you and the assistance and support of legions of angels who seek your refreshment in the spirit.

.

Scripture: *"Now is your time of grief, but I will see you again and you will rejoice, and no one will take away your joy."* John 16:22

Prayer: I thank you for placing before me your words in that I come upon "accidentally."

Response: Yes, a time is coming, a time is near – I choose this word deliberately – and you see me in your midst as this morning. You are fully engaged in community and you see it becomes a source for my words to you this morning. Yes, your friend suggests that you read the encyclical and you take from it many thoughts to ponder. And so I work in your life.

At the end of this most fruitful year, I promise that you will see more clearly my will for you in the coming days. Yes, I said days. Your grieving will cease as you ease the suffering of others. Your letter to one of your daughter's serves to ease her suffering and so your prayers uttered in the darkness of night for those near and far.

I will see you again are words to fill you with excitement and longing and of course joy. The anticipation of our meeting in the fullness of my love is to become your greatest joy, an eternal experience that you are unable to comprehend that meaning. I am stretching your capacity to love to a fullness you could not have ever comprehended.

Cultivate in your soul this expectation, the joy and excitement this generates. And share this excitement with all you meet.

In my love.

#256

Scripture: *For in this hope we were saved. But hope that is seen is no hope at all. Who hopes for what he already has? Romans 8:24*

Prayer: Dear Lord, on this first day of the New Year, I ask that you rekindle my hope in the unseen.

Response: I am going this morning to point you in the direction of New Hope. New Hope can be summed up in the hope that peace erupts to replace the violence that grips the globe. That is Safe Bold Hope because you can always point to some improvement, or if you desire to be contrary a further deterioration. In the end you have no better idea of hope, nor whether or not you have embraced it. I am not in any way suggesting that prayers for peace are meaningless. Rather I am saying that to achieve the peace you must begin within.

Yes, a hope for peace begins with you right this moment. For those areas of your life where you do not experience my peace that surpasses understanding you must pray diligently with the bold hope that your prayer will be granted, as it will be granted. This is the conversion of your spirit that I seek. You might have to begin small because I know that only now after almost 70 years you are beginning to get it, as you would say.

And it is in that hope that you truly join mystical union with me and become the body of Christ in its fully experience. The mystical union with Christ -- pretty heady concepts this early morning. There are not many souls awake both physically and consciously this early and I don't mean just the early hour.

Scripture: *If they had been thinking of the country they had left, they would have had an opportunity to return. Instead, they were longing for a better country – a heavenly one. Hebrews 11:18*

Prayer: Thank you Lord for the scriptures that you put before me each day and the instruction you provide.

Response: When you ponder this verse you understand why at times you are unsettled emotionally. The world would have you believe that your exile is only a thing of the mind – and that is how the mind would have it. Your unsettledness at times is the result from your heart consciousness, realizing that your exile is not a longing for a bigger house, more money, more fame, more health, and more popularity. No, your exile is from the new country that I am establishing for you in heaven where our reunion will be a cause of great celebration.

In these days, you are really bidding farewell joyously through your work and the love you convey. An endless celebration of departure because indeed I am preparing the new home for you. There you will be in a union in my love that will know no bounds or distinctions.

Your celebratory departure from exile serves to encourage others to look to the other country, the new country to which I am calling. This call goes out to many. You see it when someone packs up and suddenly moves to another location far distant from home in their later years. Puzzling, but not so puzzling when you see that they too hear the call from exile but have yet to raise their eyes to the horizon and see the new dawn or better the dawn star rising just before dawn.

Be refreshed and free, untangled from the worlds concerns of achievement and possessions, and continue to prepare for the new country to which you are called.

In my name this morning.

Scripture: *Even though I walk through the valley of death, I will fear no evil; for you are with me, and your rod and your staff they comfort me. Psalm 23:4*

Prayer: In reading the Pope's encyclical **Spe Salvi**, this line caught my attention as did the reference to the scripture above: *one who walks with me on the path of final solitude.* Lord, help me to become increasingly aware of your presence in my life, walking with me on this path of final solitude. And help me to draw increasing comfort from this realization.

Response: Let me speak about *final solitude*. This is an increasingly comforting time when you realize that your walk is with me. The footsteps you hear are mine and the closeness of those footsteps is to comfort you further.

This path to final solitude is a time present for all of you to be totally conscious of the meaning, your meaning. It is not a time of panic, regret, or sorrow; rather it is time for you to accept yourself as you are and are becoming and to offer this soul to me in all humility. As I have said, this path is one of increasing consciousness; it is a time of letting go of all pretenses – all pretenses. It is a time to risk honesty with yourself, if not with others, if you can be so without causing harm to others.

The valley of death represents all that you fear, and should fear, but fully accepting and believing that I am with you. It is like traversing a desert path toward an oasis that you have been told is before you. Trusting my word you continue carefully, rationing your water and your energy, but you continue forward, not allowing the temptation to cut to the left or right, or even return; you move forward keeping your eyes on the horizon.

And yes, I do suggest that you travel at night when the sun is not so intense, so consider the meaning of traveling in the dark, in the quiet. Know I am the star that you are following and I will lead you through the valley of death while your enemy sleeps, covered in thick blankets so as not to hear your footfall.

.

Scripture: *Now faith is being sure of what we hope for and certain of what we do not see. Hebrews 11:1*

Prayer: Please simplify what seems clear, yet brings my mind into action to distinguish faith and hope.

Response: The most important point to be clear on is that impregnated in you is that spark that brings into the present the future reality. In fact, let's not talk of future reality and only discuss the present reality where your consciousness is growing; and you see more clearly what once was only a faint shadow.

It is as if you are off shore and that faint outline of shore is coming into view. You hope that your sight is not distorting the horizon for you, but with each stroke the outline becomes clearer and matches the picture you hold in your heart.

Faith is a solid experience, unwavering. Hope is ever expanding as you become more aware of the dimension of my promise to you. Think back on your life when you wished for something and I don't mean a gift. When some aspect of your life changed so dramatically though you wished for the change, you could never have imagined the bounty you received.

Think of the faint hope you had before arriving in India only to see how dramatic an experience it turned out and still impacts you today with your adopted daughter and now her son. Who could have imagined? Let me stay with that point to deepen your awareness. You adopted on short notice your daughter and now your life is so enriched with her birth son.

So too the faith in me and your hope – you will experience a deepening love than you experience now. And your deepening love now, draws further dimension of my love beyond. It as if, and really is, you attract the shoreline to you as you take one stroke after another toward that shoreline.

.

#260

Scripture: *And we know that in all things God works for the good of those who love him, who have been called according to his purpose. Romans 8: 28*

Prayer: Help me this morning to see your purpose.

Response: My purpose for you is pretty clear, or is at least becoming clearer to you. I want you to use your writing skills to convey the wisdom and discernment that you are expanding into for the purpose of easing the suffering of those around you. But further, I want you to contribute to the awareness of those around you so that they can see a path that leads to great joy. It is a path of stillness. It is the path that you are on right this moment as you sit in the quiet of the darkness preceding the dawn.

This stillness allows me to speak to you and more importantly for you to hear me before all those cares and concerns intrude. While the path is more easily indicated to those who don't know you, the challenge that I ask of you is to reach those who think they know you intimately – like your children, grandchildren, close friends. These are whom I wish you to reach because once aware of this path they will become staunch in their beliefs and practices. And yes, you risk that they will think that you are going over the edge. That is the risk I ask of all. In a sense you are to become the missionary among those who love and know you and would never suspect that you spend time in deep meditation before dawn.

Be prepared to send this daily mediation to friends, family, and contacts. Make time daily and begin.

#261

Scripture: *For God did not give us a spirit of timidity, but a spirit of power, of love and self-discipline. 1 Timothy 7*

Prayer: Lord, help me to grasp exactly what this spirit is that resides within me.

Response: That's the question. It is not for you to look over the field and begin to judge those who have gathered there as if for a race. No, it is for you to explore your depth and to identify what I have touched to make you special. Take your time. In your distraction you might not have looked sufficiently deep.

Once you begin to acknowledge those special gifts it is in the acknowledging you throw off your timidity. Timidity exists only in comparison, as you once looked about judging you against another. At this point, you will find that it is like shedding a heavy woolen overcoat in summertime.

And without that overcoat, you will find that you can actually feel coursing throughout your body a spirit of power that reflects my love to others; a new confidence envelops you, not for your purpose but for mine.

Regarding self-discipline, I am not talking of a rigidity of thought or even practice, but rather I am encouraging in you self-respect for others. Though you might think you have the "word," as you might be encouraged to believe, it is through self-discipline that my spirit of power serves to touch those about you -- yes, those who are distressed and uncertain, those who ask questions that seem to go unanswered.

The spirit of power is found in the bounty of my love.

.

#262

Scripture: *We do not know what we ought to pray for, but the Spirit himself intercedes for us with groans that words cannot express. Romans 8:26*

Prayer: Please help me to understand these words.

Response: Let me begin. Indeed, there are times, perhaps at different stages in your life when you find it difficult to pray, or events that surround you are simply too difficult to understand. You wonder about what is this life experience all about. For you it is truly not about things and stuff, but the real meaning seems to escape you. Not only do you realize that there is not much you can control though you might have some small influence.

It is at times like this, however, frequent or infrequent, that I am there to influence you, prod you, counsel you, console you, support you.

And how do I do it, if it is the right word? I read the deepest recesses of your heart and give voice to that unspoken yearning in a holy groan. What an expression, but digest its meaning.

I give voice to your deepest sentiments of love that are blocked from expression as your mind seeks a rational explanation to the events in your life.

I am the groan that you utter when no one else is around and you sit in loneliness, or walk along a deserted beach at sunrise, or seek to capture on a page a mystery of life that eludes you.

Understand most clearly that not only are your prayers answered, but that I even stir those prayers within you.

.

Scripture: *Then I thought to understand this: but it was too hard for me; until I went in the sanctuary of God. Psalm 73:16-17*

Prayer: This verse I found in Dag Hammarskjold's <u>Markings.</u> Shed light for me on your sanctuary.

Response: I am pleased that you are asking about the sanctuary. Clearly, you understand that I am not talking about a structure though you can bring my sanctuary to the structure. Clearly, you understand that sanctuary is not a thing, a political, religious, or temporal facility.

My sanctuary is within each of you. It is there that I meet you. And do you know what? You don't have to be alone. Yes, you can be and I encourage you to be with others in communion. However, just as you might have been reluctant to exercise outside in inclement weather, don't blame the *weather* – lack of companions – for not coming to my sanctuary.

It is in my sanctuary within that you will hear me, that is, if you can be still in spirit, not rushing to provide words to fill a holy space of silence. It is here that you discover your heart and discover that your mind represents interests that sometimes fill the airwaves with monkey chatter.

Be still in my sanctuary. I required the prophets to take off their sandals because they were on holy ground. The sandals were not important but your attention and reverence are. Be still and listen and you will be rewarded beyond what you could have in your wildest dreams have anticipated.

In listening you will discover my path for you. No, don't get excited. Nothing is predetermined. Your path is a direction for which you can serve in the years remaining to you. Service is entwined with love and, if you have missed this, love is my message.
So enter the sanctuary – cautiously at first, if you must – but enter it and discover for yourself the nourishment of spirit that you receive, that you experience.

All for now.

#264

Scripture: *We always thank God for all of you, mentioning you in our prayers. 1 Thessalonians 1:2*

Prayer: And what of prayer?

Response: Good question for this morning. How often do you pray to have your burden eased, or to seek a clarification in the direction upon which you are committed? Today, I want to discuss the prayers that you offer for other fellow travelers on this road, some of whom, or most of whom, you do not even know.

In prayer you recognize a community of love that extends beyond the fingertips of your individual grasp or touch. In the very act of prayer your gaze rises from your toes to embrace those around you and far distant.

It is through prayer for others that you are released to become one of generous spirit. Such prayer is so generous, especially since the object of your prayer is unaware of your intention. Though you are offering so much to another you receive ten-fold in return because of this generosity and service.

In such prayer you will find that your eyes soften and you are filled with a growing compassion for those less fortunate who populate the earth, sometimes far distant. And interesting, you begin to discern signs that your prayers and intentions are having an impact on the actions and situations of others.

Prayer is most powerful, a hidden source of love of which you all have been beneficiaries, especially when you have endured much. Prayer as a sign of my love is joy to the person in prayer as it is for the recipient of the prayerful intention – even a stranger.

Prayer knits a community together and let me say there is no boundary as to how large the community can be. As I said, prayer manifests the unfolding of my love.

So take seriously and personally the power of prayer. Reflect on the prayers that might have been intended for you, and in gratitude return the favor in prayer.

Prayer has the potential to take you out of self.

.

#265

Scripture: *"I will put my law in their minds and write it on their hearts."* Jeremiah 31:33

Prayer: Give me a deep understanding of this verse.

Response: Appreciate that these words in context concern the new covenant, one that is not limited by a collection of *do's* and *don'ts*, Rather, imprinted on your heart and mind is an echo presence that serves to validate your deepest longings, especially when you bring them to action, to consciousness.

You might want to call it intuition, inspiration, conscience, the muse, or a voice not further identified, but each has the spark that can lighten your way if you choose.

The feeling, it just seems right, reflects that spark, but it is more than that. You agree, graced with the capacity that is not bounded, to embrace my love in action and service. Don't see this grace as something outlandish, or exaggerated. As with things profound, the imprint of my love is simple.

You will gain confirmation of this writing on your heart when you pause, draw a breath, and be in a moment of time, allowing your intuition to guide your reflection upon any issue that you choose. By that very deliberative action you tap into the flow of discernment for which you are searching.

What makes this discovery special is that it becomes proof for you that my covenant with you is deliberate and real.

Without exception, you all have written on your hearts this proscription. It is for you, each of you, to recognize these words and to follow the direction as it applies to your path.
If you believe only that you enjoy a special relationship with me, that is sufficient and more than enough to devote some time to fathoming the meaning for you.

All for today.

Scripture: *But those who hope in the Lord will renew their strength. They will soar on wings like eagles; they will run and not grow weary, they will walk and not be faint. Isaiah 40:31*

Prayer: Dear Lord, teach me about hope.

Response: There is much to tell you about hope. Before defining it, hope takes seed in your heart. And in the heart hope manifests your recognition of me, prompted by my grace to you. It is as if you are standing before the classroom, alone, and you proclaim your confidence in what you heart sometimes most faintly is certain.

It is like being off the coast and a deep fog settles over your craft. You hear a fog horn and know intuitively from where the sound originates indicating the narrow channel to the safe harbor.

Here is another image. Hope is moving across a rope bridge swaying above a chasm and finding a rhythm in your steps that does not move against the rhythm of the bridge as you move to the other side and safety.

Hope is, as I have said, certainty in a storm that no matter of fear or agitation that surrounds can distract you from your goal.

And see what I promise besides. In hope your strength is renewed. As you expend effort, empty yourself, you find that I fill you with strength for the arduous path, so that you soar, exhilarating and accelerating on the wind, abandoning all the constraints that those land-bound choose for themselves; you journey endlessly without any glimmer of fatigue, and let me say encouraged by the good humor you display

It is through hope that we meet. Hope is the completed circle of my love in you. In hope you raise a banner for all to see and for me to meet.

All for this day.

Scripture: *"Now is your time of grief, but I will see you again and you will rejoice, and no one will take away your joy."* Romans 16:22

Prayer: Lord, help me to understand the absence you speak of.

Response: And here I thought you would focus your question on grief and the apparent absence of joy. The absence about which I speak is only an absence that you might experience when you scurry about or should I say scamper about on fulfilling tasks that absolutely control your day, or at least your mind.

Once you catch yourself, or should I say once you catch your heart attentively, you will discover that the apparent absence has evaporated. And it has because you see I am always in you, though you talk of being with me.

Reflect upon a time of great grief and loss and think about how close you experienced my presence through clouds of tears, recall the light that flashed it seemed at the most unexpected times – and there I stood within you, consoling you.

What I am speaking to you in Romans is on several levels. But essentially I am saying that you become conscious of my presence throughout your life experience. Put another way, I return to you again and again as you become more and more conscious of my presence that never departs from you.

And as you become aware of this truth you can see that your faith and hope builds, shortening those times that you think I have departed. There is no need for you to wait for my second coming, if you will, and I mean hope. I am allowing you a foretaste of an eternal consciousness of love that awaits you in the present.

So my advice for today, though you didn't ask for advice, is to continue to become conscious of this presence, me, who lingers within you since I have no place to go in my love of you. Do your best to ease from your shoulders the distractions you carry as if a badge of honor, but more your excuse to stumble further along the path with your eyes closed. And enlightened, you will experience a joy overwhelming, one that gives you a foretaste of a joy unending in my presence.

.

Scripture: *"Do not leave Jerusalem, but wait for the gift my Father promised, which you have heard me speak about. For John baptized with water, but in a few days you will be baptized with the Holy Spirit." Acts 1:4-6*

Prayer: Lord, help me to sense deeper the presence of the Holy Spirit.

Response: Oh, the presence of the Holy Spirit, you ask. If you pause as you are at this moment, you become aware of the presence. It fills your empty room and in that presence you realize at the deepest level that you are one with that presence.

The presence of the Holy Spirit can even be distinguished in each of your lives. In fact, I prefer you to reflect when you sensed that difference. It could have been when you were a child, or when you were much older. Your consciousness distinguishes the event of the Spirit's descent into your heart.

Don't become involved in whether the Spirit has descended into that soul or the other, nor in asking why that it is so. Simply spend time with yourself and acknowledge to yourself the event, as the apostles did abiding by Jesus' command they did not leave Jerusalem, awaiting this descent.

Once you are able to describe the event ask in prayer the difference it has made in your life. Surely it made a difference in each of the lives of those who were present so many years ago. Do your best not to consider the event in historical terms of the past, but see in your lives when your consciousness deepened and you could see – almost for the first time – without the clatter of your life's sounds.

The descent of the Spirit is a quiet coming, an entrancing event that stands apart from any ceremony. It is as if you notice for the first time a garment that has been presented to you and in reflection you are surprised at the luxury and beauty of the garment.

.

Scripture: *Suddenly an angel of the Lord appeared and a light shone in the cell. He struck Peter on the side and woke him up. "Quick, get up!" he said, and the chains fell off his wrist. Acts 12:7*

Prayer: Lord, help me to wake up.

Response: Consider the painful events in life as the angel of the Lord striking you into wakefulness. You are in a prison of neglect and the angel is with you to rouse you from your slumber. Sometimes you might feel only a nudge and that might do to awaken you for a time, but it is the rousing slap that forces you to jump to your feet almost in fear.

It is the dream state that you must combat with all your energy and of course my grace. And here is another paradox – it is when you are most engaged in the task of acquiring that you are most unconscious. It is in stillness and listening that you are most awake though to an observer your *inaction* is interpreted as slumber.

Notice in this verse I am also telling you that you are struck into wakefulness for a purpose, for a mission, not one that I have selected for you but one that you see clearly as the correct path for you in my grace. You know because I speak to you, I am close, and at the deepest level of your heart you do hear me. You might even reach a point in your life when that awesome, sometimes painful strike is welcome. You see so much rests on you waking up.

Do not go back to sleep. Keep that as your refrain, especially when you find the comfort of unconsciousness as inviting as a feather comforter on a frigid night. No, wake up, dress warmly, and go out among the byways. My promise to you is that you will find me waiting for you.

Scripture: *The Sovereign Lord is my strength, he makes my feet like the feet of a deer, he enables me to go on the heights. Habbakuk 3:19*

Prayer: Is there a reason that you want me on the heights?

Response: It is from the heights that you see the landscape that I have prepared for you. It is in the journey upward that you realize how much I ask from you as you journey home. And you are to become nimble and adroit as you maneuver on those solitary paths that wind so far from the sight of those who have remained in the valley; safer it seems but in actuality vulnerable to every threat of the spirit that lurks below, at the lower altitudes.

Here again is a paradox. The higher you climb the deeper you reach and as solitary you might feel, the more in union you are with me in stillness.

Notice, I am saying that I provide you what you need for the climb both spiritually, in strength and tenacity, and in longing to leave the plain in search. And the question for you to ponder is – in search of what?

The next time you are in a mountainous area gaze at the heights and see if you can spot a mountain goat almost beyond your gaze, beyond the reach of your sight. Reflect upon its nimble frame, the power of its legs, its energy and stamina. In that sight consider your search the same as the mountain's goat – for nourishment.

And I offer you yet another paradox. As you climb in a glorious dawn on the steep and craggy ridges of the mountain slope alone, in another dimension you are in the world surrounded by those who are touched by your presence as you are touched by their presence.

Let me end today with encouragement for you to bring the confidence, independence, and strength to all your relationships below, sharing that spirit of roaming the heights alone to all those who clamor together lonely below.

CHAPTER TEN - SIGNS

They were gathered to bid farewell to a much loved pastor. One after another stood to express the impact he had upon their lives. When it came to his turn to speak, he stood and said that over the years they had heard his lengthy sermons. So for this evening his sermon would be limited to four words — "Watch for the signs!" Then, he took his seat.

Scripture reminds us to watch for signs. It is sometimes easier to look for apocalyptic signs than to watch for them in relationships, spiritual life, aspirations, and service. These signs are a barometer of fidelity to God's will in one's life.

See God in everything.

#271

Scripture: *The true light that gives light to every man was coming into the world. John 1:9*

Prayer: Speak to me more of this true light.

Response: The light is not reserved, as you know and even perceive, is not reserved for the healthy, successful, powerful, the adults, those with white skin or brown, the tall or the short. No, the light is bestowed on all without distinction. Yes, even those who do not know your scripture, who stand in silence before the rising sun on some windswept island, or forlorn desert landscape, or mountain crag.

Some embrace the light. Some are perplexed by the glow and make some effort to disguise it with a harsh or – worse – expressionless glance, or busy themselves in the activity of routine. Those that embrace the light are not routine. Each day, each moment even, is an adventure of discovery. You see once aware of the light those who accept this can do all but contain their enthusiasm to share the light with those around them and those far distant.

The light within is my light that I give to all of you. Some may call it the divine spark. Actually, many descriptions of the light prevail as people seek to explain this phenomenon. Explanations are not nearly as important as releasing the light from within for all to see.

And how do others see the light, once revealed? In your compassion, in your empathy for those who suffer, in your generosity of spirit, in your forgiveness, in your trust, in your hope, in your commitment and action to bring the light into new surroundings that are sometimes not far distant, but so isolated.

As you share the light of my love, you awaken, stir the embers of what might have been a slumbering fire into what can and does become a conflagration when joined with others, causing old fears to be swept away as you journey forward and within.
Like water so too with the light you fail to value the essential change in you once you become conscious of its Presence. It is time for you to pause and to touch, as it were, the light within you; and once touching it, send the light shimmering all around you, realizing that in the process your capacity for the light will grow exponentially.

There is much to tell you about light but so much for this morning.

Scripture: *For you have delivered me from death and my feet from stumbling that I may walk before God in the light of life. Psalm 56:13*

Prayer: On this morning the beginning of my seventieth year, speak to me, Lord.

Response: On this morning all your spirit ancestors gather and will accompany you especially this day. You are well respected. I say this to you not to inhibit you this day to become conscious of a crowd of observers. Rather, I want you to realize that in these last years, you are becoming who you are into those who could only see the outward physical manifestation.

You are holding the power of the light and in this you are experiencing at a most profound level my presence. There is no barrier or wall that you cannot climb over for my purpose. Today, I want you to take special note of all the blessings that are showered upon you.

I want you to take special care to be gentle with yourself. Let go of all those nagging feelings that seem to snare you from time to time. This day I want you to be carefree, like a kite flying in a strong breeze. See the height that it can rise and see the same for you.

I have delivered you from death, but more importantly, I have destined that you shed your encumbrances to bring my love to those far and wide.

Scripture: *Jesus answered: "It is written: 'Man does not live on bead alone, but on every word that come from the mouth of God.'" Matthew 4:4*

Prayer: Lord, this is another verse that I have read many times, brushing over the words lightly. Help me to probe a deeper meaning.

Response: You must spend your time with each of my words, especially the words that come to you from your heart. It is these words that are inscribed with special meaning for you. These words need no footnotes. Words assigned to your heart source have a potency that only you can fathom.

The word from me is truly extensive and frequent. You need no eyes to read, nor ears to hear my message spoken aloud, even no ritual in which to participate. All that is required, and I do not make light of this, is your attention, your soul attention.

Remember that your life experience, this school of learning, has little interest in you remaining seated studying various texts, but rather your receptiveness for my message and love wherever you might be. Hear me throughout your day and night. The voice you hear is not some white noise, some filtering sound. I speak to each of you directly and throughout your presence on earth.

Reassuring it is to know that I have not sent you out on this adventure, this exploration of the spirit, without a constant companion. This companion, my Spirit, is available to you as you would say 24/7 and provides you more than you even require for the arduous steps in your journey. The constancy and immediacy of Spirit means that when you awake in the depth of the night, you are present in a sound chamber, solitary, and most receptive to my word. I am not saying this to encourage you to be sleep deprived. Rather I am explaining and reinforcing the total presence of my love.

I have said this many times and I repeat: I abound in the stillness of your heart. Prepare that stillness in your lives.

.

Scripture: *Let this be written for a future generation, that a people not yet created may praise the Lord. Psalm 102:18*

Prayer: Help to connect me to those who have long since passed on.

Response: Is that your prayer, or is your attention caught by the words of the psalmist who looks out beyond the centuries and writes words that touch you?

As you are in communion and community with those around you, and even those who are far distant geographically, you are reminded this morning that you are also in communion with those who have passed on many centuries ago and even those who have yet to appear on your globe.

A theme for you this morning is to discard at least for this moment the concept of linear, single dimensional time. Discard the concept just as you would put a wristwatch in a drawer or turn the clock on the mantle-piece to face the wall.

I want you to appreciate and reverence the communion you share with all people, regardless of their era, race, culture, and any other characteristic that you would more likely use to distinguish them, to make them different, and instead to see a common bond. After all you are all on a journey and on this journey share provisions to sustain you. And in this psalm you are being offered across time sustenance that is every bit as nourishing as a drink offered by a friend on a journey through a parched desert.

And what can you do in return for this generous offering from the past which in the words become present? You can nod in thanksgiving a prayer of blessing on the gift and the one who extended to you that gift.
In this escape from dimensional time, the steps that you take that sometimes sound as those in a hollow hallway or corridor now sound like a raucous celebration of those reaching home after a long journey.

There is a reason to celebrate this and every morning.

#275

Scripture: *The Lord is gracious and righteous; our Lord is full of compassion. Psalm 116:5*

Prayer: Gracious, righteous and full of compassion. How could I not want to meet you?

Response: And you do each day. Though you are distracted so often and miss me in the crowd though I am alongside you, your constant companion. And there are those moments when you catch my glance. Yes, it might be prompted by a companion or someone you love; you might even catch my look in the eyes of a stranger; but even more powerful and direct is when you quiet and in stillness sit alongside me in attention.

Gracious here means my gentleness and patience as I observe you and encourage your dawning consciousness. It is like standing on the beach you frequent waiting for the sun to rise. I too am waiting patiently for your dawn to rise. The difference, and there are many, is that I am standing alongside you and nudging you to keep watching that seemingly blank horizon for the first pinprick of light.

Spend a moment with righteousness. No, I am not about to hurl the tablets from heaven for you to follow. I am with you to ease your dullness and obstinacy into a consciousness of love – and yes, compassion. And I am constant and consistent in this endeavor. And in doing and being such for you, I am righteous.

See me as your guide in days when the wind howls seemingly without purpose in your life; see me as your boon companion when rested you reflect on my goodness; see me as your mentor when you help the least of mine generously and with patience. Encounter me as you would a friend after a long arduous journey and in that greeting realize that the past is lost into the joy of the present.

Scripture: *Because of the Lord's great love we are not consumed; for his compassions never fail. They are new every morning; great is your faithfulness. Lamentations 3:22-23*

Prayer: These words somehow have more impact for me as the lightning flashes and the thunder rumbles through the wind before dawn off the sea. Help me to focus on your compassion.

Response: I would rather you spend a moment on faithfulness, your faithfulness. It is through your waiting, your anticipation that you are able to see my compassion in all your work and life. In the midst of this storm you await the morning and the smell and the clarity of the air. Anticipation is another word for faith – conscious anticipation, joyful anticipation.

My compassions are many and as you become conscious you also see with clarity after a storm the depth of my compassions. See the compassions that reach to the core of your being and resonate there with a knowing. All the confusion that might surround you at any point in your life seems to dissipate in those compassions and you experience a knowing that eluded you earlier.

Sit still waiting for the wind to cease, the thunder to move down the coast, the lightening to fade. In the waiting, patiently, you experience my will for you. It is in these moments of waiting that I reach you and linger within you long after the storm has fled your coast.

All you experience is cause for you to reflect in wonder upon your life. End your reflection with assurance of my compassions.

Scripture: *For I am convinced that neither death nor life, neither angels nor demons, neither the present nor the future, nor any powers, neither height nor depth, nor anything else in all creation, will be able to separate us from the love of God that is in Christ Jesus our Lord. Romans 8:38-39*

Prayer: Help me to see oneness in your love.

Response: Can you just imagine Paul grasping for words to testify to his belief, to his faith. Can you just see him looking around, looking up to draw in the analogy, the image that will convince the onlookers of the truth. Consider the question, why?

It is not to draw upon the last efforts of a work brigade to stem the flood from a crumbling dike; it is not to urge an expedition through a dense jungle or up a summit. No, Paul is saying to those in earshot, and you now two thousand years later are in the same crowd and his words are spoken to you this morning in the present. No, Paul is speaking to you these words to emphasize, if you ever doubted, that I am with you, alongside you, under every conceivable circumstance. There has not been an experience in this life that could keep us apart. In fact, it is an inconceivable contradiction of the Spirit.

So if your mind jumps around from one picture word to the next that Paul uses, realizes that he returns to the basic theme, the inalterable truth, that we are one. You might feel aloneness, but in reality, we are a crowd experiencing the torment and joy, the disappointment and celebration, the wind and the calm.

Contained in those verses for you this morning is a truth you overlook, especially when you feel overwhelmed and when you feel triumph. Do your best to pause at such times and feel my presence, a presence from which you cannot distance yourself, however hard you try. Accept "defeat," as it were, and as you have observed, victory is yours, or should I say ours?

In my peace this day.

Scripture: *But a Samaritan, who was on a journey, came upon him; and when he saw him, he felt compassion, and came to him and bandaged up his wounds, pouring oil and wine on them; and he put him on his own beast, and brought him to an inn and took care of him. Luke 10:33-34*

Prayer: Help me to see with the eyes of the Samaritan.

Response: Yes, that is the right verb: to see. And to see like the Samaritan requires you to recognize him as your guide on the lonely road you sometimes traverse. In fact, I am quick to add that the Samaritan had it easier in one sense; he was traveling alone, alone with his thoughts. His attention was fully focused. He was alert. After all he knew traveling that road could be dangerous. And he knew this long before he came upon the man at the side of the road. The Samaritan was not distracted as you can be traveling through life, attending to your affairs, meeting deadlines, accomplishing tasks. No, the Samaritan, though alert to danger, was traveling fully conscious of each step.

Thus contained in that short description that Luke offers you today – wherever you are and wherever you travel – is the simple – but not so simple to implement – stricture to be conscious of each step you take. In a sense, I want your steps not to be hurried but be aware of how you raise your foot as you take a step and how you lower your foot. Experience the weight that you put on your foot at the completion of a step and always be aware of your surroundings.

Of course, I want you to experience the full beauty that resonates in your heart and I also want you to be aware of your fellow companions who are in distress. Perhaps, you won't come upon someone literally at the side of the road in pain and near death, but surely you come upon those who emotionally are in despair, are alone, defenseless, unable to ask for help because, as the man on the side of the road, they have become unconscious.
Yes, this story holds essentially the lesson as to how you are to travel and to be conscious and your responsibility, yes I say responsibility, is to reach those not conscious, or no longer conscious, to sustain them on the journey.

And finally, consider the compassion shown by the Samaritan. In case you missed it, he represents the stranger in your midst that you are obliged to know, that is, when you have regained your consciousness.

#279

Scripture: *Brothers, I do not consider myself yet to have taken hold of it. But one thing I do: Forgetting what is behind and straining toward what is ahead, I press on toward the goal to win the prize for which God has called me heavenward in Christ Jesus. Philippians 3:13-14*

Prayer: Lord, again, I have read these words previously. This time help me to catch the meaning you intend for me this morning.

Response: There are three thoughts that I want you to focus on and listen to me explain each: what is behind, press on, and called heavenward.

How often are you thwarted or delayed in your pursuit of the goal by allowing considerations of the past to distract you? Please reduce these words to an event in your life, or a journey that proved particularly tedious and demanding. Instead of relishing that the event or experience is past you continue to dwell in the pain of it. Sometimes, your recollection inhibits your reaction to what awaits you as you sit immobilized in fear and trepidation that the experience will repeat itself. I ask that you forget what is behind and approach, indeed strain forward as one in pursuit of a goal that is to be unparalled in your life.

And that leads me to the words, press on. Yes, press on in hope with your fledgling faith. You know what is around the corner, even though you only caught a glimpse of me, because I have told you. You can hear my footsteps, if you listen, the scuffle of my sandals on the tile before you. There are even times when you seem distracted that I call softly to you. And have no concern of the exercise that awaits you because I am really calling you within where you can't help but hear me, and catch much more than a fleeting glimpse of me.

And finally, yes I am calling you heavenward. I am calling you home. Don't rush your steps; simply, and I mean this deliberately; simply take each step with meaning and purpose. Keep your focus and your attention, both of which you will see expands so that it would be hard for you to recall who you were before.

Don't look back. Those are the words I want to leave you with this morning. There are enough examples of those who did so and regretted it in scripture, literature, legend, and life. There is a reason this theme is prevalent. So take it as your motto this day.

.

Scripture: *If I rise on the wings of the dawn, if I settle on the far side of the sea, even there your hand will guide me, your right hand will hold me fast. Psalm 139:9-10*

Prayer: Help me Lord to be conscious of your presence and guidance, even when I feel alone.

Response: Yes, in the quiet before dawn you could also think that you are talking or musing to yourself. I am here alongside you, prompting you to sense my presence and love. Where might you flee, you ask, to be alone? And my answer to you is that there is no place you can be where I will not find you; no place to where I will not accompany you; and you are blessed with my companionship that does not require even acknowledgement. How is that for a thought to comprehend? I am with you and from me you learn patience. From me you learn steadfastness and commitment. From me you learn unconditional love.

And let us talk about guidance. I am there to influence you with my grace to remain on the path. Do your best to see that path as movement in service. You don't need any map; I am as it were your GPS system that informs you of the terrain around you, the roads that lie before you, in all directions. Do not trouble yourself with thoughts that you are on a treasure hunt and if you don't find the path you will lose out.

The path is not foreordained. You create the path with my grace. Consider your own path to the present moment. Reflect on the turns and challenges and how you participated, even forged the path, especially when you hit sand, or bedrock, or heights that you didn't anticipate, or for that matter, the depths that you were not sure that you could negotiate.

Let me sum up. The psalmist is talking to you today as if he were sitting alongside you over a cup of coffee. Don't be distracted by his camel's hair cloak or his scruffy beard. Just observe the intensity of his coal black eyes as he seeks to impart a message that he received and absorbed many years ago. He is telling you and others, that's why his voice sounds hoarse, I am with you always, everywhere, and I mean in any physical location, emotional trauma, at times of overwhelming joy when the last thing in your mind perhaps is to get too serious. There is no place or situation that you can evade me or disguise yourself. And I am not motivated by a desire to catch you, but only, repeat, only to love you.

So with the dawn rising consider now that I have made all known to you as the shadows of doubt evaporate.

#281

Scripture: *Then the Lord said to Abraham, "Why did Sarah laugh and say, 'Will I really have a child, now that I am old?' Is anything too hard for the Lord? I will return to you at the appointed time next year and Sarah will have a son." Sarah was afraid, so she lied and said, "I did not laugh." But he said, "Yes, you did laugh." Genesis 18:13-15*

Prayer: Lord, help me to accept your words about nothing being too hard for you.

Response: Before you can even approach me in prayer, do your best to know yourself. For prayer, for our dialogue to work, so to speak, you must be authentic. Pray as you are, and not as you think you should be.

Now, once you have identified who you are, have found your voice sometimes buried in the clutter of the tasks you think you should perform, grasp your dream and do not let go of it. Yes, it might be for a child when you are long past rearing children; it might be to embark upon an adventure that you have nourished since youth; it might involve the exploration of the soul that eluded you previously. And bring that dream to me. And let me say, if you don't have the courage to bring the dream to me, I will prompt it from you as I did Sarah, standing behind the tent flap.

You are all Sarah's, excuse me if I offend you. You are often standing behind a mask, in Sarah's case a tent flap. You are taking it all in but disguise your reaction and intent with an expressionless gaze, fearing to show your excitement. And then when you overhear, as it were, my voice in your soul you dismiss it with a laugh, until found out. Your reaction goes to a nervous laugh to fear that your disguise has not worked. Now you are confronted with my truth.

And what is my truth? I will answer with a question: *Is anything too difficult for me?* So you see in this reading, I am imploring you to dream, to grasp your dreams, and come to me with confidence in prayer. And it is OK, if you laugh nervously.

One last comment, your prayers that are connected to the dreams that resonate in your heart reflect my love for you. Now that is something for you to reflect upon.

.

Scripture: *"I have told you these things, so that in me you may have peace. In this world you will have trouble. But take heart I have overcome the world.* John 16:33

Prayer: My tongue just slips over the words that you have overcome the world. Give me a deeper appreciation of what you mean.

Response: It is difficult for you to comprehend what I mean by overcome the world. When you sit back and reflect on these words, you isolate what is unpleasant for you and cheer that I have overcome it. I would rather you reflect on the cosmic, yes cosmic, proportions of what I speak. Those words are meant to reveal to you the power I am. And instead of immediately jumping to the conclusion that the power is capable of destruction, consider love.

In this world that seems to be filling with anger, step aside and consider the power of love that is manifest. In any event that you might not want to repeat, consider the presence of love that was even sparked by what you would describe as tragedy.

Love is the rising tide that washes away sandcastles of arrogance, pride, greed, and anger of individuals, nations and even a globe. When I say that I overcome the world, I mean that my love is rising in the most unexpected regions, under the most fearsome circumstances. It is for you to nurture the peace I have bestowed upon you in my grace.

Indeed, you will experience trouble in your life of all varieties. Your only solace will eventually come when you truly accept the significance of the words that I have overcome the world, everything that fills a life from birth to death in relationship. So this morning I grant you that peace.

Scripture: *This is what the Lord says – your Redeemer, the Holy One of Israel: "I am the Lord your God, who teaches you what is best for you, who directs you in the way you should go." Isaiah 48:17*

Prayer: Lord, give me a better appreciation of your direction.

Response: What better appreciation can you have but to look back on your life, or for that matter yesterday. See me in the choices that you make that touch your whole life and I do not mean you to limit it to the scripture verse you choose or the shirt that you select to wear. In fact throw off notions that I am sitting with an open script, your script, and am giving you prompts when you forget your lines. If that were to be so I would be devoted essentially to reading a script.

No, you are writing and performing the script as it were. Staying with the analogy, I am in the audience, participating in the performance. Participating. Isn't that what an audience that relishes a performance does? Relishes the performance. Yes, I am sitting in the audience and just can't wait to read the reviews afterwards of a fine performance. And do you know who writes the reviews? You do!

So let's get back to your question. I am the director, who endures endless rehearsal sessions with you and the cast. Remember you are a member of a large cast. This is no *Off-Broadway* production. And the cast expands as you learn your lines and move to encourage others to join as they encourage you. And learning your lines is simpler than you might think. It comes from reading your heart and soul. Knowing who you are, and not some role you think you should be playing, is the lesson for you today.

So my direction has more to do with setting the stage. And even here I am a bit unorthodox. I see to it that the curtain opens on another day, as today. It is for you to walk out on stage with all the trepidation you might feel, with all the eagerness that might be stirring within, even with all the weariness you sometimes have to overcome – but walk out on the stage. The audience is waiting. The more prepared among you are those of you who have been still, learning the lines of your heart.

. And you didn't imagine that Isaiah was of the stage.

Scripture: *Be joyful always, pray continuously, give thanks in all circumstances, for this is God's will for you in Christ Jesus.* 1 Thessalonians 16-18

Prayer: These words are easier for me to understand than to apply, especially in all circumstances.

Response: You use the expression, setting the bar high. Well, this is where I set the bar – high. Consider my words as a formula to bring you peace. You see that what I ask and suggest, and you could say direct, is all within your power in my grace.

What a challenge to be joyful always. This means this very minute with no one observing, without allowing considerations of what awaits you this day, adopt a joyful spirit. You can see wherever you are and under whatever circumstances, and I stress the latter, nothing can prevent you from being joyful. I know this thought sounds bizarre to some of you, but please see that you are able to be joyful. It is your decision and one quite frankly that is easier to apply than the contrary.

About prayer, I have instructed you much. Prayer is our internal dialogue that you are asked, directed, to cultivate as if – and it is – the breath of your soul. I don't expect you to go about distracted as if in a trance. What I am asking is that you develop your consciousness, awareness of my presence in your life. For the moment, don't be distracted by thoughts of my presence in the world. Rather, I want you to consider and sense the significance of my presence in your life. And this presence is not just in passing as I pass you randomly throughout the day as if this were a game of tag. No, I am with you now, this moment, and am not watching over your shoulder to see whom I will visit next.

Now giving thanks in all circumstances seems understandable and even easy until you experience the unthinkable in your life. And do you know what? You all consider your circumstances unique and at times sobering – and they are. I am saying to you that even then, give thanks. For the mystery you will one day come to some understanding is that I work in your life in all, repeat all, circumstances. How else to fashion the unique quality you each represent.

And even when you resist, if it helps, accept that this is my will for you even if it doesn't make sense.

So begin this day with joy.

Scripture: *"Neither this man nor his parents sinned," said Jesus, "but this happened so that the work of God might be displayed in his life." John 9:3*

Prayer: How is the work of God displayed in our lives?

Response: This is almost a setup question, as if I prepared for someone in the audience to ask it – and everyone knows, or thinks they know the answer. Don't rush with words that you learned by rote or that others have given you. Instead spend some time alone and in stillness and reflect upon just exactly what works of mine are manifest in your life's purpose.

This is no easy exercise because I am asking you to go a lot deeper than the hopefully frequent acts of charity you undertake. I am asking you to go so deep that where my work ends is indistinguishable as to where your works begins. If it still seems to be an easy exercise, you must go deeper. Because you see we are united in my grace.

As you sit before the keyboard there seems to be no interval between the thought you receive and the action of your fingertips on the keyboard. I want you to do the same in exploring my works in your presence in this life.

Why do I ask this – simply to increase your consciousness, or put in another way, to help you to wake up? I am not suggesting that dreaming is not good, only that it is not conscious, and for the most of your day you are unconscious. You act in accord with that script we discussed some days ago. I want you to throw out the script and begin to touch more deeply my presence in your life. And why? Because once conscious, once out of your dream state, you will discover that we are truly working together in your environment, however narrow or widespread it is. And then what happens? Those around you, and most importantly you, will see my works displayed with clarity and force.

Many questions asked of you today to prompt deeper reflection that requires no study, simply attentiveness to my presence in you and all about as you awake.

.

Scripture: *Then he said to them: "My soul is overwhelmed with sorrow to the point of death. Stay here and keep watch with me." Matthew 26:38*

Prayer: Lord, help me enter into this season of sorrow awake.

Response: I know it is difficult and has always been difficult for you to understand, come even close to what these words mean for you. Let me see if I can help you.

As difficult it is for you to realize, accept that Jesus is divine and he fully took on your humanity, and that is the message for you today. I know that in the past you glossed over the words of overwhelming sorrow to the point of death as simply an exaggeration – that Jesus was unable to feel the full impact of humanity. And that is the key to this mystery, namely that he did experience the full dimension of humanity in order to sanctify your life with his sacrifice.

Sorrow to the point of death – each word chosen so carefully. There is no exaggeration here. He emptied himself and opened himself to the full sorrow in a special grief that encompassed you, all of you, past, present, and to come. An overwhelming sorrow took hold of his soul and in this he taught you all how to deal with such grief and loss. He resigned the loss to the Father's will, in other words he offered the real grief and sorrow to the Father.

The lesson for you today is to dwell on these words and accept them at the deepest level of meaning. As I said above, Jesus felt an overwhelming sorrow at a soul level to the point of death. Now, reflect upon who you are or to become to ease that sorrow.

All for today.

Scripture: *But Jesus remained silent. The high priest said to him, "I charge you under oath by the living God: Tell us if you are the Christ, the Son of God." "Yes, it is as you say," Jesus replied. "But I say to all of you. In the future you will see the Son of Man sitting at the right hand of the Mighty One and coming on the clouds of heaven." Matthew 26:63-64*

Prayer: Give me discernment to probe this essential truth and keep it ever fresh in my heart.

Response: Here before you is evidence of the leap of faith that I require. I am asking you to take Jesus' response into your heart. You, like the high priests of your environment have asked the question. And you have heard the answer, no matter how you have tried to phrase the question, hoping if nothing else, silence will follow so that you can go about unconscious in your dream state.

Well, I answered the question of the high priest and I have answered your question, especially when you would have almost preferred silence after the events or an event of your life. There is no denying, I have answered the question. It is as if lost you have asked for directions and I have given them plain, directly. I didn't have to draw you a map. You received and continue to receive my simple response: "Yes!" I didn't say: "No," or "Under some circumstances," "Not today, see me tomorrow," "I don't know," "That's what they say." No, I said "Yes!"

Now take that leap to the other side on faith and let's continue your journey. As I continue to answer, I ask that you continue to ask and receive my response. Each morning or evening ask the question and then receive my response with joy, relief, renewed faith, and continue your journey with the directions that bring you home.

.

Scripture: *Then the governor's soldiers took Jesus into the Praetorium and gathered the whole company of soldiers around him. They stripped him and put a scarlet robe on him and then twisted together a crown of thorns and set it on his head. They put a staff in his right hand and knelt in front of him and mocked him. "Hail, King of the Jews," they said. Matthew 27:27-29*

Prayer: These words have almost lost their bite, so often have I read or heard them. Help me to feel these words afresh.

Response: You have not presented me with much of a challenge. Take these verses and read each word slowly, pausing on the word that touches you. See the scene that is presented to you, the splendor of Rome though present in the provinces. Splendor and protocol, success and achievement represent all who serve there.

Don't linger in the past and call up visions assisted sometimes by the film industry. No, see the splendor of life for you when you would prefer not to be interrupted by the protocol of action that you have practiced, it seems for a lifetime, a protocol of action that is in truth a distraction.

Instead, if you can, see Jesus interrupting what I prefer to call a dream state. He is hauled before you and you have the opportunity to capture what is transpiring as it applies to you today. I repeat, you have an opportunity to capture the scene as it applies to you today.

You will never be the same with this experience as witness. Sense most deeply the hypocrisy disguised in the mockery, think of the clever fellow who thought up the purple robe or the one who fashioned the crown. Do not deny that there are times that you are capable of performing similarly.

These verses are meant for you today to waken you from your slumber so that you can fully appreciate where these events are leading in your life, your life, not in the script of someone playing one of the roles. And in this soft or should I say gentle recognition of what is transpiring, give thanks quietly in the deepest recesses of your heart where only you roam. If you can do this, I assure you that you have awakened.

Scripture: *After they had mocked him, they took off the robe and put his own clothes on him. Then they led him away to crucify him. Matthew 27:31*

Prayer: So few words with such import. Help me to slow the reel so to speak and catch the essential meaning for me.

Response: Yes, so few words that disguise the suffering and humiliation endured by Jesus and there was much more to come. Your inability to seize this scene adequately is a natural response, like turning away from an accident, or casting your eyes away from the bedraggled person sleeping on a grate in your city. Part of your reaction is that there seems to be nothing you can do to correct the scene. You know the ending. Jesus is on His way to be crucified. If you have your way, you would just as soon skip over the next verses and await word of the resurrection, but not so fast.

What Jesus is showing you by His acts is his overwhelming love for you in the present. Don't, if you can, linger on the historical scene but see this determination as He picks up His cross as a current event in your life. Again, if you can, don't be that passive though shocked witness, whom Jesus passes, but be the one who walks with him.

I ask you to see this journey to Golgotha as an entry way and not a destination, or a final resting place. There is much He is teaching you in these verses. Perhaps, the most important lesson is your need to plunge through all the distractions of your life, and nurture a single minded focus and determination to follow in His steps. Though you will not endure the humiliation and savagery of the crucifixion, you are being asked to commit and not to be deterred by what you might perceive to be an arduous path or one that could cause you to reveal who you really are, shed of the garments with which you wrap yourself.

Stripped of His garments has the additional more essential meaning of Jesus revealing who He is – as his words proclaimed earlier to Pontius Pilate and the chief priests. No one can claim I didn't realize who He was; but one can claim I chose to look away and not listen or observe. In looking away, these same folks failed to see the resurrection and the change made in their lives.

All for now.

Scripture: *From the sixth hour until the ninth hour darkness came over the land. About the ninth hour Jesus cried out in a loud voice, "Eloi, Eloi, lama sabachthani?" – which means, "My God, my God, why have you forsaken me?" Matthew 27:45-46*

Prayer: I am listening, Lord.

Response: It is in this instant, in uttering those words, that Jesus empties himself of the longing of humanity. Jesus' cry is so penetrating to you this day because it represents your cry at different stages and times of your life. And doesn't this recounting of Jesus' despair lend hope to you whenever you feel despair.

I am sure that you have not missed, in fact you have probably just passed over it, that Jesus so close to completing his divine mission sounds as if he has lost heart and confidence. Take these words as the encouragement he offers to you in times when you wonder what your life encounters mean. And in encouragement, as Jesus, shout your despair. I say encouragement because without doubt you will hear my word resonating in your heart as loud as any cry – that is, if you listen.

The truth that Jesus' humanity discovered, and you discover, is that you are not forsaken and Jesus' humanity discovers this also – as you will – when he follows these words with "It is consummated." That realization is for you to take into your heart and ponder.

These events, though briefly described, are there for you to ponder. They represent a special poem written concisely, no extra words included, so that you can reflect on each word as each represents a precious gem for you to carry on your journey.

.

Scripture: *"And surely I am with you always, to the very end of the age." Matthew 28:20*

Prayer: I am listening this morning.

Response: This morning I want you to focus on the word *surely*. You will, if you haven't already, discover that this is the essence of your faith. The time of debate, like on the one hand and on the other hand, is completed. You enter the next phase of your life regardless of your age, health, or disposition with a conviction that grows and matures so that you can say quietly to yourself at least "Surely, I am with you always."

Do you feel those words resonating in your bones as if those bones were a musical instrument? Whenever you doubt or seem overcome or even overjoyed by your journey, repeat these words. If you gather nothing else from the scripture let it be your conscious acceptance that I am with you always – and to the *very end of the age*.

Focus on my presence and dismiss notions and speculations as to how long the journey will be – or even on what awaits you. I await you now in companionship and love with my presence – a presence that transcends death. What a spectacular revelation, one that shocked the learned, the powerful, even those who spent their hours refuting or even proclaiming this truth in the libraries of the world. You see, I uttered these words quietly, clearly, and directly. You need no one to explain them further. You don't have to examine the vintage of the wine through the label on the bottle, simply taste the wine and discover the truth.

Indeed, there is much for you to celebrate this moment. I am with you always.

Scripture: *While they were still talking about this, Jesus himself stood among them and said to them: "Peace be with you." They were startled and frightened, thinking they saw a ghost. He said to them: "Why are you troubled, and why do doubts rise in your minds? Look at my hands and my feet. It is I myself. Touch me and see: a ghost does not have flesh and bones as I have." Luke 24:36-39*

Prayer: These verses seem more acceptable to me from an historical perspective. Help me to read the words for today in my life.

Response: Yes, tales from many years ago are easier to accept as you are entertained by myths from the past. And you are correct in your question or request that these verses are meant for you today, even more than they were meant for the original witnesses two thousand years ago. You ask why?

Today, I am asking you to put history into perspective and be in this morning. Hear my voice as I sit alongside you. I begin your day with my admonition and blessing, *Peace be with you.* Think of a time when your parents woke you gently because you were leaving on a trip and they wanted to get an early start. You are leaving on a trip this day and I want you to get an early start.

Please approach this day with this excitement regardless of how far you will go – even if you plan to stay about your home this day. Each day, if you have missed my point, is an adventure and I not only wake you with my blessing of peace, but I also accompany you.

And how often are you startled to be wakened from your slumber that sometimes extends long beyond the time you are moving about seemingly awake? And I ask you as I asked the disciples, *why are you troubled, why do you allow doubts to arise in your mind?* Let me give you some advice, doubts do not arise in your heart. So connect with your heart.
It is in your heart that you hear me most clearly once you filter out mind chatter.

Now as you might have surmised, this morning greeting I am offering you is not all about you getting ready for breakfast or for a commute into work or attending to the tasks that linger in your mind. As important as these responsibilities are, I am greeting you, awakening you so that you consciously, there's that word again, perform each task as you contribute to the unfolding of my will in your world. No, you are not robots but awakened folks who are at peace, know no fear or doubt, and are determined to cultivate your surroundings – again however confined – with my love. So I ask you why would you doubt or even be surprised by my words in your life.

.

Scripture: *"I am the Alpha and the Omega," says the Lord God, "who is, who was, and who is to come, the Almighty." Revelations 1:8*

Prayer: I approach this book with trepidation. Reveal your word to me.

Response: Take each word as you would sample a delicacy. My words are not meant to confound. In this short verse I am revealing to you timelessness, my timelessness; I know it is difficult for you to comprehend, to get your mind around a concept that has no boundaries, like time. But as I have said to you previously these lessons are lessons meant not for your mind, which is, I think you are prepared to admit even reluctantly, finite.

So first understand that when I reveal myself to you, I do so using your tablets of knowledge, your experience, even your yearnings. Just accept the mystery of what I am saying to you now. I know no beginning and no end, and that I am ever present and present to you. And in that presence, or would you prefer me say in this now, I also reveal to you eternity that as you become conscious, note I did not say more conscious, you experience to the depth of your soul eternity. Eternity is integral to your soul. It is your inheritance as it were. It, and I hesitate to attempt to define what it means, is my thrust in creating you – to become enlightened and conscious to eternity, become conscious to your soul existence that knows no boundary of space and time.

So you see, the Book of Revelations is there for you now to waken you to the realm of the eternal that is within you. You can't escape it – no way to avoid describing it differently so limited is communication through words – you are eternal. So take heart and soul, not mind, and waken to my message to you this morning. At your deepest level you know what I am saying though it takes instruction to dust off the layers of words, concepts, habits, fears, doubts that obstruct your soul vision.

I am the Alpha and the Omega and in that capacity and with that awesome power I am, I embrace you with my love.

.

Scripture: *On the Lord's Day I was in the Spirit, and I heard behind me a loud voice like a trumpet . . .I turned around to see the voice that was speaking to me. And I turned I saw seven golden lamp stands, and among the lamp stands was someone "like the son of man," dressed in a robe reaching down to his feet and with a golden sash around his chest. His head and hair were white like wool, as white as snow, and his eyes were like blazing fire. His feet were like bronze glowing in a furnace, and his voice was like the sound of rushing waters . . . His face was like the sun shining in all its brilliance. Revelations 1:10-16*

Prayer: Help me not to be distracted by the symbols, but rather be prepared to hear your voice.

Response: Allow the descriptive words to serve to underline the importance of your time alone and in the Spirit. You anticipate my presence and communication. You will never be disappointed. I will speak to you so that my words resonate as the rushing waters that John describes.

John is emphasizing the importance of the message that he is witnessing. Realize that he was not standing or sitting with a pen and paper or scroll in hand. His immediate task was to witness and recall what he was witnessing. You must admit that the imagery presented in these verses lends to total recall, especially since John was not anxious. I would say that one or two readings of these verses would allow you to do likewise; and here you are relying upon words, not events that evoke your imagination.

In the scene painted, clearly this is not an ordinary experience for John. He has not recorded similar events during his extraordinary life. So now, so many years removed, I am asking you to devote your full attention to what is to transpire. This is your prelude. Allow your mind to be still, in fact encourage your mind to be idle and allow my words and the scene that John describes to fully engage your heart. Consider yourself in a darkened theater alone and the curtain is just being pulled open. Standing before you is a worthy and respected individual whom you trust, and to reinforce this scene, I am sitting alongside to provide you insights that you might miss as your mind seeks to become engaged to solve the puzzle presented.

Realize that I tell you over and over again I am not presenting you a puzzle to solve, but rather a mystery to absorb. To the degree that you can be quiet this truth will become clear to you – if mysteries can be clear. And they can be in stillness.

All for today. I encourage you to seek understanding in this book.

#295

Scripture: *On one occasion while he was eating with them, he gave them this command: "Do not leave Jerusalem, but wait for the gift my Father promised, which you have heard me speak about. For John baptized with water, but in a few days you will be baptized with the Holy Spirit." Acts 1:4-5*

Prayer: It is difficult for me to catch the significance between water and the Spirit though I could repeat the answers I received from study.

Response: As you distinguish night and day, distinguish baptism with water and that of the Holy Spirit. As you walk on the beach before sunrise and cannot see clearly without moonlight, you see all when the sun rises.

So it is with water and the Holy Spirit. In baptism with water you were signed with my love, with the Spirit you become conscious of that love in an increasingly responsive manner and participation in that love. Baptized with the Holy Spirit is like being given an inner garment that serves you in all the climates you will encounter on your journey.

The risen Christ commands, yes that is the word used; the disciples to wait until the Spirit descends upon them prior to leaving the sanctuary of Jerusalem for points east, west, north, and south. They are to wait patiently until they receive their inner garment, their provisions, so to speak.

It is interesting that my garment increases its purpose for you as you become more conscious of its presence that is the presence of the Holy Spirit in your life. And realize that the Spirit did not descend upon you to cloth you for a life of inaction regardless as to how *mobile* or well-traveled you are or to become. As an inner garment you bring the Spirit into every venue you might visit, I repeat, every venue. And no need to think that you must shed your outer garments to reveal the inner. No, I would prefer that you reflect upon the Spirit's presence among you in those you encounter later in the quiet of your heart and recognize the fit of each person's inner garment.

.

#296

Scripture: *Suddenly a sound like the blowing of a violent wind came from heaven and filled the whole house where they were sitting. They saw what seemed to be tongues of fire that separated and came to rest on each of them. All of them were filled with the Holy Spirit and began to speak in other tongues as the Spirit enabled them. Acts 2:2-4*

Prayer: I know strong winds and in such winds feel the affect on the upper reaches of my home. Bring these words to more clarity to me since they are almost too familiar.

Response: You, like those gathered in Jerusalem, share one common trait, your attention must be seized from the events that surround your lives. The Spirit's descent is dramatic and the natural effects of the howling winds were apropos the significance of this happening. It is the rolling of the drums, the clash of symbols, or the fireworks display that has you all look up into the sky. So it was and is as the Spirit descends.

You might argue that you don't recall seeing tongues of fire pealing from a flame and resting above your neighbor, but I would think that you can recall an event in your life, events in your life, when you were at a loss for words to describe the clarity and insight you received with little or no warning.

The Spirit touches you all; its flame finds a place above you before searing you with my love. You are branded; but for so many you spend your time wondering about the *scar* and less time realizing how different, even conscious, you are becoming.

Reach across and speak from the heart and you will see that you have discovered the gift of tongues.

Do not, if you can, allow the frequency of reading a verse from scripture, dull you to the extraordinary occurrences that unfold in your life daily.

.

#297

Scripture: *Praise be to the God and Father of our Lord Jesus Christ! In his great mercy he has given us new birth into a living hope through the resurrection of Jesus Christ from the dead. 1 Peter 1:3*

Prayer: My attention lingers on the words *new birth*. Provide me a deeper understanding.

Response: *New birth* holds a special meaning of conversion of spirit. And while you might want to say that the new birth is a onetime event like the birth of a child, understand that I am signifying an event *and* the full maturation of the soul.

New birth is the path you are on now with all its joys and tribulations, with all its reflections and ponderings. This new birth is as fresh to you as a twenty year old as it is for an eighty year old. New birth is present to you this moment and in being present to you offers you daily, moment by moment, new hope.

Living hope pulsates in you and challenges you to shed all doubt, yes, all doubt. And this shedding is made possible in your new and constantly reinvigorated new birth.

And this new hope flows from the resurrection of Jesus Christ from the dead. Again words that you have heard and repeat so often; yet were you to pause sufficiently in silence, you would more appropriately be struck speechless with this reality.

Resurrection from the dead – how to explain the inexplicable? A mystery, you must conclude, but take heart, this mystery is no more inexplicable than your new birth – and that is what you should be focusing your energy on in the grace of Jesus Christ.

.

Scripture: *"The Lord bless you and keep you. The Lord makes his face shine upon you and be gracious to you, the Lord turn his face toward you and give you peace."* Numbers 6:22-26

Prayer: Let these words enfold me in my actions.

Response: Consider this greeting for whomever you encounter even if you would be hesitant to voice the words aloud lest someone think you odd, though odd you become. This blessing, if you catch the essence of my words, will be quite evident on the smile you convey, the peacefulness you promote even under tense conditions.

Requesting in prayer for someone else what you have received is the ultimate emptying that allows me to fill you with my Spirit.

Reflect upon the strength of the words *keep you, shine upon you,* and *be gracious.* And realize that my gift conveyed in your blessing of others is simply not a collection of words that are nice to the ear, rather with me turning my *face toward you* also, you receive from me what you all seek and that is *peace.*

What is peace? Rather than attempt to define peace, understand that peace is evidence that I have helped you find your way to innermost depth where I reside with you in my grace. All the scrambling to find peace and security, and in this blessing you discover that my peace is within you. One could wonder, even question, why all the wandering a field.

So, take seriously your blessing extended to others either verbally or in prayer and intention, and you will discover your own peace especially fashioned for you in your circumstances.

.

Scripture: *He will wipe every tear from their eyes. There will be no more death or mourning or crying or pain, for the old order of things has passed away. Revelations 21:4*

Prayer: On this the fifth anniversary of your wife's death, please reinforce the truth of these words.

Response: Five years, five months, five weeks – do you see that it is not a question of elapsed time, but what you bring with you on the journey unfolding before all of you who have been left to continue your quest. The passing of a loved one serves to help you distinguish what you need for the journey and what can be discarded as too weighty and burdensome.

A passing requires you to make an ascent, that is, the road seems a bit more challenging. You would hardly keep with you all the supplies and encumbrances that you carried earlier into your journey. So a passing reminds you, even requires you, if you are to make the ascent, to lighten your load, or put another way, lighten your load – as in diffusing light and love as you climb.

And what are the encumbrances about which I speak? How about anger, not forgiving, self-centeredness, self-pity, fear, despair, attachment, control, to name just a few – but if I gave you a couple of minutes your list would lengthen accordingly.

In lightening your load after a loss, some of you for the first time have taken seriously your mortality, and isn't that an interesting reflection – one not to be ignored. There is a paradox that as you lighten your encumbrances, you seem to dispense in love much more than you were carrying. Do you remember me talking about the need to empty yourself so that I can fill you? Well, here is proof of that.

So on this anniversary and any remembrance of a grievous loss, celebrate! Yes, celebrate what I send you in love and blessing into a vessel you perceived as empty. You have to do two things: accept your emptiness and accept my bounty.

All for you today in celebration.

#300

Scripture: *Above all, you must understand that no prophecy of Scripture came about by the prophet's own interpretation. For prophecy never had its origin in the will of man, but men spoke from God as they were carried along by the Holy Spirit."* 2 Peter1:20-21

Prayer: I am listening after witnessing an extraordinary sunrise that seemed to move north in its brilliant outburst.

Response: As you cannot alter the course of the planets as they circle the sun, so you can't alter the Spirit as it s rushes like the wind through your life. The Spirit carries you like a kite is carried aloft in a sea breeze. There is not much for you to do but to release your self to travel ever high and in doing so to see your life from that higher perspective.

As you can recall when you resist the flow of the air you find that your flight becomes erratic and if you are not careful results in the kite crashing to the surface. So it is in life. Catch the air currents of my grace and you will experience within a flight of unimagined proportions.

You have within you an inner guidance system, so to speak, that will give you respite when the journey seems disrupted by low energy, illusions and phantoms of the past or future that invade your space. Acknowledging the Spirit you will do well to ride the currents without resisting and in my grace and love.

For today, see the inter-connectedness in all thinks, in all my creation, and in that reflection you will bolt out of the isolation that often leads to the thought that you are on a journey apart, when in fact you are in unison and communion with those around you and afar.

You are *carried along by the Holy Spirit.*

CHAPTER ELEVEN -- AWAKENING

Oh, how I experience from time to time that I am no longer slumbering. And then, just when I delight in this awakening I fall back into slumber ruled by the mind and its control of the illusions of the past and future. Awake I sense the presence of the Holy Spirit, my listening is acute. It is as if the Lord is sitting across my desk, looking at me intensely, speaking in a whisper that I can hear distinctly. My prayer is to be awake . . . that the scales are lifted from my eyes and heart.

Scripture: *But he said to them, "It is I, do not be afraid." Then they were willing to take him into the boat; and immediately the boat reached the shore where they were heading. John 6:20-21*

Prayer: Help me to be willing.

Response: Yes, that is a key phrase – to be willing. Please take to heart those words and the scene that is described in those few words. First, I assure you in life not to be afraid even when you have not prayed to me directly nor have asked for my assistance – as the apostles in the storm tossed boat failed to do. In distress instead of seeking an immediate fix, time spent even a moment in stillness will serve you and you might even hear my assurance as I assured these frightened heart fishermen.

You can always reject my assistance and continue to rush about fruitlessly in life. It is your call, as you might say. However, if you are willing and assist me into your boat, or put another way, open the door because you see I am knocking, then I will come aboard or enter your room, whatever analogy suits you.

Now, I am just not a hungry guest – though I am hungry for your love – I come to support you in your particular situation. As you read in this verse, the results are immediate -- *the boat reached the shore where they were heading.* The verse does not say that the boat was righted and headed toward the shore where they were heading. No, the boat reached the shore. Take this in deeply. *Reached* is a powerful word. No need to report in the next chapter the journey because you know the result of bringing me aboard – you reach your destination.

Now a word about destination – you might not find it was the destination you intended. However, it is the destination you were heading despite all the distractions and detours that you explored. At the deepest level you know where you are heading. All of you must answer in the quiet of your soul. It doesn't matter where you appear to be going, even if you contribute to that impression by your life. Bring me aboard because I tell you who I am and calm you not to be afraid to discover your true heading, and you will discover before long that you have weathered the storm and reached the shore safely.

Read these words of scripture once again and take in their full meaning.

.

Scripture: *"The Spirit gives life; the flesh counts for nothing. The words I have spoken to you are spirit and they are life." John 6:63*

Prayer: I could nod in agreement but then I ask why the body is so important to me – its health, appearance, even weight?

Response: I want you to approach each verse of scripture as well as other wisdom literature, or words spoken, with that same questioning and discrimination.

Clearly, you all understand that without caring for your body you are not able, or perhaps indisposed to hear me; and equally important you are unable to add muscle, yes muscle to my service that needs torch bearers to dispel the darkness. So don't be tempted to remain reclining, listening without action to my pleas for service.

Once you understand what I am saying you should then be able to see that it is the spirit that wafts through your limbs to see the change that I urge you all to make in consciousness.

Jesus spoke with a clarity that is lost when someone takes my word and clothes it in the ego's call for respect and acknowledgement. When you serve selflessly, without concern for how the words or you look, you speak of and through the Spirit – and it is on those occasions that the darkness is dispelled.

So put into the proper perspective concerns of the flesh when they come against the inspiration of the Spirit. And equally don't denigrate the body as it performs under your direction my work.

Now having discussed the body and the spirit, ponder who you are.

All for today.

Scripture: *Then will the eyes of the blind be opened and the ears of the deaf unstopped, then will the lame leap like a deer, and the mute's tongue shout for joy. Water will gush forth in the wilderness and streams in the desert. Isaiah 35:5-6*

Prayer: Help me to comprehend more deeply the joy of which you speak.

Response: It is difficult sometimes for you to let go into the joy described, because even at an early hour you are planning your day and considering the duties that need to be performed. For a moment, however, put yourself in each of the images presented and sense the joy. In doing so, you bring the joy to the surface because it resides within you.

The eyes of the blind – don't look beyond for an image of a blind person. Distraction is your blindness as if you are determining what to avoid in a darkened room such is your dream state. Turn on the lights of your heart and feel the joy of one whose sight is restored, awakened.

The ears of the deaf unstopped – Hear me as I speak to you. There are times my words are shouted to gain your attention. You know the times, especially when an event in your life stops you still, sometimes in wonder, sometimes in grief.

The lame leap like a deer – On your solitary walks reach out and feel the energy coursing in your body, a body fashioned to serve. In acknowledging this surge you discard ponderous thinking and look forward to the next hill.

The mute's tongue shouts for joy -- And here you see praise. Yes, joy is praise. And it is for you to reflect upon the essential elements of your joy.

Water will gush forth in the wilderness and streams in the desert – This is an appropriate image given your walk on the beach just after a thunderous rainstorm. Sense the growth and cleansing that is taking place around you and within. Hear the morning birds that shuddered in their nests but now are joyous.

All the signs are there for you to see and take in, the same that Isaiah sings of. That is a connection for you that transports to a realm free of space and time constraints. And don't miss, please, the foreshadowing of the Christ in these lines; this foreshadowing is not limited to two thousand years ago but is evident for you today, if you will be the blind, deaf, lame, mute that feels the waters rush over.

All for today.

#304

Scripture: *"Whoever believes in me, as the Scripture has said, streams of living water will flow from within him." John 7:38*

Prayer: Help me to see the living water in my life.

Response: This living water of which I speak flows from me and washes over you as if you were a child sitting at the edge of the surf. As a child you will feel the splash and might even close your eyes so much is the glare of the sun and water taken together. What you sometimes, or most times do not comprehend, is that you take these living waters of grace with you and in your day-to-day actions with others and even alone in prayer. Allow the flow to come out of you.

No worry, you see, the source of the water and grace are limitless. In fact like inhaling and exhaling, you will find that the more generously you share the living waters your capacity, if it were air – lung capacity – expands.

Living waters, my grace riding the Holy Spirit, cannot be contained no matter how hard and constricted one might be. So be forewarned, once you drink in the living waters you are changed. There is no turning back, returning to who you were. You are changed and forever, for an eternity.

Sometimes it is difficult for you to realize this truth fully. Every change you experience in the external world is not forever. The most elaborate renovation will need renovation and repair in time. But I am saying to you that reception of the living water changes you forever and only your capacity to drink more of this stream of my love increases in my grace.

So sit by the shore some day and catch the meaning of the images that I have brought to you this morning.

Scripture: *For as the soil makes the sprout come up and a garden causes seeds to grow, so the Sovereign Lord will make righteousness and praise spring up before all nations. Isaiah 62:11*

Prayer: There must be a message here since I finished planting just after dawn.

Response: As you are quick to observe, there are no coincidences. Consider the knees of your jeans still wet and muddy, allowing you to retain the gardening image that I present to you this morning. All your work still waits the sprouting up that you can do nothing to hasten after your toil. And it is a continuing toil. In this simple scene whether it be of a farmer who depends upon his livelihood for the seeds to sprout up, or you gardeners who bring color around and into your home, there is a faith you demonstrate in the process and it goes further than hoping for rain.

The lesson here is to consider the preparation you make, the determination to keep to the process, your belief that indeed the blossoms will burst forth in time – and all this given witness to the mystery of life. So simple. You need no scholarly treatises to describe the process. It stands out for you each day and not only in the earth you till and plant, but in your every day activity.

Consider each day as a day in my garden. Don't be surprised, you shouldn't be, of the hard work and faith I require. Here's a challenge for you —don't even expect that you will be present for the harvest, that is, to see the blossoms. As you cultivate your faith with my grace; your knowing of the fruits that await is as real for you as wandering in a garden at the time of its richness – so great is your faith, and I should add your optimism that is reflected in your every action.

Much is written about righteousness and praise. Another word for both is love. As you grow in consciousness and love so natural to you will become full righteousness and praise. And that is the miracle that awaits you in the garden of your heart.

.

#306

Scripture: *For when I called, no one answered, when I spoke, no one listened. Isaiah 66:4*

Prayer: Bring me to a place where I do not ignore your call – where I listen to you.

Response: Call and speak have two different connotations. Both require you to be conscious and not to make as if you are only hearing the wind or a door closing, or the ambient noise living in a city. Call holds a meaning of urgency, and it is in a call that I urge you into action to serve.

And you can just imagine the diversity of service I call you to. Call is actually doing something about what I instruct you in the many lessons and events of your life. The common reaction – and you all receive my call – is to plug on even harder, unconscious, to your daily routine. Routines are established so you can go about unconscious to the activity performed. Think of your breathing. Another reason I urge you to take a deep breath and to be conscious of it, though I am not encouraging you to go about life simply being conscious of each breath. In my call, I am attempting to roust you from your slumber. I am seeking to see you awakened, yes, even enlightened through my grace.

So listen to my call. I do not get hoarse. But I do urge you not to become accustomed to the call to the point that you ignore the call to service. Even on the top of a mountain the wind ceases. Don't wait for a time when you can no longer distinguish between the howling wind and utter calm. Then you have truly fallen further into sleep.

In speaking, I am instructing you, filling your heart with my word and love. Your listening improves vastly when you respond to my call. You will find that then you can sit in stillness and you are able to hear me both in the howling of the wind – that may be turmoil surrounding you – as well as, equally, in the quiet time of meditation where thoughts of your routine do not interfere and you are totally focused on what I am saying. My teaching surely incorporates service but also and most importantly leads you to a consciousness that you never imagined possible and for which I destined you.

So you see that calling and speaking to you is all for the purpose of waking you from your slumber. No longer will you find yourself repeating the words of others, but will discover the source of your own wisdom with which I have enriched each of you.

.

Scripture: *Show us your unfailing love, O Lord, and grant us your salvation. Psalm 85:7*

Prayer: How many times have I heard the words and repeated as a refrain *grant us your salvation.* Help me this morning catch the essence in a new light.

Response: There are many thoughts and images and words imprinted in your youth that are there for you and to nourish you in your age. This verse is one. What day should not begin with this first praise? Think of a time when you can open your eyes after sleep, perhaps it is still dark, or at least only the gray of the false dawn is showing, and you begin your conscious moment with *Show me your unfailing love, O Lord, this day.* You need go no further in your morning prayer.

Those words of the psalmist are meant for you this very morning and every morning. It becomes your declaration of truth and of my steadfastness in your life. It becomes your call to consciousness after a night of slumber. Those words can serve to be your alarm clock reminding you that it is past time to declare your intention to see what I place before you each and every day.

Grant me your salvation is not, I repeat not tied to the first clause. I show you my unfailing love each moment and it is not tied to your salvation. The *and* connecting the two clauses is most important. In the past it served to unite you to the person leading the service. Now it is meant for your conscious relationship.

And a word about salvation – salvation is you becoming conscious to my love and in doing or becoming conscious every action, thought, dream, relationship reflects and is consistent with that love. So you see, salvation is a manifestation of who you are and becoming. It is your declaration and confidence in the salvation I have declared.
So open the day with that eager curiosity and expectation *Show me your unfailing love* and you will discover salvation in your midst.

.

Scripture: *I consider that our present sufferings are not worth comparing with the glory that will be revealed in us. Romans 8:18*

Prayer: Lord, in this verse please shed your light of understanding on the words *glory that will be revealed in us.*

Response: Almost unnoticed is the glory that will not so much be revealed to you as *in* you. You spend so much time looking for the light outside, and you now have discovered I mean to reveal to you that light.

When you accept this truth for the first time, beyond just nodding at the words, you will experience an enlightenment that surprises you -- intense, marked by simplicity, profound, and offering promise – all at the same time.

Realizing deeply the truth of these words reverberates throughout your whole being once you get it. With this truth there is nothing to threaten your peace – no, not illness, setbacks, even the approach of death.

How is this glory once revealed to you seen by those around you? I smile to tell you that the light cannot be contained in you once revealed. You will find, or better others will see, something quite different and yet something recognizable in the spray of the light crossing their shadow. And so the glory revealed in you prompts others to see the light within each of them in consciousness – there's that word again.

The glory that is revealed can be compared to the balance you feel standing with legs apart or sitting at a desk with your feet firmly planted beneath you. This glory is manifested as a pause – an eternal one – that needs no further declaration or explanation.
So today reach inward for the glory that is becoming manifest and allow the light to be visible in your life today.

#309

Scripture: *To one there is given through the Spirit the message of wisdom, to another the message of knowledge by means of the same Spirit, to another faith by the same Spirit, to another the gifts of healing by that one Spirit, to another miraculous powers, to another prophesy, to another distinguishing between spirits, to another speaking in different kinds of tongues, and to still another the interpretation of tongues. All these are the work of one and the same Spirit, and he gives them to each one, just as he determines."* 1Corinthians 12:8-9

Prayer: Here is another example of words with which I am familiar, yet I know that the essential meaning I sometimes take for granted. Help me to grasp the deeper meaning.

Response: Surely, you catch that these two verses outline a range of influences that the Spirit has on you all as you work your way on the path. And please do not attempt to limit the Spirit's influence by categorizing each of the gifts mentioned and believe that those gifts are representative of the whole. Think of the Spirit's influence as evidence that the Spirit each day prods you to pray, to praise, to awaken; and even provides at times the holy groans that read your heart when you are simply unable to articulate the prayer so deeply felt.

Also, do you best not to look around and say that one has this gift and the other that. The verses are to indicate to you the influence the Spirit has in your life as if a flavor added to what you might consider in yourself a bland liquid or one that needs to be invigorated. If you must, the Spirit adds flavor and carbonation to you when you are flat and stale.

However, I do want you to consider the range of gifts that are shed on you in various degrees *as the Spirit determines.* Again, don't try to figure out why he or she and not me, or why me and not he or she. It is a fruitless exercise, especially since you are attempting in that effort to comprehend with your limited mind – and no insult here – a mystery. You would do better to cultivate a spirit of thanksgiving in your heart for whatever gift or gifts you receive, and as I said above don't limit it to the gifts mentioned above. They are not, repeat not, all conclusive. For example, a mighty gift not specifically mentioned above is the gift of selfless service.

Take these gifts of evidence of the Spirit's presence and interaction in your life. Don't worry about anyone else. If you can recognize a gift within you – and you each should be able to do so – put aside false modesty – take as witness that you as well as others have been singled out. Do not consider these gifts exclusive or meant for few. Few or many, if you are focusing on your own gifts, that is more than sufficient to own the gift and to use the gift in appreciation for the grace showered on you.

Finally, these gifts serve to awaken you from your slumber. It is as if the Spirit is moving about you and slapping you awake with the gift that serves as the Spirit's rod.

Scripture: *"And afterward, I will pour out my Spirit on all people. Your sons and daughters will prophesy, your old men will dream dreams, your young men will see visions." Joel 2:28*

Prayer: Dreams, visions, what's the difference? As with so much of what I read, the words are easy to understand, but the meaning sometimes escapes me.

Response: Don't try so hard to distinguish in your mind vision from dream. As you accept your age and what you have gathered along this journey you have been on, see in your heart that dreams represent stillness where you are witness to all that is unfolding. And it is with dreams that you are peaceful, even defenseless, accepting, and vulnerable. Yet in this state you are stronger than you realize in your vulnerability.

For those that are *young*, visions are the action scenes presented and form almost as plans to bring about change. In visioning you take an active part in creating a future. In dreams you accept what is unfolding in an active manner, if that can make sense to you. There is nothing passive about dreams, but rather it is your active acceptance and surrender to my plans for you that fulfill your mission in life to serve.

Both visions and dreams have a harmony that bring to the fore what in visions you are to do and in dreams what you are to be.

In dreams you reach a place in your heart where you acknowledge my presence. In dreams, now listen carefully, you awake. That is another paradox within which meaning is buried or hidden from those who cannot yet sit still in my grace.

So let me say again, in dreams you awake. And please don't miss it is in the pouring out of the Spirit on all of you that you both have visions and dream.

.

Scripture: *All the believers were together and had everything in common. Selling their possessions and goods, they gave to anyone who had need. Acts 2:44-45*

Prayer: Lord, I read these words and can't help but think of economic and political systems that are defunct. Help me to focus on the words: *they gave to anyone who had need.*

Response: There you have it. Contained in those words is your call to service. And don't limit your call to food and shelter. Include, notice I did not say that this is an either/or call, food for the spirit.

Give a wider interpretation to *selling their possessions and goods.* You are asked to share not only your food to those who hunger in the body, but to share your message with those who hunger in the spirit, which I am sure you realize is as ravaging, even more so because that feeling of despair ravages the spirit more than the lack of food and sustenance.

So these words are not meant to make you feel guilty that you are not living in a commune. Rather I am calling you to display in action a generosity of spirit in service. Service to whom, you might ask? Service to the person who comes, maybe even stumbles, across your path, who might be quite well dressed and fed, but hungers for the word you might be able to provide; service in prayer for those in agony and sorrow scattered across the globe who have experienced deep loss; those in your midst whom you recognize by sight but not by the circumstances of their life. Be like the antenna with your alertness to catch – that is to listen to – the subtle signals, the faint signals of someone who has lost the power, if ever it was displayed, to shout a spirit need.

Selling your possessions, if you have missed it, refers much more than material goods. Selling your possessions means moving out behind the costume you wear to minister to those in need. It means revealing who you are and becoming without any regard as to what "people" say. Do I have to remind you that in appearing to the world as powerless you assume a mantle of power that you might never have envisioned?

Service is not forcing oneself on another in need. Most of all it is listening and discerning – a word that captures that pause and conclusion – where the need is, and how to provide or contribute to satisfying that need generously. You would not have to go far to find examples of what I am referring with only a brief scan of your news that reports on real and perceived needs daily.

So approach the unfolding day in a *listening* mode tied to a commitment to serve in whatever capacity needed. Notice, I did not say in whatever capacity you have time for. Ponder this line, but do so free of guilt. Look at the opportunities in both prayer and action which you can contribute. Finally, do not consider your family and those in your immediate community not worthy of your careful attention. Doing so and being so, you will find that you too live holding everything in common.

Scripture: *"For we cannot help speaking about what we have seen and heard." Acts 4:20*

Prayer: Help me to accept what I have seen and heard.

Response: How often do you attribute my hand in your life as mere coincidence? It is almost as if you fear that you will trick yourself into belief, if you were to see the intimate connection we share daily. What I propose to you is to accept a three-step process.

First be awake to what is happening in your life – everything from health issues, to financial strains or surplus, to relationships and to those who happen upon your scene, to the weather, to everything that living in this world entails – all the experiences. But do this from the vantage point of the present, not burdened by what you can recall from yesterday or even years past.

Next, be alert, some would say be awake, to those instances or incidents that catch your heightened awareness or attention because you say to yourself – *isn't that interesting*, or *what a coincidence*. And a coincidence is not always something you might consider positive. Realize in this exercise there is no positive or negative.

The third step is to leap across your doubt and cynicism and see my hand, or better my presence. No, there is not a set script for each of you, so give up assuming that I will mouth the words for the play in which you perceive you are performing. It your actions that determine the outcome of this production, or better it is you who are progressing along the path – to use another analogy – though I will whisper a word if you are stuck or provide drink to slack your thirst along the way.

What I am asking you to do is to figuratively kneel in my garden and look down at the rich earth, quietly, and in silence. Focus easily and see all that is happening just before your eyes. See the blood worms aerating the soil, the first seeds germinating, the moisture in droplets that seems to have a life of its own, smell the breeze filled with the odor of spring, sense the movement of the birds eager to discover what awaits them in the ground. And see yourself in the midst of this scene as you are in the midst of my creation.

Now when you have knelt long enough observing, not disturbing, see my connection to you in all, I repeat all aspects of your life, and give thanks, not because I need praise, but to allow yourself to witness my love for especially and specially – each day. Then, what can keep you from speaking all you have seen and heard?

.

Scripture: *"I revealed myself to those who did not ask for me; I was found by those who did not seek me. To a nation that did not call on my name, I said, 'Here am I, here am I.'"* Isaiah 65:1

Prayer: So much for me thinking at times that I found you!

Response: My love is discovered when you realize that it is spontaneous and without any merit on your part. You have many examples that point to this love around you. Remember I said point. It is for you to be reminded of the depth of my love when you see such signs in the love that a parent has for its child though the child has done nothing to merit it, In fact, often times quite the contrary is true.

Do not dwell, however, on the merit aspect of this connection to me, rather see in surprise my presence in your life precisely when you do not expect it; or more accurately you are so distracted by one crisis or another that you are not focused or still sufficiently to see me until it seems I trip you into quiet and you say "aha!"

This verse speaks to you today of my determination to find you in your circumstances. It doesn't matter where you are, how burdened or successful in the world's eyes you are, I will reveal myself to you so that you have difficulty turning away without recognizing my presence in your life. You don't even have to admit it to anyone else, simply know it in the depth of your heart.

Think of a treasure hunt with no idea of what the treasure will be and discovering all the while that you carried the treasure in your heart. It's like biting into a sandwich and discovering a note from your beloved.—that's me – who prepared the sandwich.

Feel the relief that you don't have to pore over documents in a library, or search across continents, or engage wise men in conversation – all you have to do is see how I reveal myself to you especially, even though you had not previously called to me.

.

#314

Scripture: *Break up your unplowed ground and do not sow among the thorns. Jeremiah 4:3*

Prayer: Is it my planting this spring that draws me to this verse? Provide me a deeper insight.

Response: Here I am encouraging you to discover what is unfolding and to be satisfied, declining to churn over in your mind what is of the past. Look at your life this day as an open field that needs turning, breaking up: it needs your touch. Wisely, you have identified what brings pain, even the memory of pain. I am offering you this and every day a new start.

Clearly, I am not suggesting that there is no work, effort in the project of today. The words *break up* suggests that you experience the hard labor and even strain. I will bring you relief. And once you start there is no stopping. Your field, that has been up until now unturned, is to be ploughed. Catch the excitement and the discovery that awaits you.

 And yes there is a time dimension. You are invited to plough the field and plant before the rains come. The rains also represent all the distractions that seek to encourage you to delay or avoid the challenge. I want you to greet the rains – even if they appear to be setbacks. Focus again on the surprise, the bounty that awaits you.

And about the thorns, you can understand that working among them will only remind you of the pain you suffered in the past and in doing so you lose your perspective of the present. The thorns also represent not only pain, but delay as you become engulfed among them.

Notice that in this verse I do not talk about the harvest. That will come. For the moment I want your total attention on the task at hand that begins in silence as your eyes scan over the unplowed ground, the dark earth, with all its treasures ready to be released.

.

Scripture: *For three days he was blind, and did not eat or drink anything. Acts 9:9*

Prayer: This verse is also familiar, almost too familiar, to discover a deeper meaning.

Response: The essential meaning is that Saul was required by his temporary incapacitation to be still. And note he did not know it was only to be for three days. I say this only because in retrospect you can dismiss the challenge that he faced.

If you are able, take every moment, even when you are thrashing about, to be still and listen. The dramatic circumstances of Saul's blinding and his anger, perhaps it was fear, that brought him on the road to Damascus, gave him much to consider. More importantly, his anger and fear had to subside and only then he could regain control of who he was with what turned out to be, in retrospect, a temporary blindness.

It is good to contemplate such circumstances in your own life though I am not suggesting that you stage such an event. Right not you can be "blind" to what troubles or distracts you – right now in this moment. And you can also exhibit a patience of soul by not jumping up to make a pot of coffee. Simply stay in the silence of the predawn and listen with a fullness that does not allow distractions to intrude.

You can see from the perspective of history what these three days meant to Saul, soon to be baptized Paul. Now, put history aside, and embrace the stillness that I offer with no thought of what you will accomplish or even if there is a next moment. Discover in blindness and stillness your identity and allow that identify to unfold in your purpose. So simple.

I ask you today not to dwell in the historical perspective of this verse, that is, who was it, what did he do later, what are the results today, but rather who are you, what are you doing today?

.

#316

Scripture: *When the proconsul saw what had happened, he believed, for he was amazed about the teaching of the Lord. Acts 13:12*

Prayer: A snapshot scene. Lead me to a greater wisdom.

Response: Critical for this verse is the word "saw." And that is what I encourage you to do look around you – at events in your life each day. Seek to develop a discriminating sight that catches the uniqueness of life and the manifestations of my love. Don't tread along assuming that nothing relates to you.

Consider this proconsul – and you are surrounded by proconsuls. If the truth be known, you are a proconsul. Another word could be special. You are special, though you are much more willing or inclined to observe someone else's favor. So at least for this day see yourself as special.

Next, catch the light that flickers within you and takes the form of recognition of my presence. The proconsul looked closely at what others would dismiss as madness. With courage he accepted first for himself and then aloud that the occurrences witnessed were out of the ordinary and he believed.

Those out-of-the-ordinary events did not cease two thousand years ago or earlier. They are your every day experiences. All it takes for you to see and not assume. You will find when you dismiss assumptions your life will be filled with surprise – even if some believe that there has been sufficient surprise in their lives in the form of unexpected consequences.

You are the proconsul and are asked to widen your glance, increase your peripheral vision, and in this example direct your light beyond the individual concerns you might be inclined to indulge yourself. Then, seeing almost with new eyes, I ask you to confirm, believe, and serve. Again, quite simple, requiring first and foremost keen sight to observe what is occurring on your path.

So for today, no assumptions, please. See as if your sight was restored and it is.

#317

Scripture: *But if I say, "I will not mention him or speak any more in his name," his word is in my heart like a fire, a fire shut up in my bones. I am weary of holding it in; indeed, I cannot.* Jeremiah 20:9

Prayer: I cannot recall ever reading *a fire shut up in my bones*. Help me to understand more deeply your meaning.

Response: First be prepared to have a phrase or word in scripture strike you especially one morning, though you might have come across the words previously. *A fire shut up* in your bones seeks to give expression to the divine spark that is within you, though there are times when you would seek to deny or ignore the significance of this revelation.

The essential message contained in this phrase is not really a mystery unveiled. When you are quiet, I mean soul-quiet, you realize quite clearly what I am saying. Your only difficulty is attaining that soul-quiet state when you cast aside all thought of "what would others think," if I make bold to penetrate this truth on my own.

And notice I say that my words are shut up in your bones. Think or reflect on that image – fire shut up in bone matter. What a contradiction or rather paradox. The fire you would think would consume the bones, but no, it allows, yes that is the word allows its flame to be contained in the bone matter.

It is for you to release that flame, that light, that love in your material surroundings. And here the paradox or contradiction continues, because once you release the flame you will contribute to the consummation of the material in my love.

You did not think this morning that just a phrase would lead to the conflagration of which I speak. But yes, it does and this conflagration sears away the fear and anger and hatred that up until now consumes so much of your environment.

So this morning I ask you first, to be still and feel that flame within your bones, recognize it, honor it; next, in prayer, reflection, and action release the flame into your environment. In doing so, you will discover that others will be encouraged to do likewise and what started as individual fires will spread for all to see even in the night.

.

Scripture: *Every gift and perfect gift is from above, coming down from the Father of the heavenly lights, who does not change like shifting shadows. James 1:17*

Prayer: Give me a deeper understanding of your constancy.

Response: That image is well chosen because it describes to you not only my constancy but also that I am right over you. And I remain with you and within you. There are no *shifting shadows* with which to contend or anticipate. Said another way, there is no interference in my signal to you though your life can create the static or noise that prevents you from hearing me directly. Indeed, it is your choice to turn your attention elsewhere, but I see a most constant and consistent return to the station I have set within you.

Shifting shadows also connotes unchanging. By this I do not mean or wish you to think that there is no growth allowed you or that my message is pre-canned. If you can put aside linear thinking, put aside time and space dimension which you experience, and consider that what appears to you unchanging – those heavenly lights without shifting shadows – is actually a portal to eternity that you experience now.

Think of the exhilaration of sweeping down a mountain glacier with no thought of falling or sweeping over the side of the mountain. In that experience you would no longer be concerned with every blade of ice before you, but rather you would see for the first time, you would have the capacity to take in the whole scene, without boundaries forced upon you by speed, space, and time.

So I encourage you to see that you are covered in a sense, in a real sense with my grace which is un-shifting to the light that seeks to lead you to the exhilaration of my love. And the paradox, there are so many used to confound your mind so you will be still, is that you speed down the glacier in my love when you are still, quiet, reflective, and in an ease of heart.

You would have probably chosen to have me be clearer – or perhaps not so clear – in my imagery and parables and stories and your life experiences, but then you would not have been able to acknowledge growth and even enlightenment in my love in the heavenly light that shines without any shifting shadows.

Scripture: *O God, you are my God, earnestly I seek you; my soul thirsts for you, my body longs for you in a dry and weary land where there is no water. Psalm 63:1*

Prayer: Cultivate in me that thirst that prods me to continue to search beyond a dry and weary land.

Response: One might think that I should be cultivating your taste for a fine wine, but then again I might be. You see by inspiring you, I am instilling in you a discrimination of sorts to recognize me and not to resign yourself to a dry and weary land.

Picture yourself about to give up but you recall the sound of a mountain stream, gurgling over rocks as it makes its way to the sea from the highest altitude. You can even recall the cooling and quenching taste of that experience. It is with that recollection that you stand up and continue through the dry and weary land. That recollection is my grace that urges you onward along the path.

Spend some time recalling in your life instances when you experienced the surprise of coming upon that mountain stream and the refreshment it offered even if you had never visited a mountain clime. The stream might be a chance encounter with a friend or a stranger, a visit to a bookstore and discovering a treasure just before you, hearing a musical score for the first time that enraptures you, smelling a flavor from a kitchen that recalls for you a celebration, hearing laughter from an unseen corner and recalling your own laughter.

Your thirst and longing are evidence that I surely touched you, that I beckoned and beckon you, and that I encourage you with all the signs that surround and intersect in your life daily. My presence found in those signs is there to accompany you, to sustain you, to encourage you in whatever and whenever you find yourself in a dry and weary land of your life. You will discover that your stays in such weariness become brief as you move further on the path of your life.

.

Scripture: *He said to them: "Therefore every teacher of the law who has been instructed about the kingdom of heaven is like the owner of a house who brings out of his storeroom new treasures as well as old." Mathew 13:52*

Prayer: Tell me about the storehouse and the new and old treasures.

Response: There is more to this verse than you see on first or second reading. You are instructed about the kingdom of heaven, though there are times when you might conclude that you were dozing at the time of instruction. And you are the owner of your house, that is, the temple – your body that allows you to navigate through these life experiences and lessons.

Recall a time that you had reason to investigate what was stored in a closet that was so full you avoided even opening the door. Well, imagine what you might have access to with all the gems of wisdom you have gained either as a gift from someone or from your own diligence. And even if you can't come up with an example, consider how you can access what resides untouched in that storeroom – if only you would open the door and investigate.

The treasures are much more than things to grasp or to hold. The treasures are living and spring to life – it seems – as soon as you glance upon them. In fact, you will find that once you acknowledge the truth contained in a treasure, the treasure is not external to you. You are in union. It might come as a surprise but you are in union, and yet with so many treasures you seem to roam aimlessly around and through the corridors of your heart because you are distracted by what is truly transitory and external to you.

The treasures within your storehouse are all, I repeat all, you require for your journey, the journey you are on right now though this might have even escaped you. New and old denotes a timelessness that I wish you to grasp. Old and new, new and old represent a cycle of nourishment and renewal. See this storehouse as the endless resource I provide you to meet every challenge you encounter. There is nothing awaiting you today for which I did not prepare you. Imagine me as the person you approach in planning your trip into an unknown land. I am the master logistician. You have access to all you need to endure successfully and flourish on the path. And what's more, through my grace I remind you of my presence and availability to sustain you.

And see me also this morning as the co-owner of the house who is ever eager to reveal to you treasures new and old that you have overlooked, and in the revelation you come to know the treasure as your own.

Scripture: *How priceless is your unfailing love! Both high and low among men find refuge in the shadow of your wings. Psalm 36:7*

Prayer: Help me to confound the truth of your protection.

Response: First, it is important for you to accept that the protection offered to you is that of a winged raptor, and not a pigeon nesting. See in this image fledglings are trying out flight for the first time. I want you to catch the boldness in this image and not consider yourself cowering in fear.

Next, I want you to sense the exhilaration of flight -- flight – allowing the wind to thrust you on a thermal and yet learning to control with your wings and the shift of your body flight above the clouds of your doubt.

In the shadow of my wings is intended to remind you that I am above you shielding you from all danger. That is not to say that you will not know danger, especially the danger of discouragement, or worse listlessness, sloth.

By refuge, you are to realize that if you wander off too far, scurry back quickly when you sense danger. You see, in flight you are also encouraged to use your senses to anticipate, foretell danger and to make wise decisions, namely to return to the shadow of my wings.
The shadow describes peacefulness, a knowing that all is well in my love.

So today consider the breadth of my love and protection and what awaits you if you climb in flight sufficiently.

#322

Scripture: *Within your temple, O God, we meditate on your unfailing love. Psalm 48:9*

Prayer: Let me do so in my life.

Response: Consider today that the temple I refer to is your body that carries you through each day. There is no need, in fact I would have you not reserve your prayers for a building, but you know that already. The importance in considering your place of worship to be your body is that I urge you to pray constantly. I am not suggesting that you go around as a zombie uttering prayers. Rather I ask you to maintain steady and ready access to me throughout the day.

Think of how you breathe and perform functions automatically. Well, in the instance of prayer and meditation, incorporate your life in the spirit into your conscious activity; and allow what you consider the important tasks of your life like meeting the challenges of the day to your unconscious life.

I am not looking to disrupt your life, but rather fix within you a guidance system that handles what you have considered the most important elements of your life, so that you can cherish, cultivate, and nourish the life of the spirit. What does this mean practically, you ask? It means developing routines to give your full attention to matters of the spirit. It might mean taking a period of time – you decide whether it is one minute, five, or longer, when you are fully attentive to the spirit within you. I am not suggesting that you have to be apart, or that you maintain a glazed look in your eyes. It is the consciousness that I am calling you to. Think of your alertness when you are in a darkened area and are trying to distinguish a sound. That is the sort of consciousness I am seeking for you to develop, to which to attune your sensibilities.

Now once in that consciousness, meditate, focus on the theme of this lesson, my unfailing love for you. Repeat the word unfailing because, as they say, much of the time the word is lost in translation, your translation. Unfailing love, you should repeat whenever a doubt creeps in. Why unfailing, you ask? Do I have to justify my love? Surely, you respect my power, the power of my love, to provide this love in a morning shower that might resemble for you monsoon season in India.

For today and ever after, keep the words unfailing love at the very tip of your tongue. Whisper it, shout it if you must – not on a city street and have people consider you mad. Though I must say, once you fully receive the significance of my meaning you will be considered mad by those who still churn about like robots in their daily activity.

Let me end with these words – Be conscious to my unfailing love. Awake.

383

#323

Scripture: *When you send your Spirit, they are created, and you renew the face of the earth.* Psalm 104:30

Prayer: In the recesses of my mind, I remember this verse from my youth. Bring your full meaning to me this morning.

Respond: The significance of this verse is the dispatch of the Spirit. And it is through the Spirit that the face of the earth is renewed. You are the face of the world, so it is your renewal upon which the world is restored. It is through your work guided by the Spirit that the face of the earth is renewed.

Spend a moment reflecting upon what renewal means. See renewal as not the return to old habits and rigidity but as a luster that reflects my light, like dawn, in all your activity and for all to see.

Renewal is the rediscovery of your authentic self and of authenticity in all your actions. In renewing the face of the earth means that you pause before an action or plan and ponder the consequences of your action, or better how your action contributes to the renewal.

And your action is not the world shaking events, alliances, and activities of international forums. No, I am speaking about a renewal that begins alongside of those you love. I am speaking of setting a conflagration of the heart that sears away the dense foliage and allows the planting of this crop that will bear abundance of the Spirit in all your works, aspirations, and relationships.

And remember that the *they* – of *they are created* – is you. Yes, you are created in my image and in my image you renew the face of the earth.

.

Scripture: *"The kingdom of heaven is like treasure hidden in a field. When a man found it, he hid it again and then in his joy went and sold all he had and bought that field."* Matthew 13:44

Prayer: Again with this verse, I have heard it quoted so many times. Please enlighten me to its deeper meaning.

Response: First, note that the verse does not say *a treasure* but *treasure*. Treasure encourages your imagination to expand beyond the limits of the mind. In fact, I ask you to conceive of treasure without space boundaries, without material value, and without the limitation of time.

You see, the treasure of which this verse describes is one of eternity, and, this is where you must suspend the insistence of your mind to give precise definition, because the treasure of which I speak is abundant beyond description and is within your grasp – it is within you.

If this is beyond your comprehension this moment, you have not spent sufficient time exploring the field in which you are wandering. And that field is surely the environment in which you live, those with whom you are in relationship and those farther afield – like those for whom you pray. The treasure is in the field on which you tread and my advice is to sell all that will tarnish and disintegrate through age and use, and purchase the field filled with treasure that is within you.

Experience in a quiet moment the joy that awaits your discovery. See yourself walking across this field, filled with wonder you are. And notice that this field is available to you but at a price. So as you explored for treasure, now consider the price to be paid. Yes, the field can be purchased, though it will take your sacrifice to accomplish the sale. And the sale price is set as if on a billboard set at the edge of the field – For Sale – All You Have – All You Are!

But consider what a bargain this field – the kingdom of heaven – is who would not offer all material possessions and pursuits to acquire this treasure? Are you sure?

Scripture: *In your distress you called and I rescued you, I answered you out of a thundercloud; I tested you at the waters of Meribah. Psalm 81:7*

Prayer: Speak to me of thunderclouds.

Response: First let me speak of distress. Without distress you would not pause and gain or seek nourishment. You are like the long distance runner who is maintaining a pace and discards the notion that he needs nourishment, especially water, to continue.

Keeping with this image, look around you as you move along the path and spot opportunities to refresh yourself. Remember, it is not the destination as much as the journey you are on. To avoid the nourishment and sustenance, you risk the destination.

So when you are almost overcome with fatigue, look around for the way station. It might be a book, some music, a friend, a landscape, or simply time when nothing is to be scheduled. This becomes your time and space to be nourished as you know the journey waits.

I do rescue you even when you seem to be unconscious to my presence. Sometimes the rescue is not something you would have chosen, but you must agree when you are quiet that the event or experience or even calamity served my purpose. You paused in your grief, in your loss, in your distress and you were comforted, sustained, and nourished.

You see distress does serve a purpose. It is like the alarm that announces that it is time to awake, to look about, to feel my presence that you will be surprised is always near.

How I answer you is in the surprises that await you. There would be less surprise if you were more conscious. You will discover that my surprises become a bit more subtle as your consciousness expands – like improving your ear to catch the nuances of symphony or better the flavor hidden in a special dish. So if you find that your taste for life is not much different than it was years ago, it means that you have to spend more time in silence.

And I do test you. Not for my purpose, but for you to see, to experience the *a-hah* moment of wonder and confirmation. Confirmation of what, you ask? That is what I want you to ponder this day.

.

Scripture: *In repentance and rest is your salvation, in quietness and trust is your strength, but you would have none of it. Isaiah 30:15*

Prayer: I am listening this morning for your words.

Response: Repentance and salvation are linked, despite your wish to ignore a need for correction. I have been using of late the word "awake" in my lessons. Repentance is actually a very natural experience and it begins with becoming conscious. It is what happens when you judge someone for an action, even if you say nothing to that person or even anyone else but nurture the apparent grievance in your heart. And then you discover the circumstances, or the true intent of the individual, and you realize for the first time how incorrect were you in your judgment.

You follow a path, defend a practice, and then discover your true intent hidden in an external flurry of movement. As you repent, feel the deep sorrow for your action or inaction. You are awake and conscious to your true intentions, and seek to correct – as in a course correction – your life or direction. I would say that once you become conscious there is no way to avoid repentance. The opposite is also true – if you do not feel repentance, you have still not awakened to your circumstances, to my love and salvation. Of course, you have the power to remain in slumber.

In quietness and trust is your strength. This should become for you another mantra when you are tempted to react to circumstances of your life without fully understanding what is happening. Think of the solid mountain standing amidst the fury of a storm. Quiet – not tense – allowing the storm to rage, always trusting that the winds, pelting rain, and lightning will all cease as the morning dawn in the first light of a sunrise. Apply this source of strength in your daily life when the uncertainty of a future encourages consciousness.

Until you wake, I will observe that the wisdom and grace I provide you will go unnoticed or ignored. With my grace, I assure you that your period of repose is coming to an end and you will grasp as if for the first time the aliveness in spirit that you have squandered up until now. And in this awareness you will repent deeply and sincerely.

.

Scripture: *"I'm going out to fish," Simon Peter told them, and they said, "We'll go with you." So they went out and got into the boat, but that night they caught nothing. John 21:3 He said, "Throw your net on the right side of the boat and you will find some." When they did, they were unable to haul the net in because of the large number of fish. John 21:6*

Prayer: Speak to me of the deeper meaning of these two verses.

Response: Yes, these verses are not all about fishing. First, see that the manifestation of my love is prompted by action. Peter said, "I am going out fishing." This was not a hobby but how they earned money to live. Action! And his followers, his friends, his colleagues, said that they would go with him. You can almost hear their sandaled feet on the beach dragging their boat into the water. At such times there was not much time to reflect upon. Though their inner spirit was calm at the moment of hauling the boat to the water's edge, grabbing the oars, filling the boat with the net, they were performing actions which occupied their lives from dawn to dusk and into the night.

Then they row a hundred yards out and drop the net and wait, and wait and wait. They sense that if there is a catch it is not much. Some even wonder why they acted on the spur of the moment to accompany Peter. Their fears are confirmed when they raise the net and observe nothing in the net.

And they hear the unsolicited advice of someone standing on the shore – far enough off that they are not sure who it is in the dark – but his words of authority and direction and their own frustration at not hauling in any fish causes them to comply. They are astounded at the catch that follows and recognize in that instant who is calling from the shore.

So in these two verses you are being exhorted, yes, exhorted to act, not precipitously but within the range of your experience, within the community you operate, and trust in faith, await with hope my manifestation in your lives. I am not saying that your experience and your environment will not expand. Who knows you might find yourself confidently fishing, so to speak, in deep water many, many yards from shore.

What does not change, or should not change, is your expectation; put another way, your hope. And that is what distinguishes you in my grace. Life is deciding to go fishing, hauling the dead weight of an oversized vessel to the water, rowing out sufficiently, dropping your nets, and waiting and hoping, and all this in the dark, and of course, awaiting further direction. Incidentally, the direction is always in communion with my love for you. If you hear direction that is not, then of course it is not from me and might even be the clamoring of an anxious mind. Note: I did not say heart.

So that is . A very important fishing lesson for even those who think they live far from the sea.

Scripture: *"Therefore, do not worry about tomorrow, for tomorrow will worry about itself. Each day has enough trouble of its own." Matthew 6:34*

Prayer: Help me to keep present and not drift off.

Response: Isn't it amazing how complicated you make your life. Catch the rhythm of the day; really catch it. The darkness cedes to the light and the light eases into darkness and the cycle is repeated. That is basic. To give a bit more detail, the night softens to a gray dawn and most days a brilliant sunrise awaits those who can get up on tiptoes that early, and from that the full light and activity occupies you until you slow down to accept the darkness and repose.

Where anxiety enters is when you weigh inordinate options for the day's activities, splitting moments and activities in your mind, stirring a dialogue among seeming ghosts who clamor for your time and attention. At such times, or even in that agitated stream of activity, go back to a simple description: the darkness ceding to the influence of the light and the light giving way to rest in darkness.
Take this flow or cycle into your normal day and see how it can influence you so that you are more in control and less reacting to those ghosts that flow in and out of your field of vision seeking to divert your serenity of spirit.

You will discover, if you haven't already, that this rhythm once adopted provides you a calmness of the heart that promotes your attention on what is important for this moment and you will also discover that you listen with more attention to the murmurings of your heart. It is in your heart that you discover that passion that I nourish when you are still. Ah, at such moments – you will find that your attention span expands; you will hear me and feel my pulse through all your surroundings.

Scripture: *You have made known to me the path of life; you fill me with joy in your presence, with eternal pleasures at your right hand. Psalm 16:11*

Prayer: Lord, guide my reflection this morning.

Response: The path, you have come to realize, is distinct, unique for each of you. There is a quality about it that you all experience and that is the joy that I shower on you when you let go, release your expectations and accept fully the love that I shower on you. In the letting go, you clearly are present and aware of my presence. There is no circumstance in your life that can thwart this experience of joy. Rather than attempt to challenge this statement by reviewing past events and crises, might I suggest that you simply accept the statement on face value, beginning with this moment?

Put aside, relinquish the hold of all the tasks that lay before you this day – I didn't not say ignore them as not worthy of accomplishment – rather I said relinquish the hold, the distraction each represents. And for this moment, be in my presence consciously. It is as if you are entering a protective dome of light – golden light – and there everything is revealed as to each circumstance's significance. You will find there the wisdom to distinguish the intricacies of seemingly insolvable issues related to your life.

Conscious in my presence, you experience a joy that exceeds any expectations that you might have nourished earlier. But conscious you must be, though accept that I never leave your side. This joy breaks through whatever time considerations that you generally associate with time and time constraints. And that joy, even if you can remain awake intermittently, is a hint of the eternal pleasure and joy that await you when you are fully conscious to my love. In the midst of the turmoil of your life, snatch awake this joy.

Scripture: *Be strong and courageous. Do not be afraid or terrified because of them, for the Lord your God goes with you; he will never leave you or forsake you. Deuteronomy 31:6*

Prayer: Tell me more *of them.* Who are they?

Response: Good question. For each there is a different shadow to haunt you. For some it is illness, finances, relationship, job, age, frustration, responsibility, or anxiety; for some it is a real enemy bent on your destruction as it was for the Israelites. Each shadow has the capacity to freeze you in your steps, interfere with the free flow with which I grace you; have you looking over your shoulder in fear or nodding off into slumber to escape.

And then like someone swinging a wooden hammer against a huge brass gong, I announce my presence – not my arrival – for I have never left. For those who sought solace in unconsciousness, you are jolted awake; for those looking back, your attention is riveted forward, and, yes, those who seemed paralyzed with fear, you feel the blood resuming its easy flow through your veins to supply your heart.

Repeat these last lines of the verse whenever you are so disturbed – *for the Lord your God goes with you; he will never leave you or forsake you.* Now for at least this day, apply the promise to your life even if the circumstances are not quite as dramatic – or maybe they are – as what Moses or Joshua was referring.

.

CHAPTER TWELVE -- LOVE

What an incredible power – the power of love. It's impossible to say where it resides. Love is other-worldly; wealth, health, learning, stature do not guarantee its presence. In fact, those very elements might inhibit its growth and unfolding.

Love is the desire to know and become known. In Scripture this is the constant theme – God's desire to be known by his people. He reveals himself in the burning bush to Moses, through the words of an angel who appears to Mary, as a stranger who joins the two disciples on their way to Emmaus, and in the flash of light that strikes Saul from his horse.

He is known in his compassion, sacrifice, commitment, humor, anger, focus, loyalty, patience and so much more, and ironically we too are known by the same soul elements that we cultivate in his grace.

For our part, we learn love as we become conscious and share our inmost aspirations and concerns with someone who seeks to know us as to be known whether it be as spouse, parent, child, friend, colleague, stranger, or even enemy. In risking the revelation of our authentic selves, we have the opportunity to stimulate a desire to know others.

Each morning I discover this theme of love present in the words of Scripture, encouraging me in my goal to be known by God as I seek union with Him. He, after all, is Love.

#331

Scripture: *Perseverance must finish its work so that you may be mature and complete, not lacking anything. James 1:4*

Prayer: There are times – perhaps most times – that I become impatient for perseverance to finish its work. Guide me this morning.

Response: Maybe it's not perseverance that is your challenge but the patience to await the results. Isn't the experience of life like a race on a river that you have never raced on previously? Once you settle down, because you don't know how long the race is, as there are no familiar markers to gauge your progress, you lengthen your strokes and concentrate on each single stroke -- the single act of rowing. You are focused in the present and, if I might say, you are relaxed. That is perseverance.

So your life, simply stated, is the opportunity to take one stroke, one step, one smile, one embrace, one pause, one prayer, one service, one gesture --- and on and on endlessly in the rhythm of this gracious experience of life where you discover almost unwillingly that your journey takes you through endless streams flowing left, then right, always forward. And almost contrary to your expectations you begin to exhibit that patience for which you once were most critical of yourself and others. In that moment of consciousness, enlightenment, you realize that you could continue endlessly – and will.

For today think about how perseverance calls you today.

.

#332

Scripture: *"For I know the plans I have for you," declares the Lord, "plans to prosper you and not to harm you, plans to give you hope and a future." Jeremiah 29:11*

Prayer: Whenever this verse finds me, I do not tire of its assurance.

Response: It is difficult not to see that this verse is met for you individually and not in some broad, collective sense. Wherever you are this day, the verse serves as my reminder to you this special day that I have plans for you. In the whirl of your activity, sometimes lost to you is that I care. You are like weavers in a huge hall who receive the fiber and intuitively know the pattern on which you are working. And I ask from where that intuition comes? Lost in the swirl of color, the pattern you are forming, you lose sight and appreciation for the work of art to which you are contributing. When you step back – or rather within – you sense the creation of which you are part and to which you create. This is a difficult concept for you to appreciate. Accept that you are not puppets on a string pulled by a great puppeteer, rather you are co-creators of your environment.

For you to catch a glimpse of the vision I have for you, pause for your tea break – as if you were a weaver in the mountains of Central Asia, step back or better yet climb to a higher elevation to see the interconnectedness unfolding in the tapestry of your life to those around you and afar. And as I said above, that stepping back is actually the step within where all is made clear to you, even now.

Spend a moment this day on the word prosper. I have plans to prosper you. While you might be more familiar with the noun prosperity, consider the empowerment, the blessing, the selection that the verb *prosper* conveys. Don't look around and think that I am directing my gaze elsewhere. No, I intend my words for you this very moment. All you have to do is hear the words and accept them.

Scripture: *Jesus, knowing that they intended to come and make him king by force, withdrew again to a mountain by himself. John 6:15*

Prayer: How often a verse that I have read quickly holds a meaning that I overlooked previously – as with this verse.

Response: It is like finally getting to the pastry crust and discovering a flavor missed in the filling. Yes, this verse captures for you the rhythm of Christ's movement among you – even now. Just when you have figured things out – at least you think so – the author of life takes a turn and you are left to reflect on the meaning. All the signs of the miracle on the mountainside proclaimed that a worldly kingship, freedom from worldly oppression, the satisfaction of basic needs, and the list would expand if you were to interview all present – and consider yourself present as well. And just at that moment, anticipating the answer, he withdraws to a mountain by himself. What are you to make of it?

Make of it timing, timing in your life, letting go of what you want to control, and dissolve those desires in acceptance of what is – or put another way, allow those desires to dissolve into God's will for you in this present moment. Observe the strength of character that you are witnessing in that withdrawal that he offers you in your daily life. How many times have you withdrawn to a quiet place – like now – to ponder a scene, a word, a thought, an insight before resuming your journey? So it was as Jesus withdrew again – it was not the first time, nor would it be the last – by himself.

For today, see if you can snatch a moment in time to withdraw and consider the passage of time as you journey on the path. You see in the withdrawal you greet the unfolding of who you are becoming.

Scripture: *"This is the covenant I will make with the house of Israel after that time," declares he Lord. "I will put my law in their minds and write it on their hearts. I will be their God, and they will be my people. No longer will a man teach his neighbor, or a man his brother, saying, 'Know the Lord,' because they will all know me, from the least of them to the greatest," declares the Lord. For I will forgive their wickedness and will remember their sins no more." Jeremiah 31:33-34*

Prayer: Help me to know better what is written on my heart.

Response: Consider how you would be in the world, if you accepted these words of Jeremiah literally as they are meant. Suppose you accepted that your neighbor close, and those who live far from you, because I have written it on their hearts? Is that the divine spark that you talk of when far off you come to recognize a characteristic, a trait, a sparkle in someone that you have discovered earlier within you? Is it in that moment that you put aside fear and hesitancy to find common bond? And you don't have to be far off in a less traveled land to make this discovery – you could be in a convenience store, a mall, or in the pew of a familiar house of worship.

What would it take to look boldly into your neighbor's eyes and see recognition – recognition of a traveled soul on the path homebound? How much courage would it take to put aside the pride of knowing and acknowledge in your actions that your fellow traveler will know me from the least and humble to those who occupy positions of authority, to those who speak in foreign tongues and display cultures with which you are not familiar?

You all will know me – even those strangers. I have written my message of love on their hearts.

.

Scripture: . . . *and a great crowd of people followed him because they saw the miraculous signs he had performed on the sick. Then Jesus went up on a mountainside and sat down with his disciples.* John 6:2-3

Prayer: Help me to enter the scene that John depicts.

Response: Think of a time when you hiked with friends or family and came to a spot of unmatched beauty. There was an unconscious desire on the part of all of you to prolong this moment in time, and so you paused. This is what is happening in this scene. Notice I say *is* because this scene is in the present time for you this morning. And realize that it was not the natural beauty that gave everyone pause as much as being in the company, for the disciples the select company, of someone who spoke in an other-worldly sense of matters that active people customarily overlook; and not only in words did he mesmerize his followers and the huge crowds that followed at a distance. No, he reinforced his words of love with action and service to those in need.

The great discovery of the select, who on the surface seemed fine – one might even say prosperous in matters of health and livelihood, was that his comments and instruction touched a nerve of recognition, one that they had neglected for so long. They could not get enough of his words and actions, sensing that he would not be in their midst for long. That's the scene for you to enter, and in entering you come to realize that all you need is a quiet place to be there now. It isn't as if you were successful transporting yourself back in time, but rather, and this is important even critical for you to understand, this moment on the mountain side is now. So observe and listen.

Before you give voice to what you hear and observe around you, begin with what you seek to experience in this companionship because there resides the prompt cards for you to give voice to your innermost prayers. Each assembled on the slope – whether next to Jesus or further down the slope almost out of earshot but not quite -- came with expectations that are sometimes so deeply imbued within that they hardly recognize these longings as their own, sometimes releasing them in unrecognizable groans uttered softly under their breath.

So take your seat and collect the urgings of your heart in stillness. No one is watching; they are all doing the same. .

Scripture: . . . *and a great crowd of people followed him because they saw the miraculous signs he had performed on the sick. Then Jesus went up on a mountainside and sat down with his disciples.* John 6:2-3

Prayer: Help me to enter the scene that John depicts.

Response: Think of a time when you hiked with friends or family and came to a spot of unmatched beauty. There was an unconscious desire on the part of all of you to prolong this moment in time, and so you paused. This is what is happening in this scene. Notice I say *is* because this scene is in the present time for you this morning. And realize that it was not the natural beauty that gave everyone pause as much as being in the company, for the disciples the select company, of someone who spoke in an other-worldly sense of matters that active people customarily overlook; and not only in words did he mesmerize his followers and the huge crowds that followed at a distance. No, he reinforced his words of love with action and service to those in need.

The great discovery of the select, who on the surface seemed fine – one might even say prosperous in matters of health and livelihood, was that his comments and instruction touched a nerve of recognition, one that they had neglected for so long. They could not get enough of his words and actions, sensing that he would not be in their midst for long. That's the scene for you to enter, and in entering you come to realize that all you need is a quiet place to be there now. It isn't as if you were successful transporting yourself back in time, but rather, and this is important even critical for you to understand, this moment on the mountain side is now. So observe and listen.

Before you give voice to what you hear and observe around you, begin with what you seek to experience in this companionship because there resides the prompt cards for you to give voice to your innermost prayers. Each assembled on the slope – whether next to Jesus or further down the slope almost out of earshot but not quite -- came with expectations that are sometimes so deeply imbued within that they hardly recognize these longings as their own, sometimes releasing them in unrecognizable groans uttered softly under their breath.

So take your seat and collect the urgings of your heart in stillness. No one is watching; they are all doing the same. .

Scripture: *While you were doing all these things, declares the Lord, I spoke to you again and again, but you did not listen; I called you, but you did not answer. Jeremiah 7:13*

Prayer: Lord, this verse seems as applicable to me now as it was directed to Jeremiah 2,500 years ago. Help me to keep my attention.

Response: What further reminded do you need that my word is freshly anointed? I mean that in reading my word with an attentive heart, you become the Jeremiah, the disciple, the lonely soul in the desert repeating the words silently to oneself and the words are as immediate as when Jeremiah first received them. Clearly, he thought them worthy enough to copy them down. I am not asking you to take out pen or paper, or sit before a keyboard, but I do ask you to remember the verse and respond individually to my declaration. More importantly, I ask what are you going to do about it?

Yes, I am looking for you to move on from the state described in the verse. That's the kind of doing I am asking for. Because in that doing, that action, you discover a becoming within yourself that you did not consider possible. Perhaps, you think I am suggesting that you limit your ease, or at least you consider it so – to perform at a multi-tasking pace. Well, I am. Take time to listen – and that means in stillness. You don't need any interpreter for my words, or any special acoustic devices to snatch these words from the airwaves. No, I speak to each of you individually and my voice is distinct, my message is clear. Don't ask for a summary, just take time to listen.

And do you know what? You will be surprised at how you alter your day's activities; experience the calmness that enters what might have been a house of bedlam and I don't mean structures but your interior; see sights that you might have missed in your frenzied activity.

Scripture: *But if I go to the east he is not there; if I go to the west I do not find him. When he is at work in the north I do not see him; when he turns to the south I catch no glimpse of him. But he knows the way that I take; when he has tested me I will come forth as gold. Psalm 23:8-10*

Prayer: Reassure me Lord that you do not lose sight of me.

Response: No, I do not lose sight of you. In fact your searching, sometimes frantic, as you look north and south, east and west, would be better spent looking within. You see, I have never left your side. It is, however, in your search that you, yes you, realize this thirst and it is in your thirst that your search is realized in my presence recognized.

If in a desert, you would discover that the thirst you seek to slack is immediately below you in the sand, needed only your soft tap to experience the gushing of my grace over you. Quite an incredible image for you to contemplate, when you are next dehydrated by the concerns, even anxieties of your circumstances.

This is not a game of hide and seek. In your search you learn action and service – not indulging yourself to ponder over and over your fate. Rather it is in your search for me that you shake the dust from your sandals and minister to those who also wander sometimes without purpose across your path. And you might even find that these searchers resemble you as they are members of your family or among your closest confidantes.

Scripture: *To the Lord I cry aloud, and he answers me from his holy hill. Psalm 3:4*

Prayer: With your grace keep my attention.

Response: Your prayers are the cries that indicate the depth within you is our relationship. Even before you utter the first syllable, I hear your joy, groans, murmurings. That holy hill of which the psalmist writes is within you. I have taken up residence there. So you see there are instant communications and even more instant dialogue.

If you will be patient and listen you will discover and be a participant in a vibrant exchange. You are required to be still. Sometimes, you might even say most times, you put down the receiver before I have had a chance to speak.

So my message is imbued in the circumstances around you. As you awake, you will see that our exchanges lengthen and deepen and become more meaningful. If I might say, clarity emerges and you become at ease with yourself. You will also find that you are grounded in the present time –and you are. Focus on the word *answer*, for indeed you will receive answers to your pleas and with clarity. My message you will find is fashioned for you especially because it is with you I converse in grace.

.

Scripture: *He went on to say, "This is why I told you that no one can come to me unless the Father has enabled him." John 6:65*

Prayer: What does enable mean?

Response: Perhaps you would be more comfortable with *empowered.* In my grace you awake, become conscious, and in this rousing you are enabled, encouraged, exhorted to set out on the quest. No matter where you are in your life passage; it has no import even if you have resting on the side of the path, once you are awakened and resume your journey you have been enabled. It is as if a burden was lifted from you and your steps seem lighter.

What I want you to understand and to reflect upon – it is not about you acting on your own, but rather, and this is essential for you to catch, it is about you responding. In that response you connect, tap into my grace; it is as if I was sending these random radio signals out and some isolated station picks up the signal and acknowledges receipt. As you might have imagined already, it is not about simply sending the receipt. I am asking you to embark on the path. And please do not try is distinguish whether your neighbor has been called, received the signal. In fact, each of you over the expanse of the globe can detect the signal, though only those sufficiently conscious are responding. Have confidence that others, even all, will respond in time.

See that signal as my grace and love, burst transmissions that travel a circuitry that spans the globe.

Scripture: *"My people have committed two sins: they have forsaken me, the spring of living water, and have dug their own cisterns, broken cisterns that cannot hold water." Jeremiah 2:13*

Prayer: Help me to search out the spring of living water.

Response: Your prayer should really be that you be sustained by this living water. See yourself established on the fringe of a desert where a spring of crystal clear water flows. Don't be tempted to move off further in the desert, relying upon underground chambers constructed of discarded stone and tile to hold stagnant water when you establish your temporary lodging

Identify in your life the source of living water, my grace in your life. You can recognize it because of its movement across the rocks that would interrupt your journey, but with the water serve to keep that water cool, pure, refreshing.

The movement of the living water is like the undulating waves that touch the shore, the wind that grazes across your landscape, a widening dawn at sunrise -- all reminders of my presence in grace that surround you who are sometimes pressed into shelters of your own construction.

Scripture: *"Now this is eternal life: that they may know you. . . ."* John 17:3

Prayer: Bring me to a closer knowing.

Response: The knowing that I seek for you in my grace is a knowing without qualifiers – fuller, lesser, or the like. Knowing is without words; it is a confidence like the recognition of a loved one by a walk seen in the distance, a gesture caught on a stranger that brings the loved one into your presence, a disposition that guides you yet. This knowing knows no separation; rises from a depth within that surprises you like the sun tipping through the horizon at dawn; it is familiar like a bosom friend who visits and there is no recollection when he or she was absent.

In this knowing you – the *you* who observes – changes, matures, and pulses with a capacity to love not recognized earlier. In this knowing, in this proximity, you become the love that once you observed at a distance, though you can hardly give expression to that time or that distance – like puzzling over a faded photograph as to the age and image looking out at you.

Now this is eternal life – to be one in union, transformed in and through the power of my love. No turning back.

.

Scripture: *Therefore I am now going to allure her; I will lead her into the desert and speak tenderly to her."* Hosea 2:14

Prayer: In the desert help me to hear your voice

Response: At times when your voice seems hoarse with pleas that seemingly go unheard, you might feel that you have wandered into a desolate region, sparse in its vegetation. You might realize it but you have followed all the sign posts and can't at first understand why you find yourself in a desert region. And as you look around, there is nothing to distract you other than your thirst.

And what is that thirst? The sense of assurance in my grace as I nourish you in the companions who come across your path, in the idyllic scene s of nature that touch you at that particular time, the events in your life that all seem to be progressing according to your plan, I repeat your plan. Then you seem alone. It's like running a marathon and there is no one manning a refreshment station along the route. Your prayer is bleak with your pleading, even if you don't consider yourself abandoned.

It is in the desert, the dark night, of your soul, that I embolden your heart with love for me. It is then that you continue your journey without the satisfaction of my presence though I have not left your side – another paradox. It is then that I speak to you at a decibel below the sounds around you. It is in the desert of your journey that you are strengthened in my love.

.

Scripture: *The Sovereign Lord is my strength; he makes my feet like the feet of a deer; he enables me to go on the heights. Habakkuk 3:19*

Prayer: Help me to realize that without your strength there are not many heights I would reach.

Response: By now you realize that the heights I talk of often are disguised in the depths. Ask how you penetrate or deal with the challenges that command sometimes your attention. If you find yourself figuratively closing your eyes and dashing forward, you might pause and reflect upon this verse. I am your strength; I sustain you even if you are picking your steps carefully along a mountain ridge with loose rock all about. I urge you on higher to the next level where you are surprised to discover a mountain lake high above the tree line. I encourage you especially when you are weary; when you wonder about your progress, have second thoughts about your direction.

Consider the opening lines – *The Sovereign is my strength.* Not only are those words meant to resonate in your heart in all seasons of your life, but also to be on your lips when faced with a daunting task or event in your life. Your words are not only a reminder that commands your attention, but also forewarning to those who would trifle with or obstruct your purpose. Spoken softly these words are a measure of my strength in you

For today, see if you can resume your journey higher on the slope; walk nimbly and alertly; consider even anticipate the refreshment that awaits you further on.

#345

Scripture: *My heart grew hot within me, and as I meditated, the fire burned; then I spoke with my tongue: "Show me, O Lord, my life's end and the number of my days; let me know how fleeting is my life. You have made my days a mere handbreadth, the span of my years is nothing before you."*

Prayer: Help me Lord to grasp the truth uttered by the Psalmist and not as an historical truth but meant for me this day.

Response: The psalmist is calling out to you across the centuries and he is inviting you to do likewise for those in your midst and those to follow. He invites you in the present tense to be still in my presence and experience the fire that burns especially for you. Allow that heat to envelop you even on a cold day — be it the weather or the daunting tasks, it seems, that await you. Don't rush to bring your mind of precision into the scene.

Then let me hear those words of the heart that are unspoken that lead you to even deeper truth. Embrace in my grace the answers you seek to drown out in the din of activity. You don't need an interpreter of dreams to confirm for you how fleeting this life experience is. Without getting morose, accept that truth directly and address it as it relates also to those you love.

Though your days are not much more than can be grasped as you sea shells from the sea, consider the unique treasures each represents as you hold the collection in your hands, and ponder each day especially today.

.

Scripture: "*The Lord lives! Praise be to my Rock! Exalted be God, the Rock, my Savior!*" *2 Samuel 22:47*

Prayer: Help to understand the imagery of this verse.

Response: You wake and go outside in the cold and rain and dark, and wonder. What is this all about? This question forms on your lips; you do not even utter the words aloud. And the answer, very specific, resounds around you in this time of darkness. You don't have to wake up before dawn to wonder alone. The question comes to you almost on cue.

Well, this verse is one that I will whisper within you at such times. And it is an exclamation, a shout. Notice that from declaring, shouting that the Lord lives, you are then asked to praise this Rock – this impenetrable, unchanging Presence. No, you are not being asked to worship an idol, but my Presence in your midst, at all times, in all circumstances, in all climes. My response is not affected by the wind, the rain, the frost, the sounds of fury from the sea – above and beyond all the elements I stand above as any mountain presence you have experienced.

And in case you missed it, this Rock is not unmoved but is your Savior. Now here is a mystery for you to reflect upon this day – *The Lord lives! Praise be to my Rock! Exalted be God, the Rock, my Savior.*

Scripture: *After he had said this, he went on to tell them: "Our friend Lazarus has fallen asleep; but I am going there to wake him up. John 11:11*

Prayer: Wake me up, Lord.

Response: Reflect upon the meaning you place on the words *fallen asleep.* It's temporary with a hint that you will awaken, and indeed you will. Most importantly for you now is to wake up in your physical wrapping. You nod off when you have deprived yourself of rest – so fixed you become in attending to busy duties that provide your explanation of why you can't find the time to be still. I am here to rouse you, and I accomplish this by nudging you awake, gaining your attention by an inexplicable experience you encounter whether of joy or sorrow.

Do not fail to note that you as Lazarus are my friend. I will not allow you to linger in despondency, in a desultory state, in the grip of inaction and self-absorption. Now, as your dearest friend in my Spirit I will awaken you, and urge you to rise, and in rising you will get a sense, a preview, of your rising when your physical nature slips away.

As you rise into consciousness, you will discover that you no longer nod off, or at least with the regularity you did; instead you will note a vibrancy that you have missed since the days when you played as a little child. Full consciousness, awake-ness, is measured in the endless dance of life in my grace in which you now discover the stamina to engage.

.

Scripture: *Surely you desire truth in the inner parts; you teach me wisdom in the inmost place* Psalm 51.6

Prayer: You never fail to reach me when I am still – and so now I ask in truth and wisdom.

Response: Truth and wisdom – sometime are used by you interchangeably. Truth is actually a simple concept to grasp – what you know to be true, accept and act in accordance with that truth. While easy to grasp intellectually, it proves difficult at times to act upon the truth openly without fear, especially if that truth is contradictory to the actions of your heart. And you do seek the truth and even draw that truth deep within, sometimes allowing it to mature over time, sometimes to store even confine in a hidden vault where even you have forgotten its existence.

I do desire the truth to invade your inner being and not to go unnoticed. Truth like light has the power to diffuse the darkness and ignorance that might have lay dormant, unmoving for ages. With truth, you consider yourself and surroundings with fresh heart eyes. Color has suddenly been added to what might have once been a bleak scene. Therefore, seek truth with an openness and curiosity that venerates me.

Now wisdom is what I teach as a wine steward would an apprentice. Wisdom is based on your search for truth, on patience to allow the truth to mature under my guidance and tutelage. Wisdom is a quiet knowing that one applies carefully in service, be it in a soup kitchen, interacting with contemporaries or children or those who are completing their journey. Wisdom is dispensed in measured portions and for it to be nourishing you must allow time for its assimilation, and always trusting in my grace. So for today, invite truth to invade the inner sanctum of your heart and welcome my wisdom that accompanies.

Scripture: *O Lord, do not rebuke me in your anger or discipline me in your wrath. Be merciful to me, Lord, for I am faint. O Lord, heal me for my bones are in agony. My soul is in anguish. How long, O Lord, how long? Psalm 6:1-3*

Prayer: As the season of Lent begins, help me to seek healing as I cultivate the psalmist's sense of anguish.

Response: See if you can nurture in my grace the sense of anguish that transforms into enthusiastic compassion and service. Do not linger in sorrow for missed opportunities. Rather see this moment as offering you full reconciliation in my love – right this minute. Dismiss the past and dive into the present that sorely needs your attention.

You will discover the healing you seek that transcends the human wrap, your anguish will be turned to joy, your weariness will be turned to exhilaration, and what once appeared dull and lifeless in your life will be transformed into color and vibrancy.

And all this is offered to you when you come to me in prayer, humbly offering your sorrow for transgressions of the heart with firm resolve to reach out and touch those with the mercy that I shower upon you. I desire that those who receive your grace-full love are led to wonder of the source of this love as you indeed wonder in my presence.

Scripture: *The Lord appeared to us in the past, saying: "I have loved you with an everlasting love; I have drawn you with loving kindness." Jeremiah 31:3*

Prayer: Help me to see your constancy in my life.

Response: There are times when you might feel that you are wandering in a vast field of strangers in an unknown land. At such a time, you might recall a beckoning that draws you forward and it is in that instant that you realize that you are not alone – no matter the challenge – that I go before you, never beyond earshot, or better heart-shot.

Reflect on what it means for you to experience *everlasting love*. The love that I talk of can be no other than everlasting, eternal. What you experience in your relationships represent – I trust – signposts pointing to the one true love that you actually experience now, though you must awake to catch the full dimension of the love.

Also, consider what it means to be drawn *with loving kindness*. Such love is patient, kind, trusting, not overbearing, forgiving, and tender – and all the adjectives that you would describe the intimacy of a love that is transcendent. Now, that is a word to ponder for today – *transcendent* – because you are on a transcendent path.

.

Scripture: *But we prayed to our God and posted a guard day and night to meet this threat.* *Nehemiah 4:9*

Prayer: I smile with this threat. Remind me of the need for action.

Response: The reminder for you today is that there is synergy in our relationship. Your prayer naturally leads you to action, to service – and action leads to prayer. You might find that your prayers are even prompted by your action and service, prayers of thanksgiving, compassion, sorrow, joy – the full range of heart-emotion.

My call is not one of retreat but of engagement. Indeed, I desire your prayers, to be present to hear the whispers of your heart that perhaps few hear – and I call you to action in service bolstered, emboldened by my grace.

Remember the only surrender I seek is to my love. So indeed man the ramparts and confront directly the challenges you face in daily life and do so with the knowledge of the intimacy we share and, of course, with the compassion I teach.

.

Scripture: *"Come," he replied, "and you will see." John 1:39*

Prayer: Give me the grace to accept the invitation.

Response: This is an open invitation to you and it doesn't even require an RSVP – you can be spontaneous and show up without fanfare or announcement. "Invitation to what?" you ask. Well, would you drop all your responsibilities and you come, if I replied, "To a lecture series, to a briefing, to an admonition on conduct, to a donors' conference?" Perhaps not. No, my invitation is for you to enter into my presence and see to the full capacity of your heart – and listen quietly. No need to respond or even comment, if you are not so inclined. Just come and see.

And it is what you experience and will experience that will spur you to return. As you reflect upon your life to date, you will recall the fullness of spirit, your spirit that you recognize, each time as if for the first time, in my presence. Linear time – moving in a straight line from past thru present to future – dissipates, and you are in an eternal moment where mind-thoughts of age, illness, finances, loss, or any other cause for worry or anxiety fade as the credits of a film you are previewing.

Come and see is to listen at a heart level what I reveal and the discernment I share, yes share with you, and most importantly to witness by service to those who are still sitting on their invitation. And in witnessing, you are not to judge why others have not responded to the invitation with alacrity. Only describe what you see allowing my grace to influence all in time. So I repeat, *Come and see.*

.

#353

Scripture: *The true light that gives light to every man was coming into the world. John 1:9*

Prayer: Deepen my understanding of this light.

Response: It is not surprising that this short verse contains a mystery that you push to grasp. Think back when you traveled in a car late at night alone on your way to Montana. You intended to drive through the night when you perceived a single light approaching you in the winter air, by then you were in North Dakota. You pulled to the side of the road to confirm that it was a train approaching, but more importantly that it was not heading down the center of the highway. And you waited and waited and waited – and then many minutes later confirmed that the approaching light signaled a locomotive that passed you on tracks to the right of the road.

Well, excuse me for reaching back into your memory bank to allow you to catch a glimpse of the excitement of the Light that comes into the world for every man. If you think your attention was gripped so many years ago – was it from fear that you would be run over by the train having inadvertently strayed onto the tracks or fatigue from driving non-stop from New York – so should this verse freeze your attention on this event in your life. *True light – to every man – coming into the world.*

So before you look around you and take a head count of who is included in *every man*, look within; pull off to the side of the road and receive the light that comes most especially for you.

.

Scripture: *You have made known to me the path of life; you will fill me with joy in your presence, with eternal pleasures at your right hand. Psalm 16:11*

Prayer: I am struck by the majesty of the words of this verse and tend to miss the essential meaning.

Response: It is the majesty as you name it that catches your attention. Surely, by now you understand what is the path of your life? Without filling the specifics of tomorrow – after all there is only today – you recognize the path. It is a path trod by those who preceded you and energetically followed by those behind. And to open your heart, see if you can eliminate for this moment the notion of linear, surface time and singular path.

You are approaching the Godhead and were never distant – another paradox. And this truth serves as the foundation, the basis of your joy as you are enlightened to this truth. Imagine the joy of reunion with one long absent, only to discover you have never been separated. In this moment be the person who recognizes my presence now and for evermore.

Eternal pleasure begins with the realization that the silence of the moment resounds with my presence. Yes, I am just here, just now. The king you sought out from afar to petition is alongside listening intently to that petition though you speak in whispers. Now that is joy for you to experience.

.

Scripture: *A bruised reed he will not break, and a smoldering wick he will not snuff out.* Isaiah 42:3

Prayer: From my youth this verse is familiar. Help me to fathom its deeper meaning. Look about you this day and minister gently and secure in my love. This verse contains a jewel for you to snatch and keep close on your journey.

Response: I ask you to stay for a moment with the words presented and not rush off to the interpretation that you have learned. Delve into the spirit of the One who is all powerful yet with no need to show that power or to dismiss the intention of the weary. This verse is meant for you today as a sign of encouragement. Bruised and smoldering at times, you are encouraged to seize responsibility, endure, and to nurture the smoldering wick – if that is how you appear or better someone with whom you are in contact.

You see, the question to ask is if the all powerful does not break a bruised reed or snuff out a smoldering wick, why should you? You are called to encourage those who falter, are bruised, seem to be losing their flame. Be not dismissive or impatient. Allow the bruised reed the time in your patience with my grace to be restored, the spark to flame once more.

.

Scripture: *In God we make our boast all day long, and we will praise your name forever.* Psalm 44:8

Prayer: I need help with the words *all day long.*

Response: If it helps, the verse is guiding you to an inclination of the spirit. Just beneath the hum of daily activity – some quite meaningful, some automatic responses to daily routines – you are being asked, directed even, to be conscious. Sounds like another paradox doesn't it? This inclination of which I talk is to be nurtured on the path so that you do not miss what is vital to your awakening. In a real sense I am asking you to be alert to the surprises that await you. In praise – silent praise as well as praise uttered aloud – you acknowledge my presence and that serves to raise you to another state of consciousness.

And why boast? Well, in your boasting you embolden your faith; you are more prepared to face adversity – perhaps not a battlefield – but surely required as you face what you once considered – and maybe even still do – daunting challenges. Boasting serves to bring forth a deep roar – even if subdued – to the surface of your being, manifesting a confidence in my grace, bolstered by my love.

For today be alert to your every challenge whether in the home or work environment or in chance encounters; and as you approach the challenge boast of my support and discover the relief that you experience.

.

Scripture: *Now faith is being sure of what we hope for and certain of what we do not see. Hebrews 11:1*

Prayer: Give me the courage to hope and the certainty from faith.

Response: This is a special verse that in its brevity commands your attention. The verse challenges you to take a huge step not reserved for the timid. Yes, I am not asking you to put your foot forward hesitantly – so to speak. I am asking you instead to proceed down what appears to be a darkened corridor with confidence. If it helps, my grace is there to embolden you, and if you listen carefully in the silence, you will hear a melody that is familiar to reassure you.

Aside from stepping forward, I want you to fashion in your heart what you hope for. Again, this is not an exercise that is beyond you, rather one that you tend to avoid for fear that you are alone in this darkened corridor. Your hope expressed in silence or aloud is a deep set prayer that you are sometimes not accustomed to utter. Well, I ask you to do so, realizing that hope represents a special prayer, one that goes beyond the safe prayer of generalities. I say safe because whether or not the prayer is answered, no one is really the wiser. So I ask you to bring into consciousness your deepest most private hope – and let me remind you, if I must, that you will find that such prayer often does not involve circumstances that surround you but might truly affect those you love or those you have yet to encounter.

Now the third step in your awakening is to cultivate that certainty of what you do not see in that darkened corridor. Such certainty is that of someone who is certain that you walked along this corridor previously – know the designs carved on the walls, the curvature of the corridor, its height, and even – in your certainty – its length.

For today, pray with this faith, hope, and certainty.

Scripture: *For you have been born again, not of perishable seed, but of imperishable through the living and enduring word of God. 1 Peter 1:23*

Prayer: On this my birth day, help me to understand re-birth.

Response: Your life to date on this journey has witnessed a rebirth into the spiritual realms. Rebirth is awakening and not reserved to one event in your life. Rebirth is similar to the ribbon of light you witnessed this morning far out to sea on the horizon as it burned its way to the surface, seemingly an inch at a time. That is rebirth – you awake to my bounty. In expanding your awareness, you serve, not wearing your rebirthing as some badge of honor. Rather I am calling you to service, to exhibit compassion to those lingering in the shadows of neglect, to learn about those you fear and do not understand, to be courageous without bias and prejudice, to be indefatigable in my word, and most of all to be joyful in all, I repeat, all adversity.

You are imperishable and you are on a path of discovery. Look around you; you are moving through an exotic land; take in the sights, smells, sounds, melody that encompass you, as you once did arriving in India for the first time. Maintain a spirit of adventure and discovery that promote and encourage my consciousness. No need to travel to some foreign shore; my love and grace are found on the streets of the cities, in the redoubts of poverty, on campuses searching for answers, in seminaries of doubt, on ball fields seeking victory and consoling defeat, and in the corridors of power. Bring my love and light to wherever you are.

You are *imperishable through the living and enduring word of God.*

.

Scripture: *But I would not have you to be ignorant, brethren, concerning them which are sleep, that we sorrow not, even as others which have no hope. For if we believe that Jesus died and rose again, even so them also which sleep in Jesus will God bring with him. 1 Thessalonians 13-14*

Prayer: Help me to take in deeply this scripture.

Response: Don't make it any more cryptic and esoteric than it is. Simply, you are called to nurture hope in my grace. Yes, you are called. Take the message as written for you today though you are in good health, though you grieve for others who have passed. These two verses bring you together and challenge you to cultivate hope in those who are without hope.

I also implore you to rise from your ignorance. Listen to me in stillness; reflect upon my word; catch the meaning, the need, of someone around you who lingers without words; be bold in a gentle way to share the path – the path you are on and have trod; encourage the lonely and the despairing.

Hope is essential. It is the surprise finale to a great meal – and I know about meals – and that finale is an eternal beginning. How simple is that? My words are not meant to puzzle. Smile wide when those without hope choose to scowl or embrace despair. And do not separate yourself from them but seek to touch them. Instead embrace them in my love. Give them hope in my grace.

Scripture: *His heart is secure, he will have no fear; in the end he will look in triumph on his foes.* Psalm 112:8

Prayer: Help me to fathom a heart secure.

Response: The psalmist provides you a description of full or perhaps dawning consciousness – a worthy aspiration for you, but you must awake first. If you rise from the bed or cot, from your chair alongside your desk or from your seat in the sand and doubt, or hold apprehension, or anxiety seizes your attention, you can be assured that you have fallen back asleep.

There is much for you to consider in these last words. Coming into my consciousness does not mean that it is accumulative and no longer requires your attention. Quite the contrary, as you progress in the awakened state, I am asking you to nurture this awareness. This is no time to sit back figuratively or literally, else you will be in slumber before you finish this sentence.

My consciousness, the consciousness that I shower upon you in my grace, is marked almost by a 360 degree panorama, around, up and below you; it is where you sense first the inner stirring within you and you apply this heightened awareness to those with whom you come in contact – yes, those in need, disconsolate, in poverty of the body and spirit; those who turn to you for sustenance; and those who offer understanding, consolation, and forgiveness. Whether you dance or not, you are in a spirit dance with those around you and afar – and the only way to hear the music and to learn the movement is to awake this moment.

Scripture: *But with you there is forgiveness. Psalm 130:4*

Prayer: Teach me of forgiveness.

Response: Yes, you have touched an essential theme in my message of love. Forgiveness is looking over the wall of your fear and discontent, and offering a gift of peace and reconciliation. I did not suggest jumping over the wall – just yet. The offering that you are capable of providing is a gift and is pulled together with what you have available at the moment. Withholding the offering until a time when you are more affluent and secure, when the memory of the affront has faded in your memory, will not provide the healing that awaits you – to say nothing of the offender. And as a gift, you are not to calculate the response, the thank-you, you seek. As the offering is a surprise, so is the return, if there is a return.

Forgiveness surges from the heart – not the ego. Forgiveness is acceptance; even acceptance of a culpability that might have gone unnoticed within you. One of the first fruits of forgiveness is peace – peace for you first and perhaps that peace will invade the inner precincts of the one you once perceived as the offender. Peace is a freedom to enjoy in spirit the splendor of an expansive field in spring without distraction, a community of spirit without comparison or competition. It is a transformative experience nurtured in silence and stillness.

Peace promotes a remembering that emboldens the risk of offering forgiveness.

.

#362

Scripture: *And when he had given thanks, he broke the bead . . . 1 Corinthians 11:24*

Prayer: Help me to catch moment of these words that are so familiar to me.

Response: As you live by the sea and sometimes reflect upon the silence between waves as they crash on the shore, be filled with the same expectancy in hearing these words. Giving thanks and then breaking the bread – two actions seemingly distinct and yet in silence and reflection they serve as the door post to enter into an eternal consideration.

Would that you incorporate thanks and action into your life; not limiting yourself to a few words before a meal. It is in thanks that you respond to your soul urgings that recognizes my presence in your life beneath all the turmoil, our interconnectedness. Accept that you are not a random appearance on this earth without purpose. It is in thanks that you also declare a hope, a conscious hope, that my will for you, your purpose, will become ever more manifest.

And then he broke the bread. Reflect upon how his audience was almost mesmerized by these deliberate purposeful acts. Thanks and the breaking of the bread – the pause between two thunderous waves shocking the shore into wakefulness. You are the shore, awaiting the incoming waves, hear me, awake.

#363

Scripture: *All your words are true. Psalm 119:160*

Prayer: Help me to accept your truth.

Response: A short verse and an almost shorter prayer. Interesting how profound meaning is contained in few words. Notice how you are not directed to read a long treatise on the subject of truth; no footnotes are given to clarify meaning. A simple declaration is made – *my words are true.*

Now the first thing you must do is to be still and hear my words. Following that simple direction ensures that you receive my word with the clarity that can be lost in the cacophony of voices that surround you. This simple direction is the challenge you have faced in youth and now as you wonder where youth has fled. But don't spend time wondering about the process. Simply take a moment in your day – and don't bind the moment in elapsed time. Rather take a moment and allow the moment to unfold.

My promise to you is that when you follow this proscription, you will find that you could have written those words of the psalmist and will now in the fabric of your heart. And you will also discover that you no longer need *help* in accepting my truth because you become that truth as it is manifest in you.

.

#364

Scripture: *Teach me your ways that I may know you. Exodus 33:13*

Prayer: Lord, I repeat the words please *teach me your ways.*

Response: There are many ways that I reveal myself to you. When you are looking elsewhere and are distracted or intense about a matter lingering in the future or hopelessly embroiled in a dispute of the past, I reveal myself in a special encounter with someone special, an event unplanned, a moment of overwhelming beauty, or in an experience of great joy or even sadness. All of the latter experiences register in your deepest consciousness and for a time – it doesn't matter how long the experience lasts –that moment is eternal.

Now there is another way – and there are many ways for you to know me – is when you are attentive, that means conscious, awake, and you hear my teaching. Please don't consider that I am speaking at such times from a prepared text from which you have been preached or that I am setting the dimensions of your confinement. At such times, you become intuitive to my words however they reach the you who watches alert within. And it is then that you truly perceive who I am.

It is as if you've been sitting at the back of a large lecture hall, listening to the teacher drone on in a language foreign to you, and then suddenly you awake to find yourself in the front row and the teacher is speaking softly and clearly, and he is looking directly at you. If you are still in a large cavern of learning, you are unaware of it. All you know is that you hear with an awareness and in a light unmatched previously.

So for today, take note – or should I say notes – of those moments when the teacher pulls you up unaware to the front row of the hall. Don't worry about taking notes literally – the lesson will be repeated; rather spend your time as an artist would sketching as if to determine who this teacher is. And if you missed it, I am that teacher.

#365

Scripture: *When he had received the drink, Jesus said: "It is finished." With that, he bowed his head and gave up his spirit. John 19:30*

Prayer: The words, *It is consummated,* resounded in my heart last night as they related to a dear friend. I discovered later that he passed just hours previous. Help me to penetrate the deep meaning of completion.

Response: You will need a book of completions, so to speak, to even approach the depth of meaning you seek for completion. Consummation, completion, to use a sports metaphor, is rowing across the finish line knowing that you applied all your skill and strength to the endeavor. Yes, there were times in the race that you contributed to the shell going off keel or balance for a moment; yes you dipped your oar too deep on a stroke and *caught a crab* that nearly tossed you out of the boat; yes you allowed thoughts to distract you so you were not in synch with the team; and I could go on.

Yet, as the finish line came upon you – though only the coxswain was facing it – and he shouted, exhorted and beat against the gunwales with the wooden chocks, there was a sense of exhilaration, triumph that all the training, all the determination, all the resiliency despite the setbacks, brought you to this moment – crossing the finish line to savor in absolute exhaustion the peace, yes peace of completion. And please notice that I said nothing about *winning* the race against any competition.

So for today and much longer into your race, see yourself approaching the finish line; concentrate on taking each stroke as you have trained; just cover the blade with the water; sustain your balance; pull through with vigor but evenly; breathe deep; in recovery shoot your hands out ready to take the next stroke. Such is life and consummation.

.

EPILOGUE – DAY IS DONE

It is appropriate that I am sitting at my desk just after sunset. The birds are bidding me adieu, the wind has calmed, the rain has ceased, and the ocean quieted. I have just finished entering the last edits from friends and family who encouraged me in this project; to share with you, the reader, a practice that I have enjoyed for years. What I have discovered in prayer and in reflecting upon Holy Scripture and listening in the stillness before dawn is a gift that awaits you all.

Breinigsville, PA USA
04 September 2009
223597BV00002B/1/P